New Perspectives on

MACROMEDIA®
FLASH™ MX

Introductory

LUIS A. LOPEZ
St. Philip's College

THOMSON

COURSE TECHNOLOGY™

Australia • Canada • Mexico • Singapore • Spain • United Kingdom • United States • Japan

THOMSON

COURSE TECHNOLOGY

New Perspectives on Macromedia® Flash™ MX–Introductory
is published by Course Technology.

Managing Editor:
Rachel Crapser

Product Manager:
Donna Gridley

Production Editors:
Christine Spillett, Daphne Barbas

Senior Product Manager:
Kathy Finnegan

Associate Product Manager:
Brianna Germain

Composition:
GEX Publishing Services

Product Manager:
Karen Stevens

Editorial Assistant
Emilie Perreault

Text Designer:
Meral Dabcovich

Technology Product Manager:
Amanda Shelton

Marketing Manager:
Rachel Valente

Cover Designer:
Efrat Reis

Developmental Editor:
Kim T. M. Crowley

Preface

Course Technology is the world leader in information technology education. The New Perspectives Series is an integral part of Course Technology's success. Visit our Web site to see a whole new perspective on teaching and learning solutions.

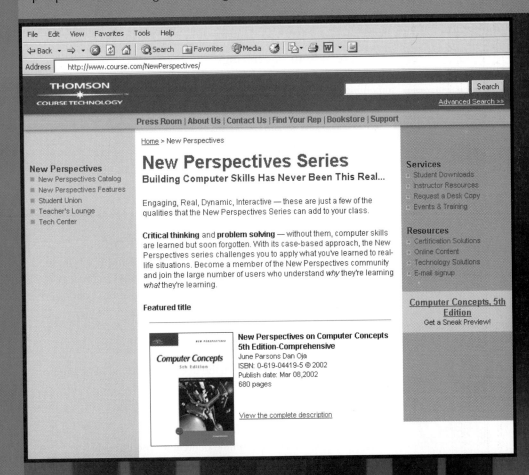

New Perspectives—Building Computer Skills Has Never Been This Real

Why New Perspectives will work for you.

Critical thinking and **problem solving**—without them, computer skills are learned but soon forgotten. With its **case-based** approach, the New Perspectives Series challenges students to apply what they've learned to real-life situations. Become a member of the New Perspectives community and watch your students not only **master** computer skills, but also **retain** and carry this **knowledge** into the world.

New Perspectives catalog
Our online catalog is never out of date! Go to the Catalog link on our Web site to check out our available titles, request a desk copy, download a book preview, or locate online files.

Brief
Introductory
Comprehensive
Advanced

Complete system of offerings
Whether you're looking for a Brief book, an Advanced book, or something in between, we've got you covered. Go to the Catalog link on our Web site to find the level of coverage that's right for you.

Instructor materials
We have all the tools you need—data files, solution files, figure files, a sample syllabus, and ExamView, our powerful testing software package.

SAM XP and TOM

How well do your students know Microsoft Office?
Experience the power, ease, and flexibility of SAM XP and TOM. These innovative software tools provide the first truly integrated technology-based training and assessment solution for your applications course. Click the Tech Center link to learn more.

Get certified
If you want to get certified, we have the titles for you. Find out more by clicking the Teacher's Lounge link.

Interested in online learning?
Enhance your course with rich online content for use through MyCourse 2.0, WebCT, and Blackboard. Go to the Teacher's Lounge to find the platform that's right for you.

Your link to the future is at
www.course.com/NewPerspectives

What you need to know about this book.

- Macromedia Fundamentals interactive training

- Students will appreciate the detailed, real-world scenarios that provide the context of the case problems in each tutorial.

- Each tutorial includes planning material that the student can use as a guide in creating a Flash document.

- Students will gain confidence as they learn how to use Flash MX to create graphics, animations, and movies for Web sites.

- In addition to teaching how to use Flash, this book provides information about the underlying technologies of Web media, and the impact of different Web media on Web page development.

- The multiple methods of accomplishing different tasks in Flash are presented, giving the student a wide perspective on how to work in the Flash environment.

- A wealth of graphics and figures provide support and reinforcement to the concepts being presented.

- Each tutorial includes four running case scenarios in which the student puts knowledge into practice to create rich Flash animations for realistic business Web sites.

CASE	TROUBLE?	SESSION 1.1	QUICK CHECK	RW
Tutorial Case Each tutorial begins with a problem presented in a case that is meaningful to students. The case sets the scene to help students understand what they will do in the tutorial.	**TROUBLE? Paragraphs** These paragraphs anticipate the mistakes or problems that students may have and help them continue with the tutorial.	**Sessions** Each tutorial is divided into sessions designed to be completed in about 45 minutes each. Students should take as much time as they need and take a break between sessions.	**Quick Check Questions** Each session concludes with conceptual Quick Check questions that test students' understanding of what they learned in the session.	**Reference Windows** Reference Windows are succinct summaries of the most important tasks covered in a tutorial. They preview actions students will perform in the steps to follow.

TABLE OF CONTENTS

Acknowledgments

The author wishes to thank:

I would like to thank all of the people at Course Technology who have made this book possible. I am very grateful to Donna Gridley, Product Manager, for her support and to Christine Spillett, Daphne Barbas, and John Freitas for their wonderful work getting the book through the production process. The reviewers of this text, Barbara Burns, Nancy Peaslee, Tamara Davis, and Pat Hathaway, provided valuable feedback on the text.

I would especially like to thank my Developmental Editor, Kim Crowley, for her support, guidance, and encouragement throughout the development of this book. Her thoroughness and her insightful comments and suggestions have made this a much better book.

And finally, this book would not have been possible without the love and support of my wife, Gloria, and our daughter, Alyssandra. Thank you both for your patience and understanding as I spent many nights and weekends in front of the computer.

Luis A. Lopez

New Perspectives on

MACROMEDIA
FLASH MX

Read This Before You Begin

To the Student

Data Disks

To complete the tutorials, Review Assignments, and Case Problems, you need **five** Data Disks. Your instructor will either provide you with these Data Disks or ask you to make your own.

If you are making your own Data Disks, you will need to copy a set of files and/or folders from a file server, standalone computer, or the Web onto your disks. Your instructor will tell you which computer, drive letter, and folders contain the files you need. You could also download the files by going to www.course.com and following the instructions on the screen.

Before creating your Data Disks, check with your instructor to find out where you will be storing your data files. If you will store your data files on drive A, you will need **five** blank, formatted high-density disks. The information below shows you which folders go on each of your disks so that you will have enough disk space for the files for all the tutorials, Review Assignments, and Case Problems.

Label these disks as follows:
Data Disk 1: Tutorials 1-3

Copy the **Tutorial.01**, **Tutorial.02**, and **Tutorial.03** folders onto Data Disk 1.
Data Disk 2: Tutorial 4 Tutorial and Review

Copy the **Tutorial.04\Tutorial** and **Tutorial.04\Review** folders onto Data Disk 2.
Data Disk 3: Tutorial 4 Case Problems

Copy the **Tutorial.04\Cases** folder onto Data Disk 3.
Data Disk 4: Tutorial 5 Tutorial and Review

Copy the **Tutorial.05\Tutorial** and **Tutorial.05\Review** folders onto Data Disk 4.
Data Disk 5: Tutorial 5 Case Problems

Copy the **Tutorial.05\Cases** folder onto Data Disk 5.

It is assumed that you are working from the hard drive of your computer; if you are working from a removable disk then you'll need to substitute the appropriate drive letter when instructed to navigate to a location.

When you begin each tutorial, Review Assignment, or Case Problem, be sure you are using the correct Data Disk. Refer to the "File Finder" chart at the back of this text for more detailed information on which files are used in which tutorials. See the inside back cover of this book for more information on Data Disk files, or ask your instructor or technical support person for assistance.

Installation Information

We assume a default installation of Macromedia Flash MX and Macromedia Flash Player 6. The screenshots in this book were taken using a machine running Windows XP Professional and, when showing a browser, Internet Explorer 6. If you are using a different operating system or a different browser, your screen might differ from the figures in these tutorials.

The data files used with this book were saved using Flash MX. If you are using Flash 5 you will not be able to open the data files. To convert the files to Flash 5 format, open them in Flash MX and use the Save As command. Select Flash 5 Document (*.fla) from the Save as type list in the Save As dialog box.

Using Your Own Computer

If you are going to work through this book using your own computer, you need:

- ■ **Computer System** A text editor and a Web browser (preferably Internet Explorer or Netscape Navigator, versions 4.0 or higher) must be installed on your computer. If you are using a non-standard browser, it must support frames and HTML 4.0 or higher.

- ■ **Data Disks** You will not be able to complete the tutorials or exercises in this book using your own computer until you have your Data Disks.

Visit Our World Wide Web Site

Additional materials designed especially for you are available on the World Wide Web. Go to www.course.com/NewPerspectives.

To the Instructor

The Data Disk files are available on the Instructor's Resource Kit for this title. Follow the instructions in the Help file on the CD-ROM to install the programs to your network or standalone computer. For information on creating Data Disks, see the "To the Student" section above.

You are granted a license to copy the Data Disk files to any computer or computer network used by students who have purchased this book.

OBJECTIVES

In this tutorial you will:

- Refresh your knowledge of the Internet and the World Wide Web

- View and navigate Web pages using Internet Explorer

- Compare vector graphics and bitmap graphics

- Explore examples of Web media

- Learn about Internet animation

- Learn about factors in Web media transmission

- Discover what Macromedia Flash is

- Start Flash and explore its main elements

- Use Flash Help

INTRODUCTION
TO MACROMEDIA
FLASH

Researching Flash Graphics for
Clients of Actions Web Design

Actions Web Design

Actions Web Design is a fast growing Web site design and development company that specializes in building Web sites for small to medium-sized businesses and organizations. Since the founding of Actions Web Design in 2001, the company has established itself as an innovative Web design company meeting the needs of a growing list of clients from various industries, including a national sports equipment company and a local pet store. The company's rapid growth and success has largely been due to its energetic and creative employees and their dedication to the company's clients.

Actions Web Design is co-owned by Gloria Adamson and Jim Torres, both graduates of a Web design and multimedia program at a local college. There are three other full-time employees at Actions Web Design: Aly Garcia, Chris Johnson, and Raj Sharma. Each of the partners and employees is responsible for a different aspect of the company's operation. Gloria handles the bulk of the business decisions and also oversees the Web site design and development projects. Jim is responsible for marketing and manages the company's finances. Aly is the graphics designer, and Chris and Raj are the site designers responsible for developing the content for the clients' Web sites.

Recently, Aly has begun exploring Macromedia Flash, a Web-authoring tool for developing Web graphics, Web site navigation controls, animations, and even entire Web sites. With this tool the company can enhance its clients' Web sites to include more visually exciting and interactive components, such as animated logos, and online interactive advertising. Gloria and Jim are excited about Flash and they have approved the hiring of an intern, you, to help Aly develop Flash graphics and animations.

In this tutorial you will begin your new position at Actions Web Design by learning the basics of Macromedia Flash from Aly. In the remaining tutorials in the book, you will work on projects assigned to you. These projects range from creating simple nonanimated logos to creating more complex animations such as ad banners with sounds and buttons for user interaction.

SESSION 1.1

In this session, you will review the basics of the Internet and the World Wide Web. This review will prepare you for your tasks at Actions Web Design incorporating Macromedia Flash graphics into Web pages. In this session you will also use a browser to open and navigate Web pages.

The Internet

A **network** is formed when two or more computers are connected together for the purpose of sharing information and resources. Networks can themselves be connected together for the same purpose, thereby connecting a larger group of computer users. Networks connected together are known as an **internetwork**, or internet. The most widely known and largest internet, the **Internet**, has evolved from an experimental network connecting a few United States research and military organizations in the late 1960s to its current form as a vast web of networks and subnetworks connecting millions of individual computer users to each other around the world.

One of the most common configurations for a computer network is the **client/server architecture**. In a typical client/server network, one computer is the **server**, and acts as the network's central controller. The server, or **host**, stores and distributes information and resources across the network to individual computers, which are considered **clients**. The Internet employs a variation of a client/server architecture in which there is no single controlling server. Servers on the Internet coordinate and communicate with all the other computers connected to them, which may be either their own clients or other Internet servers—and their clients—around the world. Each server stores information and responds to requests for information. It is important to note that there is no one server that controls the entire network just like there is no one organization that is in charge of the Internet. Figure 1-1 shows how the networks that make up the Internet are connected by a combination of fiber-optic cables, satellites, and phone lines.

Figure 1-1	THE INTERNET

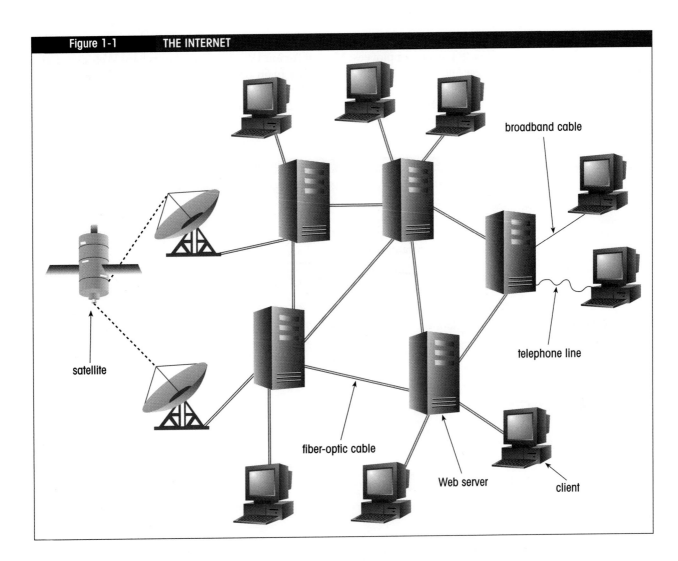

A client computer's request for information may travel only a short distance between that client and its server, if that is where the requested information is stored. It may also be passed along from that server to other servers on the Internet, traveling through many different servers before finally reaching the server which actually holds the desired information. When information travels back from a distant server, it need not follow the same path as the request. Both request and response are able to reach their destinations because each client and server on the Internet has an IP (Internet Protocol) address, which is simply a unique number assigned to it. You will learn more about IP addresses later in this tutorial.

The World Wide Web

The **Web**—short for **World Wide Web**—is a collection of Internet servers that store a system of **hypertext documents** called **Web pages**. Web pages are electronic files that contain **hyperlinks** or just **links**. A hyperlink can be a word, phrase, or graphic that targets a location on the same Web page or on another Web page. When a user clicks the hyperlink, the information at the target location is displayed. The computers on the Internet that store Web pages are called **Web servers** or **Web hosts**. A **Web site** is a collection of hyperlinked Web pages stored on a Web server belonging to an organization or individual. Web sites can be used to provide information about an organization or an individual. They can also be used by businesses to sell or advertise their products and to communicate information to their customers or employees. Most of Action Web Design's clients have Web sites designed for these purposes. Each Web site has a main or initial Web page called the **home page** which contains links to the rest of the Web site. Figure 1-2 shows the home page for *Amazon.com*, one of the world's busiest commercial Web sites, and shows some of the common features of a commercial home page.

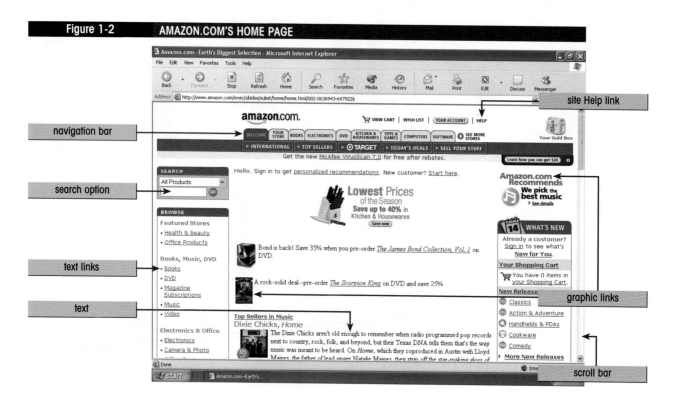

| Figure 1-2 | AMAZON.COM'S HOME PAGE |

A program designed to retrieve, display, and enable a user to navigate Web pages is called a **Web browser**. The *Amazon.com* home page shown in Figure 1-2 is displayed in **Microsoft Internet Explorer**, a popular Web browser. Another commonly used Web browser is **Netscape Navigator**. When you are viewing a Web page in a browser, you can click with your mouse to navigate to another point in the same Web page, to open another page, or to play a video or sound file, depending on the nature of the link. The contents of each page can include information ranging from simple text to complex multimedia. Web pages are intended primarily to be viewed on a screen rather than printed on paper, so they are not limited to any particular length. Users can use the scroll bars in the browser window to scroll the Web page to view contents that extend beyond the edge of the browser window.

In order to access the Internet and view Web pages using a Web browser you must have a connection to the Internet. If you are enrolled at a university, you might be connected to the Internet by the university's computer network. If you are working from a home computer, you might connect to the Internet using a modem and your phone line. This is called a **dial-up connection**. You may also be connected using a DSL (Digital Subscriber Line) connection which uses your phone line or your cable TV connection. Both of these are known as **broadband connections** and offer faster access than a dial-up connection. Regardless of the type of connection you use for your home computer, you need to have an account with an ISP (Internet service provider), a company that sells Internet access. An ISP can guide you in configuring your computer to connect to one of their servers via a telephone or cable modem. When you are logged on to your ISP account, meaning you are connected to your ISP's server, you can use the software on your computer to access files, e-mail, and other resources located anywhere on the Internet.

Hypertext Markup Language

Web pages are created using a special language called **Hypertext Markup Language (HTML)**. An HTML document contains a combination of Web page text along with markup codes called **tags**. Web browsers are designed to interpret these tags to display the text, graphics, and hyperlinks on your computer screen. HTML code can contain many kinds of instructions. These instructions are used to display and format the text, link to other Web pages or to specific locations within those Web pages, to place images to illustrate the text being displayed, or to set up interactive forms that visitors can use to communicate with the owner of the Web site. Hyperlinks can also be included to link to a sound or video file that plays when visitors click the link or to link to an e-mail address to allow visitors to send e-mail messages. Figure 1-3 shows a simple Web page displayed in a Web browser, and its corresponding HTML code.

Figure 1-3	SIMPLE WEB PAGE AND ITS HTML CODE

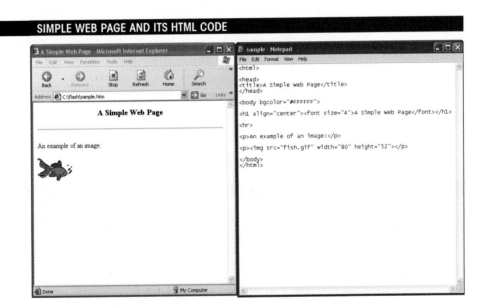

You will be working with existing Web pages from various clients of Actions Web Design and using Macromedia Flash to modify these pages. To view these Web pages, and to view your completed Flash enhancements to them, you will use the Web browser, Microsoft Internet Explorer. Therefore, you should make sure you are familiar with Internet Explorer and the various elements in the browser window.

Starting Internet Explorer

You can start Internet Explorer by clicking the Internet Explorer button on the Quick Launch toolbar, by clicking the Internet Explorer icon on the Windows desktop, or by clicking the Start button on the taskbar, and then clicking Internet Explorer on the All Programs menu.

When you first start Internet Explorer, the browser window typically opens a Web page designated as your browser's home page. "Home page" in this case refers to the page the browser is set to open when the program is first started. Internet Explorer by default designates the

Microsoft Network (MSN) Web site as the home page, but you can choose to designate any Web page you want as your home page in Internet Explorer. For example, if you are a student at a university, you might designate your university's Web page as your browser home page. Coincidentally, this university Web page is also referred to as a home page—the university's home page. This page typically contains information about the organization to which the site belongs, hyperlinks to other Web sites, and associated pictures and sounds.

If no home page has been specified, then a blank page appears, or a default Web page is opened from your computer's hard drive when you start Internet Explorer.

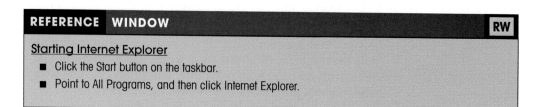

REFERENCE WINDOW   **RW**

Starting Internet Explorer
- Click the Start button on the taskbar.
- Point to All Programs, and then click Internet Explorer.

This book assumes you are using Internet Explorer as your Web browser. If you are using a different Web browser, such as Netscape Navigator, your instructor will provide you with specific instructions for its use. In this case, the appearance of your screen might differ from the figures in these tutorials, but these variations should not impact your work with Macromedia Flash.

To start Internet Explorer:

1. Make sure that your computer is turned on and that the Windows desktop appears. See Figure 1-4.

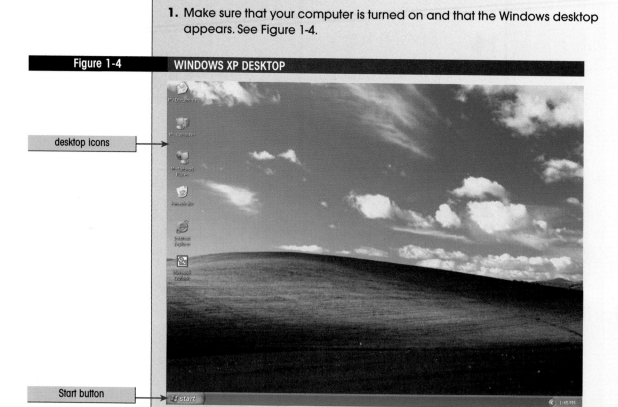

Figure 1-4   WINDOWS XP DESKTOP

desktop icons

Start button

TROUBLE? Your desktop might look different from the one shown in Figure 1-4; it may display different icons on the desktop and on the taskbar.

2. Click the **Start** button [⊞ start] on the taskbar. If you don't see Internet Explorer on the Start menu, then point to **All Programs** to display all the programs installed on your computer.

3. Click **Internet Explorer** on the Start menu or on the All Programs menu. The Internet Explorer window opens, and displays the home page currently designated on your computer. The default browser home page for Internet Explorer is the MSN Web site. Depending on your system configuration, your browser's default home page may be different. See Figure 1-5.

Figure 1-5	INTERNET EXPLORER PROGRAM WINDOW

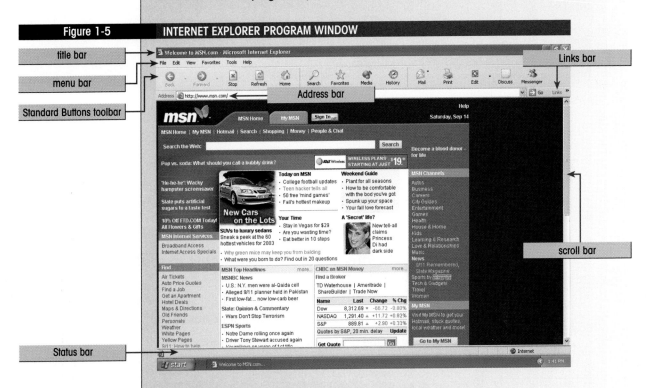

title bar
menu bar
Standard Buttons toolbar
Links bar
Address bar
scroll bar
Status bar

TROUBLE? Your computer may not automatically connect to the Internet. If so, the default home page may not display or a saved version of the home page may be displayed. You do not need to be online to complete the rest of this tutorial.

TROUBLE? The icons on the Standard Buttons toolbar in Internet Explorer might appear larger or smaller than those shown in Figure 1-5. The size of these icons is an option that you can customize in Internet Explorer.

Figure 1-6 describes some of the elements of the Internet Explorer window.

Figure 1-6	ELEMENTS OF THE INTERNET EXPLORER PROGRAM WINDOW
INTERNET EXPLORER ELEMENT	**DESCRIPTION**
Title bar	Displays the Web page title
Menu bar	Lists the menu options File, View, Edit, Favorites, Tools, and Help; these menu options include commands to open, save, and print Web pages, view a page's HTML, create a list of favorite Web sites, and customize the browser window
Standard Buttons toolbar	Lists buttons to the more frequently used browser commands
Address bar	Lists the address of the Web page currently being displayed; you enter a Web page's address in the address bar to open the page
Scroll bar	Use to move the view of the displayed Web page when the page is longer or wider than the browser window
Status bar	Displays the location information when you move the pointer over a link on the displayed page; also shows the download status of a Web page being opened
Links bar	Displays links for frequently visited Web pages

4. If necessary, click the **Maximize** button 🗗 on the Internet Explorer title bar to maximize the browser window.

It will be easier for you to work through the steps in this tutorial if your Internet Explorer window matches the window shown in the figures. In the next set of steps, you will set up your Internet Explorer window to match the figures shown in this tutorial.

To set up the Internet Explorer window to match the figures in this tutorial:

1. Click **View** on the menu bar, and then make sure the **Status Bar** option is checked. If it is not checked, click the **Status Bar** option to select it.

2. Click **View** on the menu bar, point to **Toolbars**, and then make sure the **Standard Buttons**, **Address Bar**, and **Links** options are checked. These are the three toolbars you will use most in working with Internet Explorer. To ensure the buttons on the Standard Buttons toolbar are easy to use, you will customize these buttons so that each appears with a text label identifying its purpose.

3. Open the **View** menu again, if necessary. Point to **Toolbars**, and then click **Customize**. In the Customize Toolbar dialog box, click the **Text options** list arrow, and then click **Show text labels**.

4. Click the **Close** button to close the dialog box. Your Internet Explorer window should appear similar to that shown in Figure 1-7.

Figure 1-7 HOME PAGE DISPLAYED IN INTERNET EXPLORER

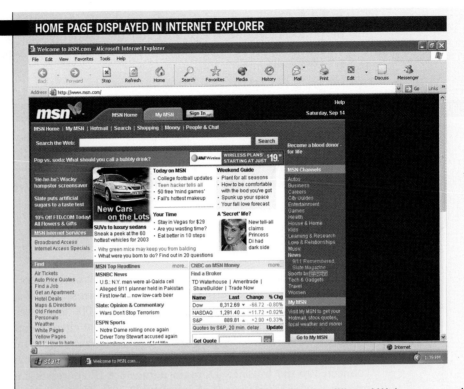

TROUBLE? If your Internet Explorer window shows a different Web page and the Address bar shows a different address, your default home page is different from the one shown in Figure 1-7.

Next you will open a Web page using the Address bar.

Opening a Web Page with a URL

When you use a Web browser to access a Web page stored on a Web server, the browser software locates and retrieves the Web page content and downloads it to your computer. Web documents transmitted over the Internet use **Hypertext Transfer Protocol (HTTP)**, a communications protocol for transferring information. A **protocol** is a standardized procedure that computers use to exchange data. A **Uniform Resource Locator**, or **URL**, is the Web page's address and identifies where the Web page is stored on the Internet. A URL begins with the communications protocol identifier followed by the address of the server that stores the Web page, and ends with the file pathname to the Web page.

The URL shown in Figure 1-8 indicates the communications protocol HTTP. Notice that the protocol identifier is separated from the rest of the URL by **://** (a colon followed by two forward slashes). Forward slash symbols are also used to separate the folder and file names in the pathname.

Figure 1-8   **COMPONENTS OF A TYPICAL URL**

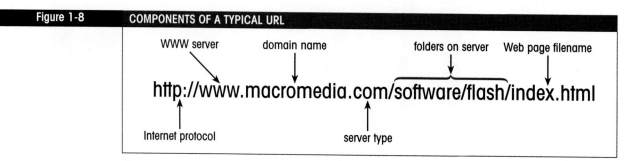

The server address portion of a URL may consist of numbers or letters. Every computer on the Internet has an **Internet Protocol (IP) address**. An IP address is a unique number consisting of four sets of three-digit numbers from 000 to 255 separated by periods (such as 216.035.148.254) that identifies the specific server or client computer. Because most people would have a hard time keeping track of IP addresses for the multitude of Web sites they access, domain names were created as another means of identifying computers and servers connected to the Internet. **Domain names** are IP addresses consisting of letters (such as *www.macromedia.com*) instead of numbers. Domain names provide more meaningful identification of a Web site, and therefore are most commonly used in the server address portion of a URL. The URL address shown in Figure 1-8 has the domain name *macromedia.com*, which indicates the specific address of the server or computer on which the page resides, and the type of organization that operates it. In the URL, *www* indicates that the server is a Web server; *macromedia* is the identifying name chosen by the organization to whom the Web site belongs; and *.com* indicates that the server is operated by a commercial entity. Other common types of servers in the United States are education (.edu), organization (.org), and government (.gov).

In addition, all Web pages and referenced media files stored on Web servers have unique pathnames, just like files stored on a disk. The pathname in a URL includes the folder name(s), filename, and filename extension for locating the Web page. The extension for most Web pages is either *.htm* or *.html*. In the example URL shown in Figure 1-8, the pathname that follows the domain name *www.macromedia.com* specifies a file named *index.html*, which is stored in a folder named *flash* which is in a folder named *software*.

If the URL does not include a filename as the last element of the path, your browser will assume a default filename of *index.htm* (or *index.html*), or *default.htm* (or *default.html*) and open that file if it exists at that location.

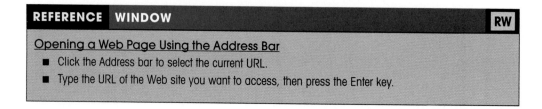

REFERENCE WINDOW   **RW**

Opening a Web Page Using the Address Bar
- Click the Address bar to select the current URL.
- Type the URL of the Web site you want to access, then press the Enter key.

As you know from your first meeting with Aly at Actions Web Designs, she designed the graphics on the company's Web site and on the Web sites for the company's clients. Before you begin your work with Aly, she wants you to examine the Web sites to become familiar with their graphic elements. As you work through the tutorials in this book, you will use the Macromedia Flash authoring program to enhance or create more visually exciting graphics for some of the client Web sites. The files for the Actions Web site are stored on your Data Disk. Therefore, the URL to the Web site includes a pathname to the files stored on your disk, instead of a URL to a Web page stored on a Web server.

To access a disk-based Web site in Internet Explorer:

1. Make sure that Internet Explorer is open and that your Data Disk is in the appropriate drive.

   TROUBLE? You must have a Data Disk to complete the tutorials in this book. If you do not have a Data Disk, ask your instructor or technical support person for help.

   TROUBLE? This text assumes your Data Disk fits in the A: drive. If your Data Disk fits into a drive designated by another drive letter, then substitute that drive letter when asked to type A: in the following steps.

2. Click the text that appears in the Address bar to select it.

   TROUBLE? If the text is not selected, then you may have double-clicked the text currently in the Address bar, thereby changing to editing mode. Click and drag to select the text in the Address bar, and then continue with Step 3.

3. Type **A:\Tutorial.01\Tutorial\Actions\index.htm** in the Address bar. This is the address for the home page of the disk-based Actions home page stored on your Data Disk. Note that for a disk-based Web page you use backslash symbols instead of forward slash symbols.

   Internet Explorer has an AutoComplete feature that guesses the address you are typing and finishes typing it for you, or displays a menu of the addresses for previously opened Web pages. The suggested match appears highlighted in the Address bar. If this is the correct address for the Web page you are attempting to access, you can press the Enter key to open the Web page. Otherwise, you can click another address in the list of previously opened Web pages, or you can continue typing the address on your own.

4. Press the **Enter** key. The home page for Actions Web Design opens. See Figure 1-9.

Figure 1-9   ACTIONS WEB DESIGN HOME PAGE

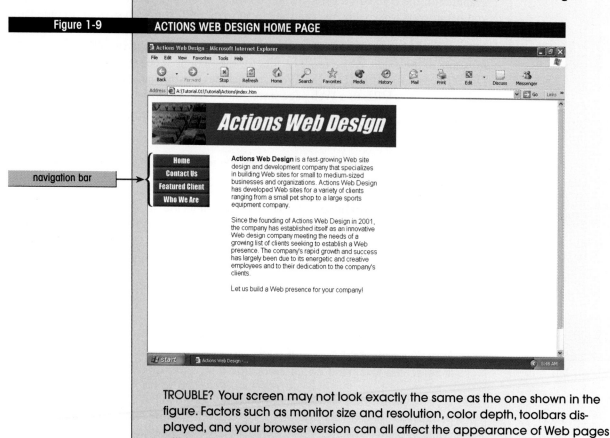

TROUBLE? Your screen may not look exactly the same as the one shown in the figure. Factors such as monitor size and resolution, color depth, toolbars displayed, and your browser version can all affect the appearance of Web pages within your browser window.

Next, you will explore the Featured Client page on the Actions Web Design Web site to view a sample of the current Web site for one of the company's clients.

Navigating Web Pages

Text links in a Web page can appear in one of several ways. The text may be underlined, colored and underlined, appear in a different color, or it may have some other visual clue indicating it is a hyperlink. Many Web pages include a navigation bar containing links that open other pages on the Web site. These navigation bars may be text only or they may consist of graphic elements such as buttons. The home page for Actions Web Design contains several links to other pages in the Web site. These links are in the form of a navigation bar made up of a series of buttons.

Because you will be creating graphics for client Web sites using Macromedia Flash, Aly wants you to review the featured client site to see its current design.

To follow a link to another Web page:

1. Make sure the home page of the Actions Web Design site is open in your browser window.

2. Point to (but don't click) the **Featured Client** link in the navigation bar. The mouse pointer changes to a hand shape, and the pathname for the linked page appears in the lower-left corner on the status bar.

3. Click the **Featured Client** link. The Featured Client Web page opens in the browser and replaces the home page. See Figure 1-10.

Figure 1-10   ACTIONS WEB DESIGN FEATURED CLIENT PAGE

4. Click the **Flounders Pet Shop** link. The Flounders Pet Shop Web page opens in the browser and replaces the Featured Client page. This is the current Web site home page for one of Actions' clients.

Notice the company banner on this page which is the top graphic element. In later tutorials you will be creating a new banner using Macromedia Flash. In addition to the banner and text, there are several graphic images of pets. Notice that you have traveled several hyperlinks from the main page, navigating deeper into the content on the Web site. This is referred to as "drilling down."

5. Click the **Actions** logo link at the bottom of the page to return to the Featured Client page.

6. Click the **Home** link in the navigation bar to return to the Actions Web Design home page, and then click the **Close button** to close Internet Explorer.

You have completed the first part of your training by examining the Actions Web Design Web site and its Featured Client page. In the next session, you will learn about the different types of Web media found on Web pages.

Session 1.1 QUICK CHECK

1. The _____ is a vast web of networks and subnetworks connecting millions of individual computer users to each other around the world.

2. What is the communications protocol for transferring information on the Internet?

3. What is an ISP?

4. How many sets of three-digit numbers are in an IP address?

5. In an IP address, each set of three-digit numbers can range from 000 to
   _____ .

6. The Internet is composed of client and _____ computers.

7. What is the difference between a domain name and a URL?

8. What is the difference between a Web page and a Web site?

9. The first page a browser opens when it starts is called the browser's
   _____ page.

10. The top-level entry page of a Web site is called the Web site's
    _____ page.

11. What information appears in the Status bar when you point (without clicking) to
    a hyperlink?

12. What happens when you click a hyperlink?

SESSION 1.2

In this session, you will learn about the different types of Web media, and the Web media that you can create using Macromedia Flash. You will also learn about the differences between bitmap and vector graphics.

Defining Web Media

Web pages are made up of the following elements:

- Text
- Graphics
- Animations
- Sounds
- Videos

These elements are referred to as **Web media**. The different types of Web media are created by a variety of programs, and then pulled together through HTML to work as a cohesive whole on a Web page. The most common types of Web media found on Web pages, besides text, are graphics and animations. Macromedia Flash excels at creating these types of media and they are the focus of the discussion in this session.

Types of Graphics: Bitmap and Vector

There are essentially two types of graphics: bitmap and vector. Each has its advantages, disadvantages, and appropriate uses in Web page design.

A **bitmap graphic** is a row-by-row list of every pixel in the graphic, along with each pixel's color. A **pixel** is the smallest picture element on the monitor screen that can be controlled by the computer. A 100 × 100-pixel bitmap graphic is simply a grid containing 10,000 colored pixels. As a result, bitmap graphics cannot be resized without unattractive side effects. If you enlarge a bitmap graphic, for example, the edges become ragged as the pixels get redistributed to fit the larger grid. There is also no simple way to take a bitmap graphic apart to modify only one portion of the image. Bitmap graphics, however, provide blending and subtle variations in colors and textures. A common example of a bitmap graphic is a photograph that has been scanned or captured by a digital camera. You can also create bitmap graphics using imaging software such as Macromedia Fireworks or Adobe Photoshop. The two most common file formats for bitmap graphics used in Web pages are JPEG (Joint Photographic Experts Group) and GIF (Graphic Interchange Format). Bitmap graphic files stored in these formats have a file extension of .jpg or .gif, respectively.

A **vector graphic**, on the other hand, is a set of mathematical instructions that describe the color, outline, and position of all the shapes of the image. Each shape is defined by numbers which represent the shape's position in the window in which it is being displayed. Other numbers represent the points that establish the shape's outline. As a result, vector graphics scale well, which means you can resize a vector image proportionally and the quality remains the same. Vector graphics also appear uniform regardless of the size or resolution of the monitor on which they are displayed. Individual shapes within a vector graphic can also be modified independently of the rest. Vector graphics excel at sharp lines, smooth colors, and precise detail. Also, an advantage of vector graphic files over bitmap graphic files is that they are generally smaller. This means that vector files take less time to download than bitmap files. Common examples of vector graphics are images created in drawing programs such as Macromedia Freehand and Adobe Illustrator. Images created in Flash are in the vector format, although bitmap images may also be imported into Flash movies.

Figure 1-11 shows an image of a basketball in the two different formats. The one on the left is a bitmap graphic. The one on the right is a vector graphic. Notice how the enlarged version of the bitmap graphic becomes distorted while the enlarged version of the vector graphic retains its quality.

Figure 1-11	BITMAP GRAPHIC COMPARED TO VECTOR GRAPHIC

original bitmap graphic	original vector graphic
bitmap graphic enlarged	vector graphic enlarged

Animation Types

Animation is accomplished when a series of still images is displayed in sequence giving the illusion of motion. Animation can be accomplished with both bitmap and vector images.

Bitmap animation consists of putting bitmap still images into motion for Web viewing. This can be accomplished by creating a file consisting of a sequence of bitmap frames. The playback of the frames produces a perception of smooth motion as long as the frame frequency is high enough and the changes from frame to frame are gradual enough.

Each change in what the viewer sees on the screen requires changing the colors of pixels in the frame. A significant amount of information is required to keep track of all of the pixel changes even for small images of short duration. The amount of information that must be stored increases dramatically for larger frame sizes, longer sequences, or smoother motion. Because of the importance for rapid transmission over the Internet, bitmap motion graphics are usually limited to small frame sizes and short sequences.

Vector animation consists of a listing of shapes and their transformations. These too are played back in sequence to provide the perception of motion. The amount of information required to describe the modification of shapes in a vector animation is usually less than the amount of information required to describe the pixel changes in a bitmap animation. Also, because vector graphics are resolution independent, meaning that they always appear with the optimum on-screen quality regardless of image size or the screen resolution, increasing the display size of the shapes in a vector animation has no effect on the file size.

Factors in Web Media Transmission

Web pages are plain text files consisting of HTML code. These files do not contain any images or sounds. Instead, the HTML code contains references to the image or sound files. Any Web media other than formatted text in the Web page must be referenced in the HTML code by specifying the media's filename and its location on the Internet using its URL. Just as each Web page has a URL address, so does each of its Web media components. Downloading a Web page that contains images to display on your computer screen involves downloading more than just the HTML file. Each of the image files has to be downloaded separately. It is then the job of the Web browser to collect all the referenced graphics and display them on the page along with the text. Web media such as bitmap graphics stored as GIF and JPEG files are typically displayed within the page and positioned according to the HTML code, as shown in Figure 1-12.

Figure 1-12	WEB PAGE WITH WEB MEDIA AND CORRESPONDING HTML

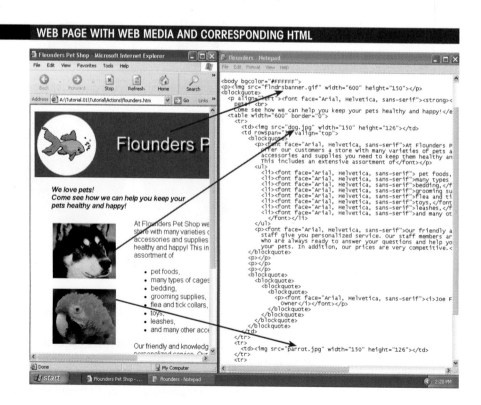

Other Web media types require additional software that is capable of reading and displaying the media. This additional software is called a **plug-in**. Many plug-ins have been developed to support specific media file formats that extend a Web browser's capabilities. It is usually up to the user to locate and install the required plug-in to display or listen to that media.

Web media that require a plug-in can be displayed in one of two ways. Ideally, a plug-in enables the associated media to appear embedded in the Web page where it is referenced, allowing it to appear seamless with the other elements on the Web page. Some plug-ins however, also display the media in a separate window created by the plug-in. This window typically has its own controls and menus which the user can use to control how they view the Web media. Figure 1-13 shows an example of Web media displayed in a separate window created by a plug-in.

| Figure 1-13 | WEB MEDIA DISPLAYED IN A SEPARATE PLUG-IN WINDOW |

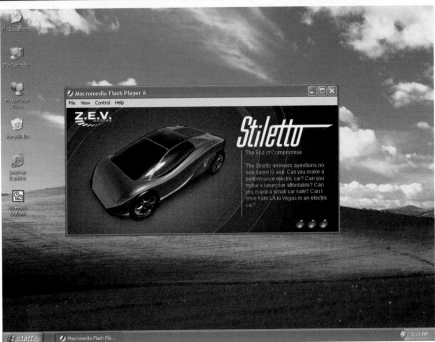

The speed with which an end user is able to view a Web page can be affected by a number of factors—the client computer and operating system, the browser, the quality of the connection to the local ISP, the number of other users browsing the Web at the same time, even the speed of the Internet on any given day. All of these factors are beyond the Web page developer's control. A Web page developer does, however, have control over several factors related to the Web media files used in the Web page which directly affect the speed with which each page is displayed. These factors are bandwidth, compression, streaming, and media weight.

Bandwidth

Because every element of a Web page must be downloaded as a separate file from a remote server, there are some limitations to the use of media on the Web. Research has shown that people browsing the Internet do not wait very long for a page or graphic to appear. Media files are inherently larger than the HTML text files that reference them. In particular, animation and sound media require a great deal more bandwidth to be acceptable to end users. **Bandwidth** refers to the amount of data that can be transferred in a given timeframe. Low bandwidth is associated with small amounts of data and slow speeds, high bandwidth with large amounts of data and high speeds. Movie trailer files, for example, typically require high bandwidth for satisfactory results. Figure 1-14 shows two different Web pages, one that requires low bandwidth and one that requires high bandwidth. Notice that the low-bandwidth page contains mostly text and only simple graphics, while the high-bandwidth page contains many more graphic elements.

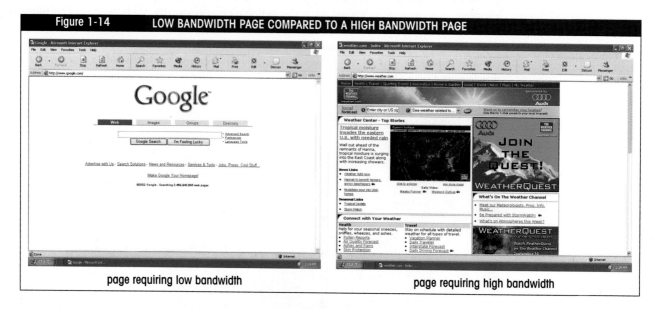

Figure 1-14   LOW BANDWIDTH PAGE COMPARED TO A HIGH BANDWIDTH PAGE

page requiring low bandwidth   page requiring high bandwidth

Compression and Decompression

In order to reduce the size of media files, and, consequently, the amount of time end users must wait to view information while browsing, various strategies have been pursued. In the case of media files, **compression** can be applied to produce smaller files that take less time to transfer over the Internet. The media files are compressed before they are stored on Web servers, and then they are **decompressed** on the client computer after they have been downloaded but before they display in the browser window.

Compression techniques may be lossy or non-lossy. **Lossy compression** actually throws away information and reduces the level of detail from the original media, though in ways that are inconspicuous to the end user. **Non-lossy compression** employs programming techniques that maintain the level of detail of the original media while processing it to reduce file size.

All methods of compressing media files for Web pages involve processing twice: once when the data is compressed for transmission from the server, and again when it is decompressed for display on the client's computer. One drawback to this technique is that the decompression on the client's computer requires processing time that can again slow down the display of the Web page and its various media.

Streaming

Another way to speed up the display of media is to employ **streaming** techniques that allow end users to begin viewing or listening to media files while the remainder of the file continues downloading in the background. Several movie and sound formats have built-in streaming capabilities. As shown in Figure 1-15, a common feature of media player interfaces is a **streaming status area** to indicate the status of the download process. Streaming media can begin playing when enough of the video has downloaded. A **media player** is a plug-in such as the Microsoft Windows Media Player or Real Player from Real Networks that is used to play videos and music.

Figure 1-15	WINDOWS MEDIA PLAYER

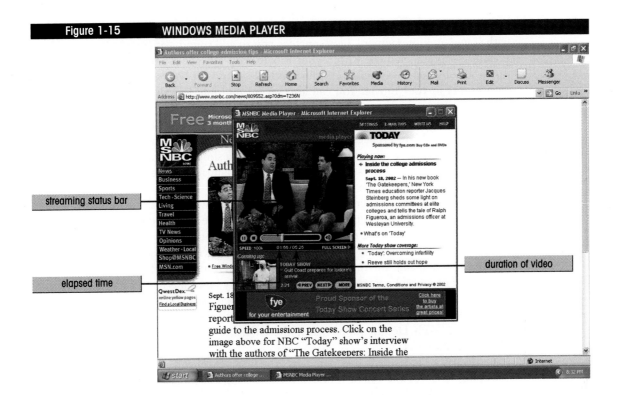

Media Weight

Another way a Web page developer can impact the speed at which a Web page downloads and displays is in the selection of the type and format of the graphical media. The file type and format is directly related to the size in bytes of the graphical media. This is often referred to as the **weight** of the media. Recall that vector graphics generally are smaller in size, or have a lower weight, than bitmap graphics. Therefore, vector graphics transfer and display faster than bitmap graphics in a browser window. Using vector graphics for a Web site instead of bitmap graphics is one way to reduce the file size of graphics and speed up their display on the client without using compression and decompression.

What is Macromedia Flash?

Macromedia Flash is a program developed by Macromedia, Inc. that was initially developed as a way to create small, fast loading animations that could be used in Web pages. Over the years, it has evolved into a full Web page production tool that allows developers to create interactive media ranging from animated logos to Web site navigational controls and even entire Web sites. Flash allows developers to create media-rich elements that integrate with Web pages and that download quickly. Flash media also has streaming capability, which allows Web media such as animations to start playing even before they download completely.

Web media created in Flash are called **movies** whether they are static images or animations. The graphics that are created in Flash are primarily vector graphics. Flash animations are created when you create a series of vector graphics and then sequence them. The Flash program also supports a wide variety of import formats so that developers can include media from a broad range of sources without having to convert them to vector graphics first.

Bitmap graphics can also be imported and used in Flash. Bitmap images often provide a realistic compliment when combined with vector graphics. For example, bitmap images such as photographs often appear as the background to Flash vector animation sequences. They tend to soften the overall effect, and add a little realism to Flash movies.

The completed movie can include anything from silent still imagery to motion graphics with sound and interactivity. Flash enables you to add sound—as sound effects, voiceovers, or music—to any element within your movie. You can choose to have sound play all the time, be activated by a mouse click, be turned on and off by the user, or be synchronized with events in your movie. You can also set up multiple sounds to play simultaneously if your movie requires that. Like any other media file, a Flash movie must be referenced in an HTML file in order to be viewed in a Web page. As a Flash developer, you can publish the HTML files and references automatically from within the Flash program. Alternately, although the syntax is a bit more involved than for a simple graphic image, if you are experienced with HTML, you can insert the reference manually, or create your own HTML file to reference and control the Flash movie.

While developing content using Flash, you work with a Flash authoring document, referred to as a **FLA** file. That is, Flash documents have a file extension appended to their filename of .fla. When you're ready to deliver that content for viewing by end users, you convert the Flash document to a published movie known as a **Macromedia Flash Player movie**. The filename for these movies have an extension of .swf, which stands for **small Web file**. For example, if your first assignment as Aly's intern is to create an animation to be used on Actions Web Design's own Web site, the document you create and develop in Flash might have the name AWDanimation.fla. Once you finish the animation and publish it to the Actions Web Design home page, the filename for the published movie would be AWDanimation.swf.

To display a Flash movie in a Web page, the browser must have the **Flash Player** plug-in. This plug-in is free and can be found at *www.macromedia.com/downloads*. All current versions of the major Web browsers come with the Flash Player plug-in already installed. Besides allowing Flash movies to be viewed in your browser, the Flash Player plug-in provides controls for zooming in and out, rewinding, playing individual frames, and other functions. The controls can be accessed by right-clicking the animation to display a **shortcut menu** (called a **context menu** by Macromedia). See Figure 1-16.

Figure 1-16   **FLASH PLAYER PLUG-IN CONTEXT MENU**

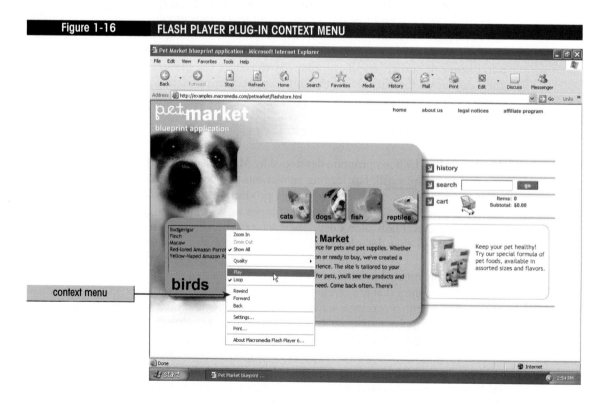

context menu

Finally, another element of Flash is **ActionScript**, a scripting programming language that allows you to add interactivity to buttons and other Web media that a user can click or select to control the Flash movies or animation they are viewing. You will learn more about ActionScript in Tutorial 4.

Viewing Examples of Macromedia Flash Movies

In order to get a feeling for what you can create with Macromedia Flash, Aly wants you to look at several examples of Flash movies she has created. She asks you to look at these examples located at the Actions Web Design Web site.

Opening a Flash Web page is no different than opening any other page in your browser. If you have the Flash Player plug-in installed, the streaming capability of a Flash movie allows the player to begin playing the movie as soon as enough of the file has been downloaded.

To view examples of Flash movies in your browser:

1. Make sure that your computer is turned on, and the Windows XP desktop is displayed.

2. Start Internet Explorer and make sure the Address bar, the Links bar, and the Status bar are displayed in the browser window.

3. Type **A:\Tutorial.01\Tutorial\Actions\sample.htm** in the Address bar, and then press the **Enter** key. The Actions Web Design sample page displays in the browser window. This page contains several examples of Flash movies that are available for Actions' clients to review.

4. Right-click one of the animations on the screen. The context menu containing controls for the Flash movie opens. See Figure 1-17.

Figure 1-17	SAMPLE FLASH MOVIES

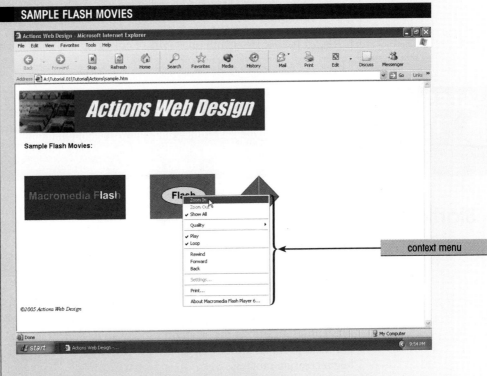

TROUBLE? If the context menu does not appear as shown in Figure 1-17, right-click a different graphic on the screen.

5. Click **Play** on the context menu to remove the check mark from this command and deselect it. The animation stops. Open the context menu again, and click **Zoom In** to increase the movie's magnification level. Continue to use the context menu controls to rewind, zoom out, and step forward and back through the movie.

6. When you are done reviewing the sample Flash movies, click the **Close** button ☒ to close the browser window.

In this session you learned about the different types of Web media and about Macromedia Flash, which is a program designed for creating Web media. In the next session you will become familiar with the Flash program and its different elements.

Session 1.2 QUICK CHECK

1. Macromedia Flash creates _____-based images.

2. What file extension does a Flash movie have after it has been published for Internet delivery?

3. List three things you might find in a Flash movie.

4. Flash allows you to synchronize sound with events in your movie. True or False?

5. Bitmap graphics store information as a grid of _____.

6. How does a vector graphic store image data?

7. Does the term "resolution independent" apply to bitmap graphics, vector graphics, or both?

8. What are two common results of enlarging a bitmap image?

SESSION 1.3

In this session, you will start Macromedia Flash and become familiar with the program window and its elements. You will preview a movie with a simple animation. You will see how the movie uses frames and you will change the animation and play back the results. In this session you will also learn about the tools found in the toolbox and you will learn about panels and how to customize them.

Starting Macromedia Flash

You start Flash by clicking the Start button on the Windows taskbar, and accessing the Macromedia submenu from the All Programs menu. If the Flash program icon appears on the desktop you can also double-click it to start the program.

The Flash program window is made up of several components. The program allows you to organize its various elements to suit your work style and needs. Aly suggests you start the Flash program and set the program window to its default layout so she can help you identify the main program window components you need to become familiar with before you can begin creating movies.

To start Macromedia Flash and set the program window to its default layout:

1. Make sure that your computer is turned on and that the Windows desktop is displayed.

2. Click the **Start** button ⟨*start*⟩ on the taskbar, and then point to **All Programs** to display all the programs installed on your computer.

3. Point to **Macromedia** and then click **Macromedia Flash MX**. The Macromedia Flash program window opens. If necessary, click the **Maximize** button 🔲 on the title bar to maximize the Flash program window.

   TROUBLE? If this is the first time you have started Flash, the Flash Serialization dialog box may open. Enter your name and the serial number provided to you when you purchased Flash, then click the OK button. If you do not know your service number, ask your instructor for assistance.

   TROUBLE? If the Please Register Now dialog box opens, click either the Don't Remind Me button or the Register later button to close this dialog box.

   TROUBLE? A small window may appear with the title of Welcome, What's New, Lessons, or Tutorials. If that is the case, click the Close button to close it.

   The Flash window is customizable, which means you can easily change the way different panels are arranged in the program window. To ensure your screens match those shown in these steps, you can change the layout of the Flash program panels to their default layout.

4. Click **Window** on the menu bar, point to **Panel Sets**, and then click **Default Layout**.

5. Click **Window** on the menu bar, and then point to **Toolbars**. Make sure that the options **Main**, **Status**, and **Controller** do not have check marks next to them. If one of these menu options has a check mark, then click it to deselect it.

6. If necessary, click the **Maximize** button 🔲 on the document window's menu bar to maximize the document window.

   The Flash program window arranges its various panels to look like that shown in Figure 1-18.

Figure 1-18	FLASH PROGRAM WINDOW DEFAULT LAYOUT

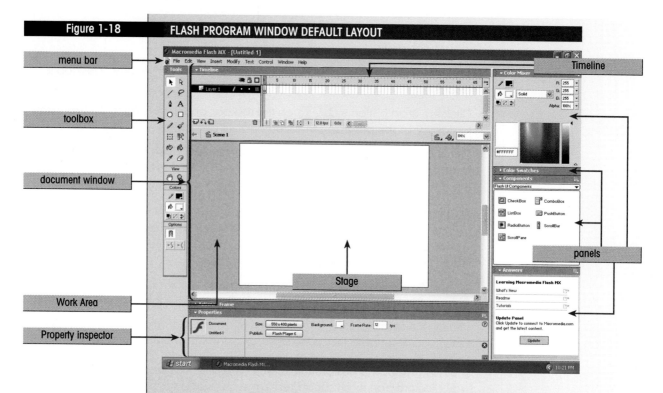

Figure 1-19 briefly describes each of the main components of the Flash program window.

Figure 1-19	MAIN COMPONENTS OF THE FLASH PROGRAM WINDOW

FLASH COMPONENT	DESCRIPTION
Menu bar	Lists the menu options such as File, Edit, View, Insert, and Help; these menu options include commands to access most of the features of the Flash program
Toolbox	Contains the Flash tools; the toolbox includes tools for drawing and painting lines and shapes, selecting objects, changing the view of the Stage, and choosing colors
Stage	Located in the document window, the area where you assemble and position all of the objects that are part of a Flash movie
Work Area	Located in the document window and used to place objects that are not part of the viewable Stage; also used to position objects that move onto or off the Stage as part of an animation
Timeline	Located in the document window; displays and controls the Flash instances that make up an animation and organizes the objects that are part of the movie
Panels	Contain controls for viewing and changing the properties of objects
Property inspector	Provides easy access to the most common attributes of the currently selected tool or object

Later in this session we will discuss in greater detail the five elements of the Flash window you will use most frequently; the Stage, Work Area, Timeline, toolbox, and panels. Next, Aly wants you to preview a simple movie she has created.

Previewing Movies

As you are developing a Macromedia Flash movie, you often need to preview the movie to check the results of your changes. There are several ways to preview your work in Flash. You can preview or play the movie within the Flash program window, publish the movie to play in a separate Flash Player window, or publish it to play in a Web page in your default Web browser.

Previewing the movie in the Flash program window is the quickest method, although some animation effects and interactive functions only work in the published format. You will view Aly's movie from the Flash program window. The SimpleKite.fla file is a Flash movie consisting of a simple animation and is stored on your Data Disk.

To preview the sample movie in the Flash progam window:

1. Make sure that your Data Disk is in the appropriate drive, click **File** on the menu bar, and then click **Open**. The Open dialog box is displayed.

2. Click the **Look in** list arrow, select the drive containing your Data Disk, open the **Tutorial.01** folder, and then open the **Tutorial** folder. Click **SimpleKite** from the list of files, and then click the **Open** button. The SimpleKite movie opens on the Stage.

3. To see all of the movie, click **View** on the menu bar, point to **Magnification**, and then click **Show All**. The Flash program window should look like that shown in Figure 1-20.

Figure 1-20	SIMPLEKITE MOVIE

4. Click **Control** on the menu bar, and then click **Play**. As the movie plays, notice that the Timeline tracks the movie's progress. You will learn more about the elements in the Timeline later in this session.

You can also preview the published movie in a separate Flash Player window or in a browser window.

To preview the published movie in a separate Flash Player window and then in a browser:

1. Click **Control** on the menu bar, and then click **Test Movie**. Flash creates a file in the SWF format, opens it in a separate window, and then plays it with the Flash Player as shown in Figure 1-21.

Figure 1-21 | PUBLISHED MOVIE PLAYING IN A SEPARATE WINDOW

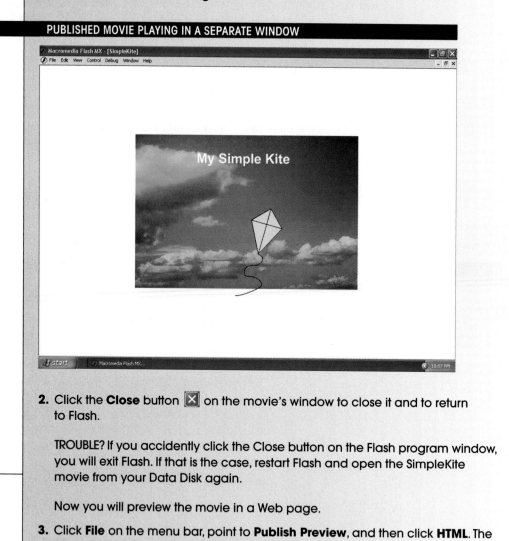

2. Click the **Close** button ⊠ on the movie's window to close it and to return to Flash.

   TROUBLE? If you accidently click the Close button on the Flash program window, you will exit Flash. If that is the case, restart Flash and open the SimpleKite movie from your Data Disk again.

   Now you will preview the movie in a Web page.

3. Click **File** on the menu bar, point to **Publish Preview**, and then click **HTML**. The default browser on your computer opens and the movie plays in a Web page. See Figure 1-22.

Figure 1-22   MOVIE PLAYING IN A WEB PAGE

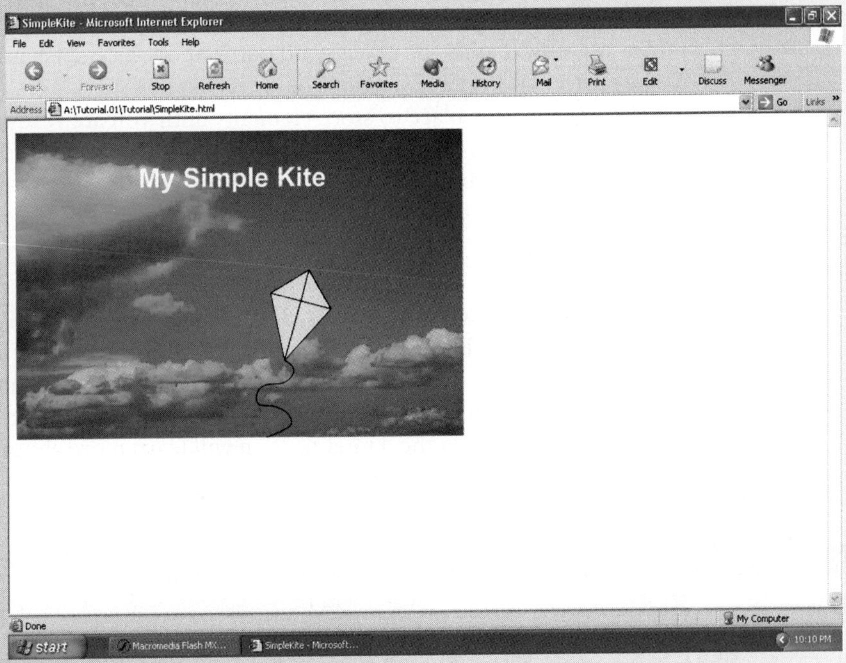

4. Close the browser window to return to Flash.

Before you can work with Aly's simple movie, or create movies of your own in Flash, you need to learn more about the Flash program window components.

Macromedia **Flash Program Window Elements**

The main elements of the Macromedia Flash window are the Stage, Work Area, Timeline, toolbox, and panels. The Stage, the Work Area, and the Timeline make up the document window.

Stage

The **Stage** is the central area of a document window where you assemble and position all the elements of your movie.

It is important, however, to understand that the Stage only shows the objects that are visible at a particular point in a movie. In fact, the Stage in Flash is just like the stage in a dramatic production. As the production progresses, actors appear and disappear, and move around from place to place on the Stage.

Because Flash may be used to create animations, you would expect different objects to be visible at different times during playback. While you are working on a project, therefore, the Stage only displays those objects that are associated with the currently selected frame. Flash movies are divided into frames and each frame may contain different images or different states of the same image. If you select a different frame, different objects may appear or disappear, or objects may be in different positions or be changed in appearance.

Work Area

Surrounding the Stage is a gray area called the **Work Area**. When you complete a Flash movie and view it, only the objects and portions of objects that are within the Stage will appear in the movie. Objects and portions of objects in the Work Area will not be shown. The Work Area is a convenient place to store elements until you are ready to add them to the Stage, or for storing notes and other information you want to refer to as you develop the movie. You can also place a graphic in the Work Area and then animate it to move onto the stage.

Timeline

The **Timeline**, shown in Figure 1-23, is used to control and coordinate the frames and layers that make up a Flash movie. **Layers** are used to organize the images, animations, and other objects that are part of a movie. A **frame** represents a unit of time. Another key element of the Timeline is the **playhead**. The playhead is a marker that indicates which frame is currently selected on the Timeline. You will learn more about these and many of the other Timeline elements in later tutorials.

Figure 1-23	FLASH TIMELINE

Flash movies are divided into frames similar to a motion picture film. The Timeline is used to coordinate and control the timing of the animation by determining how and when these frames are displayed. Each frame may contain different images or different states of the same image. As the movie is played over time, the playhead moves from frame to frame and the contents of each frame are displayed in succession, thus achieving the perception of motion. You can also play the movie manually by dragging the playhead back and forth through the frames with your mouse. This is called **scrubbing** and is useful when testing the movie during development. When you first start a new movie in Flash it contains one frame. You add more frames as you build your movie.

In addition to frames, layers are also controlled using the Timeline. The layers are listed in a column on the left side of the Timeline. Each row within the column represents one layer. The frames for that layer are shown to the right of the layer. A new Flash movie starts with one layer. As you add more layers, additional rows representing the layers are inserted into the Timeline. You can then place different objects on the different layers. When you draw on a layer or change something on a layer, the objects on the other layers are not affected. Only the contents of the active layer are changed.

To explore the frames, layers, and playhead in the Timeline:

1. Scrub the playhead back and forth by clicking and dragging it with your pointer to see how the movie on the Stage changes based on the contents of the different frames. The animation changes as you scrub the playhead.

2. Click **Frame 15** in the Timeline header to make it the current frame as shown in Figure 1-24. The Stage displays the contents of Frame 15.

Figure 1-24	SELECTING A FRAME IN THE TIMELINE HEADER

Frame 15 in the Timeline header

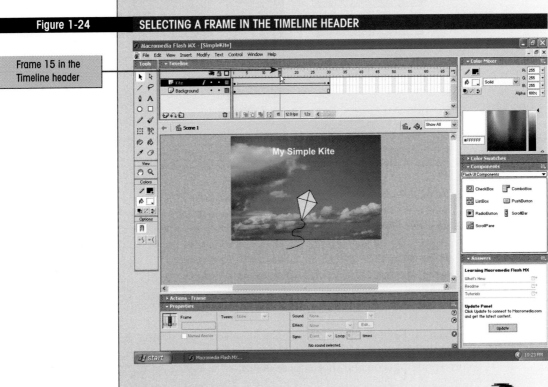

3. Click the dot in the Kite layer under the Show/Hide All Layers icon. The dot changes to a Hidden Layer ✕ icon and the contents of the Kite layer are temporarily hidden.

4. Click ✕ to unhide the contents of the Kite layer.

Now learn about the toolbox.

The Toolbox

The **toolbox** located on the left side of the Flash program window contains the tools that let you draw, paint, select, and modify Flash graphics. The toolbox, as shown in Figure 1-25, is divided into four areas. These areas are tools, view, colors, and options.

Figure 1-25   TOOLBOX TOOLS

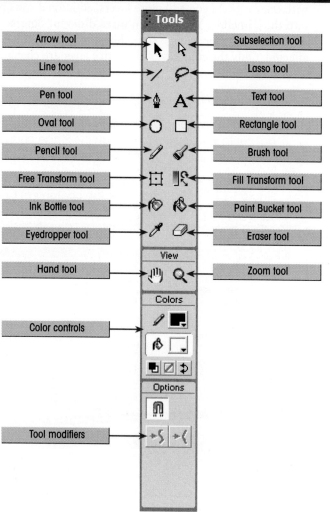

Each of the tools in these areas may be selected by clicking the tool's icon or by pressing the tool's keyboard shortcut. The function of each of the tools under the tools area and its corresponding icon and shortcut are described in Figure 1-26.

Figure 1-26	TOOLBOX TOOLS AND THEIR FUNCTIONS		

TOOL NAME	BUTTON	SHORTCUT KEY	FUNCTION
Arrow		V	Selects objects on the Work Area; an object must be selected before it can be modified
Subselection		A	Modifies specific anchor points in a line or curve
Line		N	Draws straight lines (strokes) of varying lengths, widths, and colors
Lasso		L	Selects objects or a group of objects
Pen		P	Draws lines or curves by creating anchor points that connect them. Clicking will draw points for straight lines. Clicking and dragging will draw points for smooth, curved lines
Text		T	Creates and edits text
Oval		O	Draws ovals of different sizes and colors
Rectangle		R	Draws rectangles of different sizes and colors
Pencil		Y	Draws lines and shapes in a free-form mode
Brush		B	Paints fills with brush strokes
Free Transform		Q	Use to move, scale, rotate, skew, or distort objects
Fill Transform		F	Use to transform a gradient or bitmap fill by adjusting its size, direction, or center point
Ink Bottle		S	Applies color, thickness, and styles to lines
Paint Bucket		K	Fills enclosed areas of a drawing with color
Eyedropper		I	Picks up styles of existing lines, fills, and text and applies them to other objects
Eraser		E	Erases lines and fills
Hand		H	Moves the view of the Stage and Work Area
Zoom		M,Z	Increases or reduces the view of the Stage and Work Area

The first area of the toolbox, **tools**, contains tools that are used to create and modify the lines, shapes, and text that make up the graphic images of a Flash movie. For example, you can draw ovals and rectangles, you can draw lines and curves, and you can fill in shapes with color. These tools also allow you to select specific parts of the graphic and then resize, rotate, and distort them to create new shapes.

The **view area** includes the **Hand tool** and the **Zoom tool**. The Hand tool converts the pointer to a hand that can then be dragged to move the view of the Stage. This is especially useful when you want to see a different area of a movie that has been magnified. The Zoom tool changes the view of the Stage by reducing or enlarging it. Neither of these tools affects the way the movie is displayed to the user.

The **colors area**, as shown in Figure 1-27, includes options to specify the colors for strokes and fills. **Strokes** refer to the lines that make up a Flash graphic and **fills** refer to the areas enclosed by the lines.

Figure 1-27   COLORS AREA

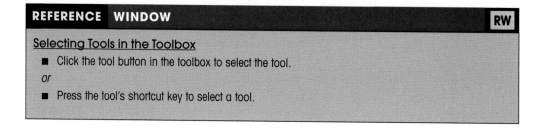

The Stroke Color control is used to set the stroke color. The Fill Color control is used to set the fill color. In either color control you select a color by clicking its color button and then choosing a color from the Color pop-up window. The bottom of this area has three additional icons. The Black and White button is used to change the stroke and fill colors to their default of black and white. The No Color button specifies that no color be used. This may be applied to either the stroke or the fill color. And the Swap Colors button swaps the current stroke and fill colors.

The last area of the toolbox is the **options area**. This area displays tool modifiers that change the way a specific tool functions. The modifiers in this area change to reflect the tool that is currently selected. For example, when the Zoom tool is selected, the Enlarge and Reduce buttons are displayed in the options area.

As you create movies in Flash, the tools you use most often will be those found in the toolbox. Always look carefully at which tool is currently selected before you click an object on the Stage. You can tell which tool is selected by seeing that its button is depressed in the toolbox. The mouse pointer also changes to reflect the function of the tool that is currently selected. For example, when the Zoom tool is selected, the pointer appears as a magnifying glass.

REFERENCE WINDOW   **RW**

Selecting Tools in the Toolbox
- Click the tool button in the toolbox to select the tool.

or

- Press the tool's shortcut key to select a tool.

Aly wants you to try using some of the tools in the toolbox to modify the SimpleKite document.

To use tools in the toolbox:

1. Click **Control** on the menu bar, and then click **Rewind** to make Frame 1 of the movie the current frame.

2. If necessary, click **View** on the menu bar, point to **Magnification**, and then click **Show All** from the Magnification menu to display all the movie's elements.

3. Click the **Arrow** tool in the toolbox. Click the **kite** in the Work Area to the left of the Stage to select it. Notice that a light-blue line surrounds the kite to indicate that it has been selected as shown in Figure 1-28. This is called a **selection box**.

Figure 1-28	KITE SELECTED

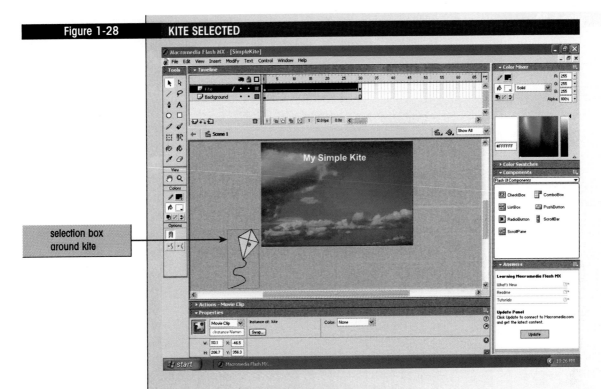

selection box
around kite

TROUBLE? If you accidently double-clicked the kite, the rest of the movie will
fade and you will be in a different editing mode. Click Scene 1 in the Work
Area's Address bar and repeat Step 3.

4. Click and drag the **kite** to a different position on the Stage.

Now preview the movie to see how moving the kite on the Stage has changed
the movie.

5. Click **Control** on the menu bar, and then click **Play**. Notice that the animation
has changed based on the different starting point of the kite.

Aly points out that there are many kinds of graphic objects you can create in Macromedia
Flash, and each object has different properties that you can control. Flash puts most of the
controls you need into panels that you can keep handy as you work.

Panels

Flash panels contain controls for viewing and changing the properties of objects. There are
also panels for aligning objects, transforming objects, and mixing and selecting colors. To
display a list of all of the available panels, you can click Window on the menu bar. Those
that appear with a check mark next to them are currently displayed in the Flash program
window. Panels can be organized according to your needs. You can close panels you do not
use often; you can reposition panels according to how you work; if desired, you can also
group several panels together. Once you customize how you want the panels arranged, you
can save the layout. Then next time you start Flash you can select your saved panel layout to
arrange the panels according to your customized arrangement. See Figure 1-29.

Figure 1-29   **PANELS IN THEIR DEFAULT LAYOUT**

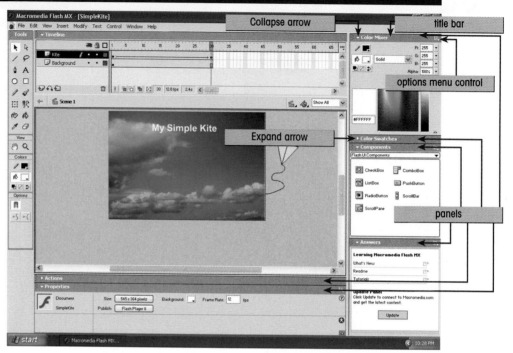

Organizing Panels

Each panel has a title bar with the name of the panel. Most panels also have an options menu that is accesible by clicking the options menu control located on the right side of the title bar. A panel can also be collapsed by clicking the Collapse arrow next to the panel's name in the title bar. When you collapse a panel, only the title bar is visible and the Collapse arrow changes to become an Expand arrow. When you click the Expand arrow, the panel is expanded again. To move a panel, you position the mouse pointer on the left edge of the panel's title bar until the pointer changes to ⟷, and then drag the title bar to the new location. To group panels into a set, you drag one panel into another or into an existing group.

To collapse, expand, and reposition a panel:

1. Click **Window** on the menu bar, point to **Panel Sets**, and then click **Default Layout**. The Color Mixer panel should be opened in the upper-right corner of the program window.

2. To collapse the Color Mixer panel, click the **Collapse** arrow ▽ as shown in Figure 1-30. The Color Mixer panel collapses and only the title bar is visible.

Figure 1-30	COLOR MIXER PANEL

3. To expand the panel click the **Expand** arrow ▷ in its title bar.

   Now reposition the Color Mixer panel.

4. Position the pointer on the left border of the Color Mixer title bar until the pointer changes to ⊕. Click and drag the panel to the middle of the screen. Release the mouse to place the panel in its new position.

   You can also group the Color Mixer panel and the Color Swatches panel together.

5. Click the **Expand** arrow ▷ in the Color Swatches panel's title bar to expand it if it is not already expanded.

6. Drag the Color Swatches panel and place it inside the window containing the Color Mixer panel. The Color Swatches panel and the Color Mixer panel are now grouped together as shown in Figure 1-31.

Figure 1-31 | GROUPED PANELS

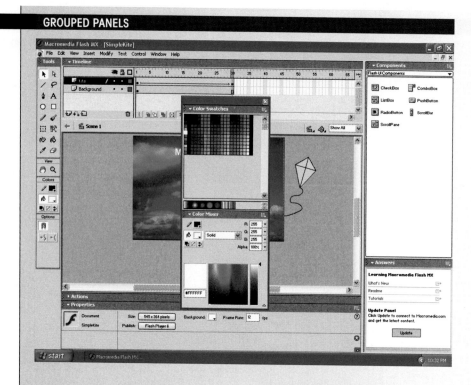

7. To move the panels back to their default layout, click **Window** on the menu bar, point to **Panel Sets**, and then click **Default Layout**.

Many of the most frequently used options are located in a special panel called the Property inspector. You will work with that panel next.

The Property Inspector

The **Property inspector** is a panel located at the bottom of the Flash program window. It provides easy access to the most common attributes of the currently selected tool or object. The contents of the Property inspector change to reflect the tool that is selected. For example, if you select the Arrow tool, the Property inspector displays information about the movie such as the background color or the frame rate, as shown in Figure 1-32.

Figure 1-32   PROPERTY INSPECTOR WHEN THE ARROW TOOL IS SELECTED

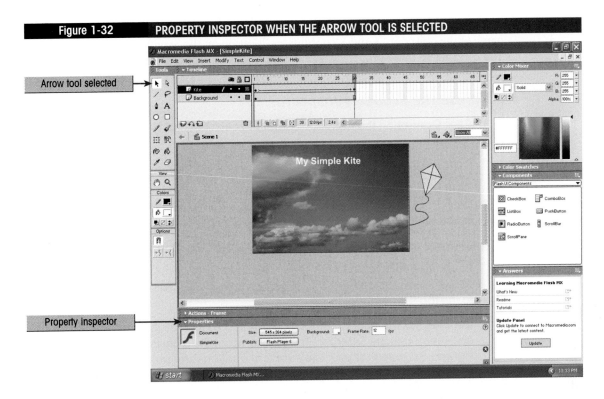

Arrow tool selected

Property inspector

If you select an object on the Stage such as the kite, the contents of the Property inspector change, as shown in Figure 1-33.

Figure 1-33   PROPERTY INSPECTOR WHEN AN OBJECT IS SELECTED

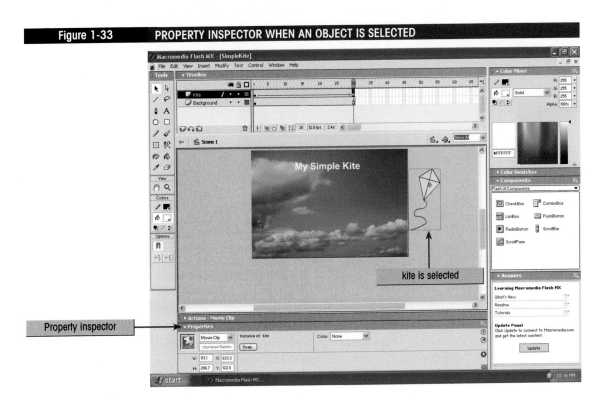

kite is selected

Property inspector

In this case the Property inspector displays properties specific to the object, such as the name of the object, its X and Y coordinates (location on the Stage), and its width and height. You can change these properties within the Property inspector.

To use the Property inspector:

1. Click **Control** on the menu bar, and then click **Rewind** to make Frame 1 the current frame.

2. If necessary, click **View** on the menu bar, point to **Magnification**, and then click **Show All**.

3. If the Properties inspector panel is not visible, click **Window** on the menu bar, and then click **Properties**.

4. Click the **Arrow** tool in the toolbox, and then click the **kite** to select it.

   To change the kite's position, you will change its X and Y coordinates. These values represent the horizontal (X) and vertical (Y) position of the kite relative to the top-left corner of the Stage.

5. Double-click the value in the **X:** text box in the Property inspector, type **100**, and then press the **Enter** key. The position of the kite changes horizontally. See Figure 1-34. Note that your kite's vertical position may be different from that shown in Figure 1-34.

| Figure 1-34 | KITE IN NEW POSITION |

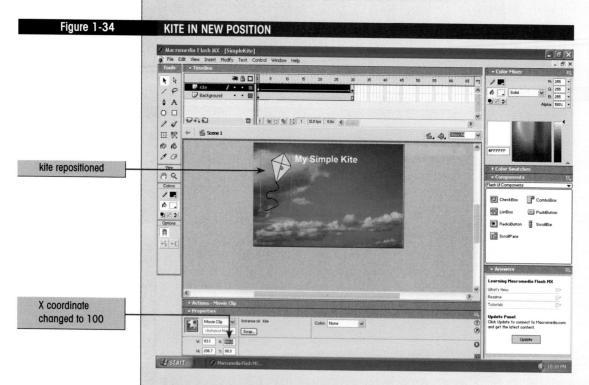

kite repositioned

X coordinate changed to 100

6. Double-click the value displayed in the **Y:** text box, type **100**, and then press the **Enter** key. The kite changes position vertically.

   You can also change the kite's dimensions by changing the width (W) value and the height (H) value.

7. Change the value in the **W:** text box to **100** in the Property inspector. The kite gets skinnier.

8. Change the value in the **H:** text box to **100**. The kite now appears shorter.

   Now you will play the SimpleKite movie to see the effect of the changes you made to the properties of the kite.

9. Click **Control** on the menu bar, and then click **Play**.

   The kite starts in its new position and moves to its end position as before. Notice that the kite gradually changes back to its orignal dimensions. Because you only changed the dimensions of the kite in Frame 1, Flash automatically adjusted the rest of the frames to change the kite to its original dimensions in the last frame. This feature of Flash will be covered in Tutorial 3.

Getting **Help in Flash**

There are several ways to access the Flash Help system. You can click Help on the menu bar, and then click Using Flash. You can press the F1 key on the keyboard. You can also click a panel's options menu control icon and then click Help from the options menu. Using a panel's options menu automatically displays the help information associated with that panel.

Regardless of the method you choose, the Macromedia Flash Help system displays in your default browser as a Web page with two panes. The pane on the left includes three tabs, Contents, Index, and Search. By default, Contents opens and displays a selection of three main categories, Using Flash, ActionScript Dictionary, and Tutorials. You click one of these categories to display a selection of subcategories, each of which contains a list of help topics. When you click one of the help topics, a page displays on the right pane with the associated help information. The help pages in the right pane also contain links to related topics. Clicking one of these links displays another page for that help topic.

The Index tab in the left pane will display a selection of letters linked to the various help topics. Clicking a letter displays the topics available for all items that start with that letter. For example, if you are looking for information on the Property inspector, you click the letter P. A list of all topics that begin with the letter P then display. You click the listed topic to open its help page in the right pane.

The Search tab opens a separate window in which you can type a keyword. The Search feature lists all the help topics containing the keyword. You then click a topic to display its help page in the right pane of the browser window. When you are done using the Search feature, you close the Search window.

Using the Contents option in the Flash Help system is an easy way to get Help. Aly wants you to try this method to obtain more information about the Property inspector. She wants you to gain experience with the Help system and also learn more about the Property inspector.

To use the Flash Help system to get more information about the Property inspector:

1. Click **Help** on the menu bar, and then click **Using Flash**. Your default browser opens and displays the Flash Help system. You can select a help category from the topics listed in the left pane.

2. Click the **Using Flash** category. A list of subcategories displays. Now you can select a subcategory.

3. Click the **Working in Flash** subcategory. A list of topics displays. Aly wants you to learn more about the Property inspector so you will select the appropriate topic in the list.

4. Click **Using the Property inspector to change document attributes**. The help page for this topic displays in the right pane as shown in Figure 1-35.

Figure 1-35   FLASH HELP SYSTEM

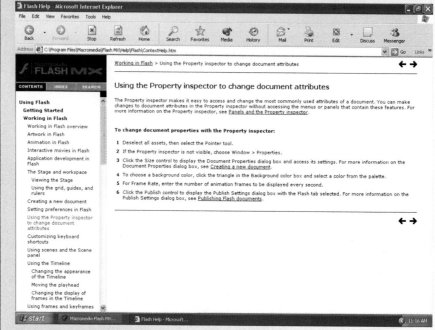

The help page provides information about the Property inspector and includes links to other related help pages.

5. Read through the information on the page, and then exit the Flash Help system by closing the browser window. You are returned to the Flash program window.

You have completed your exploration of the Flash program window. Now you will learn how to close a movie and exit Flash.

Closing a Movie and Exiting Flash

Once you finish working with a movie in Flash, you should close it. If necessary, first save the movie before you close it. Flash movies are saved in the FLA format.

To close a movie and exit Flash:

1. Click **File** on the menu bar, and then click **Close**. When prompted to save the file, click the **No** button. Because you have just been experimenting with Aly's SimpleKite document as you explored the Flash program window, you do not want to save the changes you made to it.

2. Click **File** on the menu bar, and then click **Exit** to exit Flash.

With Aly's help, you have spent some time with Macromedia Flash, and have begun working with the Flash program and become familiar with the program's main features. She has shown you the basic elements of the Flash program window including the tools and panels that you will be using as you create and modify movies.

Session 1.3 QUICK CHECK

1. What is the name of the area in which you position the objects that will appear in your movie?
2. What is the name of the area which displays your movie's frame and layer information?
3. What is the Hand tool used for?
4. Dragging the playhead back and forth in the Timeline to test a movie is called _____ .
5. A new Flash movie starts with _____ frame and _____ layer.
6. Which special panel changes to display different options depending on which tool or object is selected?
7. What are layers used for?

REVIEW ASSIGNMENTS

To review what you have learned with Macromedia Flash, Aly would like you to explore some of the sample Flash movies that are installed with the program and view other samples stored on the Macromedia Web site. She would also like you to modify the SimpleKite movie. By practicing these skills you will be better prepared to use Flash to develop graphics for Actions Web Design's clients.

If necessary, start Flash, insert your Data Disk in the appropriate drive, and then do the following:

1. Click Window on the menu bar, point to Panel Sets, and click Default Layout to place the panels in their default positions.
2. Click Help on the menu bar, and then click Samples. Internet Explorer opens and displays a Web page with a list of Flash sample movie files. To view a sample movie, click its link. Read the information provided with the sample movie, and then experiment with the interactive components, if available, of the movie. To return to the list of sample movies, use the browser's Back button.
3. Connect to the Internet. With your browser still open, type **http://www.macromedia.com** in the Address bar, and press the Enter key to open the Macromedia home page.
4. Look for the link for Products, and click it to open the Products page. Locate the link for Macromedia Flash MX and click it to open its page. On the Flash product page, look for a link or category called Showcase. If necessary, click Showcase and look for a Case Studies link. Click the Case Studies link to view a list of Web sites that use Flash.
5. Click one of the case study links in the Macromedia Showcase page to view a page with more information about the particular Web site. This page should include a graphic related to the case study and a link to its associated Web site. Click this link to go to the actual case study Web site. The site should open in a separate browser window.
6. As you navigate to some of the sites showcased, study and compare the animation effects you see. Listen for sound effects, music, and voiceovers. See if you can distinguish between bitmap and vector graphics. To view other showcased Web sites, close the browser window that opened in Step 5, and use the Back button on the browser window displaying the Macromedia Web site to return to the list of showcased links. When you are done exploring the showcased sites, close Internet Explorer.
7. Return to Flash and open the SimpleKite file stored in the Tutorial.01\Tutorial folder on your Data Disk. Make sure the magnification level is set to Show All. Click Control and then click Rewind to make Frame 1 the current frame.

Explore   8. Click the Collapse arrow for the Color Mixer panel to collapse it. Also collapse the Components and Answers panels if they are expanded.

Explore   9. Click Window on the menu bar, and then click Library to open the Library panel. This panel contains the objects that are part of this movie. Drag the Library panel window to the right side of the program window under the collapsed panels.

10. Click the Arrow tool in the toolbox to select it, and then click the kite.

Explore   11. Click the Swap button in the Property inspector. In the Swap Symbol dialog box, click balloon to select the balloon symbol, and then click OK. The yellow kite is now replaced by a red balloon.

Explore   12. Click Control on the menu bar, and then click Go To End to move the playhead to the last frame (Frame 30). Select the kite on the Stage, then click the Swap button in the Property inspector, and select the balloon symbol to replace the kite symbol with the balloon.

13. Play the movie to test the changes you have made.

Explore   14. Rewind the movie. Change the image in the background of the movie by first clicking the sky bitmap graphic on the Stage to select it. Swap the sky bitmap with the sky2 bitmap using the Swap button in the Property inspector.

Explore   15. On the Stage, double-click the text My Simple Kite. Change the word Kite to **Balloon**. When you are done editing the text, click the Arrow tool in the toolbox.

16. Click File and Save As to save the revised movie. Name the file **SimpleBalloon** and save it to your Data Disk in the Tutorial.01\Review folder. Exit Flash.

CASE PROBLEMS

Case 1. Exploring Web Media on the Internet Noh Boarders is a small windsurfing equipment company located in Santa Rosa, California. They design custom sailboards and sails for windsurfers in the San Francisco Bay area. Started by designer-craftsman Andy Murakami ten years ago, Noh Boarders has succeeded in establishing a solid base of regular customers, both by word of mouth and by their Web site. A few years ago, Andy was joined by Meg Harrison, a graphic designer who shared his love of windsurfing and Japanese art. They often employ motifs derived from Japanese designs in their boards and sails. Andy and Meg are aware of the potential that animation holds for helping their Web site actively convey the elegance of their company's designs around the world. As a result, they have hired you to improve their Web site with Macromedia Flash animation.

Because the Web site will be improved with Flash, you decide to find Flash resources on the Internet and to explore examples of Web media that may be used for the Web site.

If necessary, start Internet Explorer, connect to the Internet, and do the following:

1. Open the home page for Macromedia at **http://www.macromedia.com**. Click the Support link, and then select Macromedia Flash to go to the Flash Support Center. Within this page there are many links to tutorials, sample files, and technical updates. Look for a section on "More Resources," and then look for a link to "Web sites devoted to Macromedia Flash and Macromedia Flash developers." Follow this link, and then look for a list of Web site links. Navigate to several of the sites and explore the resources they provide. Look for examples of Flash movies and other Web media. Each site opens in a separate browser window, so to get back to the Macromedia site, be sure to close the window that the site opens in. Record the URL of the two sites you like best. Record what you like best about each site (e.g., resources, Web media, etc.).

2. Open the home page for the Flashkit site at **http://www.flashkit.com**. At the home page for this Web site, look for a list of hyperlinks, usually located at the top of page. In this list of hyperlinks, click the link to "Featured" sites. Follow the links to several of the featured sites to see examples of how Flash is being used. Each site opens in a separate browser window, so to get back to the Flashkit site, be sure to close the window that the site opens in. Record the URL of the two sites you like best. Record what you like best about each site (e.g., colors, sound, pictures, navigation, etc.).

3. At the Flashkit site, look for and click the link for the "Gallery." This leads to a page where you can see different types of Web media. Scroll down and look for a category that you like. Click the category's link. At the category's page, scroll down to see a list of graphic images available for download. Notice that each image has information such as its width, height, size in number of bytes, and its format, such as .jpg or .gif. If an image has a link, click it to see the image displayed in its actual size. Find at least three examples of .jpg images and three examples of .gif images. Record the information provided about each of these images (name, width, height, size, and format). Based on the images you saw, record what you think are the main differences between the .jpg and .gif formats.

4. Close Internet Explorer and close your Internet connection, if necessary.

Case 2. Customizing the Flash Program Window Orkney Sportswear specializes in a wide variety of outerwear, sportswear, footwear, and accessories. They pride themselves in developing innovative products that are functional and stylish. Their chief designer is Moira Shapiro. The recent discovery of an early Viking treasure boat off the Scottish coast has inspired her to create decorative motifs for a new line of shirts based on some runic symbols and other designs found in the wreck.

As a result, Moira is commissioning you to develop a Macromedia Flash animation to promote the new shirts on their Web site. The animation is expected to integrate the ancient symbols—and their history—with her new clothing designs.

In preparation for this new request, you decide to practice with Flash to learn how to customize the panels you will use regularly.

If necessary, start Flash, insert your Data Disk in the appropriate drive, and then do the following:

1. To learn how to organize the panels and to save the customized settings, start by setting the panels to their default layout. Click Window on the menu bar, point to Panel Sets, and then click Default Layout.

2. Click Window, and then click Align to open the Align panel. The panel opens in its own window. Move this window to the left side of the screen by clicking and dragging the window's title bar. Also open the Info panel and the Transform panel. Note that as you open new panels, they may cover panels that are already opened.

3. To group these three panels into one window, you start by dragging the Info panel out of its own window and into the Align panel's window. Point to the left edge of the Info panel's title bar to the left of the Collapse arrow. When the pointer changes to a 4-headed arrow, drag the panel and drop it inside the Align panel's window. The two panels should now be grouped into one window.

4. Repeat these steps to drag the Transform panel into the window with the Info and Align panels. All three panels should now be grouped together.

Explore 5. Click Window on the menu bar, and click Save Panel Layout. Name the saved layout **My Layout**.

6. To test this setting, return the panels to their default layout. Click Window, point to Panel Layout, and click Default Layout. The panels return to their original arrangement.

7. Click Window, point to Panel Sets, and this time click My Layout, which now appears on the list of panel layouts. The panel arrangement should reflect the changes you made.

Explore 8. To get a printout showing your panel arrangement, first copy the screen image to the Windows clipboard. Do this by pressing the Print Screen key on the keyboard. Start the WordPad program by clicking the Start button, pointing to All Programs, pointing to Accessories, and then clicking WordPad. In the WordPad document window, type your name as the first line on the document. Press the Enter key. Click Edit on the menu bar, and then click Paste to paste the image of the Flash program window below your name. To print this WordPad document, click File on the menu bar, and then click Print. In the Print dialog box, click Print again. Once you have your printout, close Wordpad. You do not need to save the document.

9. Exit the Flash program.

QUICK CHECK ANSWERS

Session 1.1

1. The Internet is a vast Web of networks and subnetworks connecting millions of individual computer users to each other around the world.
2. HTTP is the communications protocol for transferring information on the Internet.
3. An ISP is an Internet service provider.
4. An IP address consists of four sets of three-digits numbers.
5. Each three-digit number in an IP address can range from 000 to 255.
6. The Internet is composed of client and server computers.
7. A domain name uniquely identifies a server computer on the Internet (without specifying a protocol). A URL (Uniform Resource Locator) uniquely identifies a file on the Internet, including the protocol, domain name, and path.
8. A Web page is a single HTML file on the Internet. A Web site is a collection of related Web pages that are linked to each other.
9. The first page a browser opens when it starts is called the browser's home page.
10. The top-level entry page of a Web site is also called the Web site's home page.
11. A hyperlink's URL appears in the status bar when you point to the hyperlink.
12. When you click a hyperlink, the browser attempts to locate the linked resource on the Internet (typically a Web page or a specific location in a Web page), and open it in the browser window.

Session 1.2

1. Flash creates vector-based images.
2. A completed Flash file published for Internet delivery is called a Macromedia Flash Player movie and is in the SWF format.
3. Three things you might find in a Flash movie include any of the following: still imagery, sound, animation, hyperlinks, buttons, text, and scripted programming.
4. True. Flash allows you to synchronize sound with events in your movie.
5. Bitmap graphics store information in a grid of pixels.
6. Vector graphics store image data as a set of mathematical instructions that describe the color, outline, and position of all the shapes of the image.
7. The term "resolution independent" applies to vector graphics.
8. A bitmap image that has been enlarged looks jagged or blurred.

Session 1.3

1. The area in which you position the objects that will appear in your movie is called the Stage.
2. The area which displays your movie's frame and layer information is called the Timeline.
3. The Hand tool is used for moving the view of the Stage and Work Area.
4. Dragging the playhead back and forth in the timeline to test a movie is called scrubbing.
5. A new Flash movie starts with one frame and one layer.
6. The Property inspector changes to display different options depending on which tool or object is selected.
7. Layers are used to organize the images, animations, and other objects that are part of a movie.

OBJECTIVES

In this tutorial you will:

- Set the document's properties

- Display grid lines, guides, and rulers

- Select objects and modify them

- Draw lines, curves, ovals, and rectangles

- Apply stroke and fill colors

- Modify strokes and fills

- Transform graphic objects using the Free Transform tool

- Create text blocks

- Export a graphic for use on a Web site

USING THE TOOLS IN THE TOOLBOX

Creating a Banner for the Flounders Pet Shop Web Site

CASE

Actions Web Design

Actions Web Design has developed a number of different Web sites for its clients. The focus of the company has been to design easy-to-use, informative, and effective Web sites. Each Web site has been designed with the needs of the client in mind and the clients have been very pleased with the results. Now several of the clients have requested some enhancements to their Web sites. One of these clients is Flounders Pet Shop, a small business specializing in selling pets and related pet supplies. The owner of the pet shop, Joe Flounders, has requested that a new banner be developed for his Web site to promote a special sale on fish and aquariums. As a result, Gloria Adamson has asked Aly to work on this request along with Chris Johnson, one of Actions' Web designers.

Aly and Chris hold a planning meeting with Joe Flounders to discuss his request. You are invited to the planning meeting because you will be working under Aly's supervision to create the banner. At the meeting, Joe expresses his wish for a colorful banner with graphic images of fish. Aly suggests the banner resemble an aquarium with several fish and plants inside the aquarium. Joe is very excited about this idea and Chris thinks that such a banner will blend well with the current design of the pet shop's home page. Aly sketches a draft of the banner so everyone can see what it will look like. After further discussion and revisions to the sketch, everyone is in agreement and you are assigned the task of creating the banner using Macromedia Flash according to the sketch shown in Figure 2-1.

Figure 2-1   SKETCH OF THE BANNER FOR THE FLOUNDERS PET SHOP WEB SITE

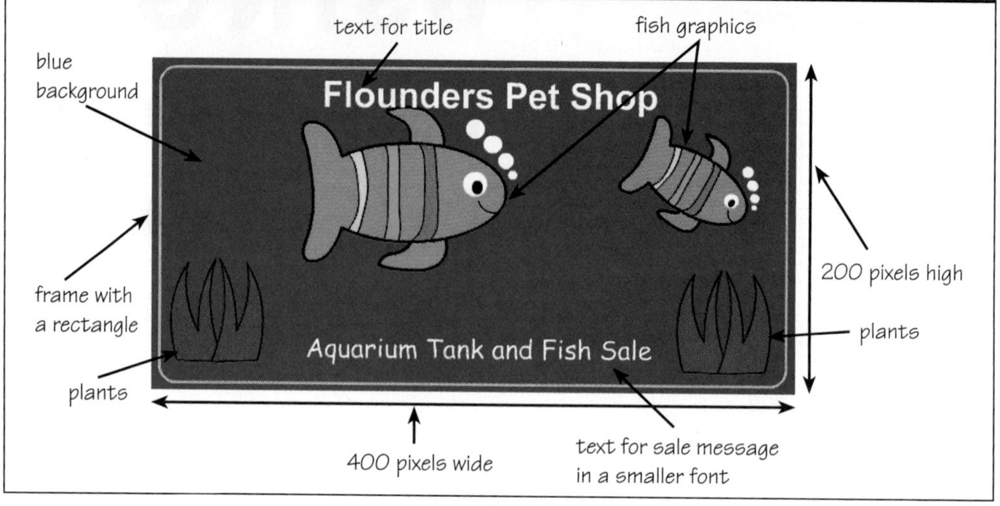

As you use Flash to create the banner for the Flounders Pet Shop in this tutorial, you will learn how to use the selection and drawing tools, text tools, and tools for modifying graphic objects. You will also learn how to select and apply colors. You will modify existing graphics, create new graphics for the banner, and then export the banner for use on the Flounders Pet Shop's Web site.

SESSION 2.1

In this session you will learn how to adjust the view of the Stage and Work Area to make working with Macromedia Flash graphics more efficient. You will see how to change the dimensions and background color of the Stage, and you will learn how to add a grid, guides, and rulers to the Stage to help align graphic objects. You will also learn the difference between strokes and fills. You will learn how objects connect with or split existing objects when drawn or moved to overlap each other, and how to avoid these effects by grouping objects together. Finally, you will use the selection tools to select individual objects or a group of objects.

Setting the Stage

When you start Macromedia Flash, the program creates a new document. This document will be called a movie once it is published for display on the Web. Recall from Tutorial 1 that the document is displayed on the Stage, which is where you create, import, and assemble all of the graphic objects for your document. The Stage is the central area of the document window and is within the Work Area. The Work Area is a convenient place to store elements until you are ready to add them to the Stage; it is also handy for storing notes and other information to which you want to refer as you create your document. Any graphic object that is to be part of your movie must be on the Stage, whether it is a static object or one that is animated.

Changing the View of the Stage

As you develop graphics on the Stage, you at times need to change your view of the Stage by adjusting the magnification level. You do this by using the Zoom tool in the toolbox. When you select the Zoom tool the **Enlarge** and **Reduce** modifiers display in the options area of the toolbox. The Enlarge modifier is selected by default. If you want to use the Zoom tool to reduce the magnification level of the Stage, then click the Reduce modifier. Once you select the Zoom tool, you click the part of the Stage that you want to enlarge or reduce. You can also click and drag the pointer over a certain area of the Stage to draw a rectangular selection marquee around it. This selects the area to enlarge. A **marquee** is a temporary outline drawn around an object to select it. The concept of selecting objects in Flash is covered in more detail later in this session.

In addition to the Zoom tool, you can also use the **Zoom In** or **Zoom Out** commands on the View menu. The Zoom In and Zoom Out commands change the view of the Stage accordingly. Another command on the View menu is the Magnification command, which has a submenu of percentage levels that can be applied to the view of the Stage, and the commands Show All, and Show Frame. Selecting the **Show All** command changes the view of the Stage to display all of its current contents including objects in the Work Area. Selecting the **Show Frame** command displays the entire Stage. The commands found on the Magnification submenu are also available on the Zoom control located in the upper-right corner of the Stage window.

Once you have magnified the view of the Stage, some graphic objects may no longer be visible within the Stage window. To move the view of the Stage without having to change the magnification you can use the Hand tool. You select the Hand tool from the toolbox and then click and drag the pointer on the Stage to move it so that the graphic objects you need to work on become visible within the Stage window.

REFERENCE WINDOW   **RW**

Changing the View of the Stage:

- Click the Zoom tool in the toolbox.
- In the options area of the toolbox, click the Enlarge or Reduce modifiers.
- Click a part of the Stage to enlarge or reduce it, or click and drag the pointer to draw a rectangular selection marquee around the part of the Stage you want to enlarge or reduce.

or

- Click View on the menu bar.
- Click the Zoom In or Zoom out command, or point to Magnification, and click a percentage level. Or click Show All, or Show Frame.

Before you begin working on the banner for the Flounders Pet Shop, Aly suggests you start Macromedia Flash and familiarize yourself with the various ways to change the view of the Stage. You will use a document of Aly's that contains sample objects she has drawn in Flash.

To open the Sample document and change the view of the Stage:

1. Make sure that your computer is turned on and that the Windows desktop is displayed. Also make sure that your Data Disk is in the appropriate drive.

2. Click the **Start** button 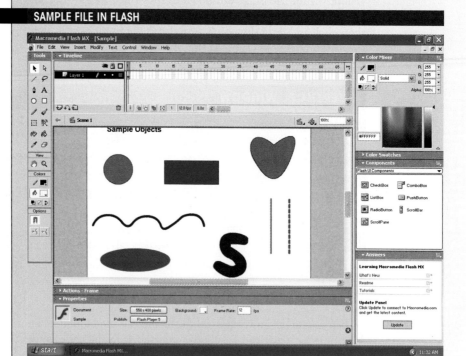 on the taskbar, point to **All Programs**, and then point to **Macromedia**. Click **Macromedia Flash MX** to start the program.

3. To position the panels to match the layout shown in the figures in this book, click **Window** on the menu bar, point to **Panel Sets**, and then click **Default Layout**. The panels are repositioned to their default positions. Now you can open Aly's document of sample objects drawn in Flash. The file is named Sample.fla and is stored on your Data Disk.

   TROUBLE? If the Panel Sets menu is not available on the Window menu, click File on the menu bar, click New to create a new document, and then repeat Step 3.

4. Click **File** on the menu bar, and then click **Open**. In the Open dialog box, select the drive containing your Data Disk from the Look in: list box, double-click the **Tutorial.02** folder, and then double-click the **Tutorial** folder in the **Tutorial.02** folder on your Data Disk. Click **Sample.fla** in the file list, and then click the **Open** button to open the file in the program window. See Figure 2-2.

   TROUBLE? If the Sample file does not include the FLA extension in its filename, your computer's operating system may not be configured to display file extensions. If this is the case, just click the file named Sample in the file list.

Figure 2-2   **SAMPLE FILE IN FLASH**

You should close the Timeline panel because you will not be using it in this tutorial, and closing it will provide more room for your work on the Stage.

5. Click **Window** on the menu bar, and click the **Timeline** command to remove the check mark and close the Timeline. Now display the entire Stage in the program window.

6. Click **View** on the menu bar, point to **Magnification**, and then click **Show Frame**. The zoom level changes to make all of the Stage visible.

7. Click the **Zoom control** list arrow in the upper-right corner of the Stage window, and then click **50%**. The view of the document on the Stage changes as shown in Figure 2-3.

Figure 2-3	STAGE VIEW AT 50% MAGNIFICATION

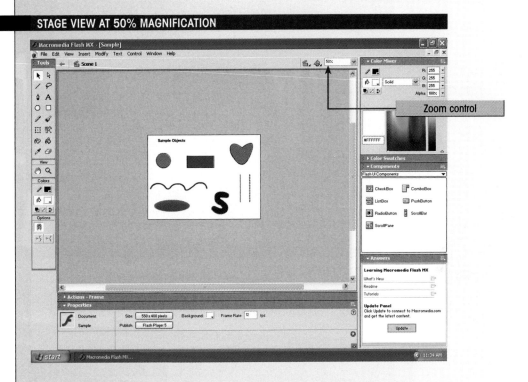

Next use the Zoom tool to change the magnification of the Stage.

8. Click the **Zoom** tool 🔍 in the view area of the toolbox, and then click the **Enlarge** modifier ⊕ in the options area of the toolbox. The pointer changes to ⊕.

9. Click the middle of the **heart-shaped object** on the Stage, and then click the **heart** one more time. The magnification level of the view increases each time you click the heart. The heart also appears in the center of the Stage window each time you click it.

You can also use the Hand tool to adjust the view of the Stage. This tool is useful when you want to focus on a particular portion of the Stage without changing the magnification level. Try that next.

To use the Hand tool to view a different portion of the Stage:

1. Click the **Hand** tool 🖐 in the view area of the toolbox. The pointer changes to a hand 🖐 as you move it over the **Stage**.

2. Using the 🖐, click and drag the **Stage** to the right until you see the red circle in the middle of the Stage as shown in Figure 2-4.

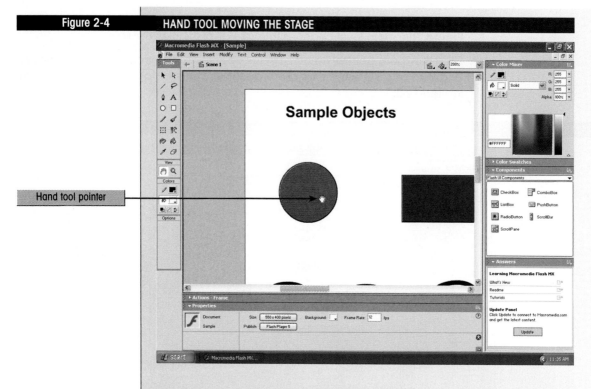

Figure 2-4   HAND TOOL MOVING THE STAGE

Hand tool pointer

Now reduce the magnification of the Stage.

3. Click 🔍 and then click the **Reduce** modifier 🔍. The pointer changes to 🔍.

4. Click the center of the **rectangle**, and then click the **rectangle** one more time. The magnification level of the Stage reduces each time you click.

When working with a Flash document, as you enlarge, reduce, or move the Stage view you will often want to quickly return to a view that shows all of the Stage centered in the Stage window. You can easily do this by double-clicking the Hand tool. This can also be accomplished by clicking the Show Frame command on the View menu.

5. Double-click the **Hand tool** 🖐 in the toolbox. The view changes to show all of the Stage centered in the Stage window.

The Stage also includes some features designed to aid you as you create your documents. These features are the grid, the rulers, and guides.

Displaying the Grid, Rulers, and Guides

When working with Macromedia Flash you can lay out objects on the Stage more precisely if you display the Grid. The **Grid** appears as a set of lines on the Stage behind all of the objects you place or draw on the Stage. The grid lines do not become part of your document. They are only visible while you are developing your document. The Grid menu offers several commands for controlling the grid, and is located on the View menu. For example, to display the grid on the Stage, you use the Show Grid command. The Grid menu also includes the Edit Grid command which opens the Edit Grid dialog box in which you can change the color of the grid lines and change the spacing between the lines. You can also select the Snap to Grid option if you want objects to snap to the grid lines as you move or draw them on the Stage. This can help you align different objects vertically or horizontally. Changes you make to the grid are saved with the currently active document.

Aly suggests that you practice with the Sample document and explore how to change its settings. You will first display the grid.

To display and edit the grid:

1. Click **View** on the menu bar, point to **Grid**, and then click the **Show Grid** command to place a check mark next to it. The grid lines are displayed on the Stage. See Figure 2-5.

Figure 2-5	GRID DISPLAYED ON THE STAGE

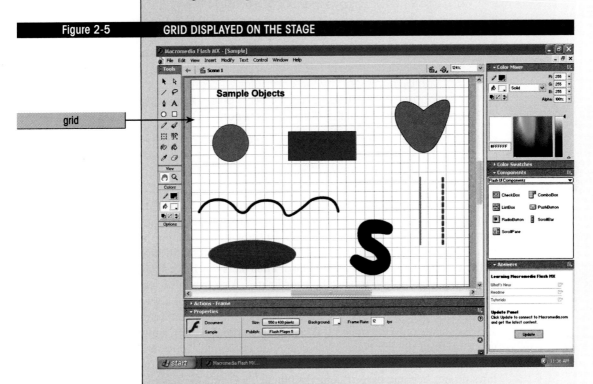

grid

You can modify how the grid is displayed on the Stage to better suit your needs and work habits. To do this you access the different options for the grid from the Edit Grid dialog box.

2. Click **View** on the menu bar, point to **Grid**, and then click **Edit Grid**. The Grid dialog box opens as shown in Figure 2-6.

Figure 2-6	GRID DIALOG BOX

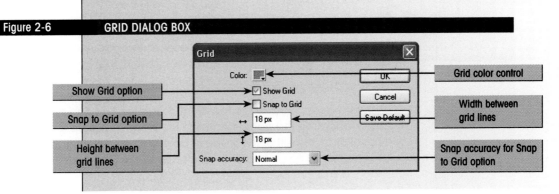

Show Grid option

Snap to Grid option

Height between grid lines

Grid color control

Width between grid lines

Snap accuracy for Snap to Grid option

In this dialog box, you can select a specific color for the grid lines. This may be necessary if the background color of the document is similar to the grid lines color, in which case the grid lines may be hard to see.

3. Click the **Color list arrow** to open the color pop-up window. The pointer changes to an eyedropper ✎.

4. Click the **yellow color swatch** located in the first column, tenth row of the color pop-up window.

Also, you can use the grid lines as you draw or move objects on the Stage. By turning on the Snap to Grid option, objects will snap to, or align with, the nearest grid line when you move them or as you draw them.

5. Click the **Snap to Grid** check box to select that option.

The width and height values are expressed in pixels. A **pixel** is a unit of measurement that represents the smallest picture element on the monitor screen that can be controlled by the computer. Web graphics and other elements on Web pages are commonly measured in pixels. In the grid settings the width and height represent the distance between the lines.

6. Click **OK** to close the dialog box. The Grid lines now reflect the settings you selected in the Grid dialog box.

Another option that can be very helpful when you are developing your graphics is to display the **rulers**. These rulers are vertically displayed on the left edge of the Stage window and horizontally displayed on the top edge. To show the rulers, you select the Rulers command on the View menu. The rulers show the unit of measurement, such as pixels, that is specified in the Document Properties dialog box. The rulers can be very helpful when placing objects on the Stage according to specific coordinates. Also, when the rulers are displayed you can create vertical or horizontal guides. A **guide** is a line used to align objects that can be moved to a specific part of the Stage using the rulers for reference. To create a guide, click a ruler and drag a line onto the Stage. If you drag from the top ruler, a horizontal guide is created. If you drag from the left ruler, a vertical guide is created. You can also edit the guide lines to change their color, to have objects snap to them, and to lock them into place. Just as the grid lines do not become part of your document, the same applies to the guide lines as they are only visible while you are working with your document. Also, guide lines can be created whether the grid is displayed or not.

Aly wants you to practice creating guide lines using the Sample document. You will need to display the rulers first before creating guide lines. You will also practice changing the guide line properties.

To display the Rulers and create guides:

1. Click **View** on the menu bar, and then click **Rulers**. The rulers are displayed in the Stage window.

2. Make sure the **Arrow** tool ▸ is selected in the toolbox.

3. Click the horizontal ruler at the top of the Stage window. The pointer changes to ▸₋. Click and drag the pointer down to the Stage to create a guide. Use the vertical ruler on the left of the Stage to position the horizontal guide so that it is approximately 50 pixels from the top border of the Stage. It should snap to the closest grid line. See Figure 2-7.

Figure 2-7	HORIZONTAL GUIDE LINE

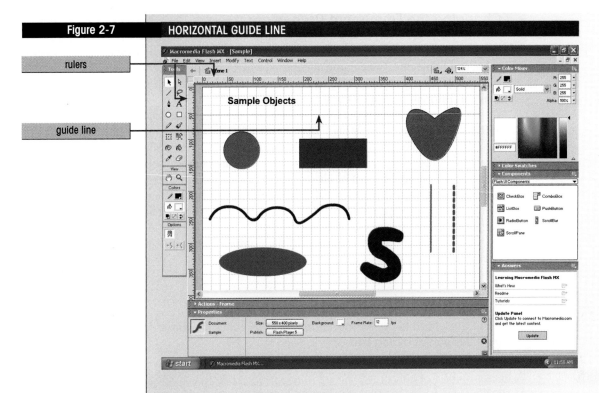

rulers

guide line

Next you will create a vertical guide.

4. Click the vertical ruler on the left edge of the Stage, and drag the pointer to the Stage to create a vertical guide. Use the horizontal ruler at the top of the Stage to line up the guide so that it is approximately 100 pixels from the left border of the Stage. It should snap to the closest grid line.

5. Click **View** on the menu bar, point to **Guides**, and then click **Edit Guides**. The Guides dialog box opens as shown on Figure 2-8.

Figure 2-8	GUIDES DIALOG BOX

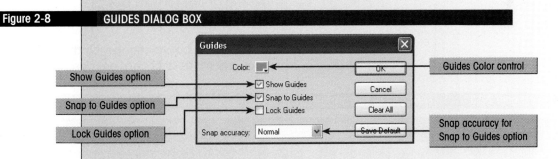

Show Guides option

Snap to Guides option

Lock Guides option

Guides Color control

Snap accuracy for
Snap to Guides option

If necessary, the color of the guide lines can be changed to make them easier to see against the background color.

6. Click the **Color list arrow** to open the color pop-up window. The pointer changes to an eyedropper ✐.

7. Click the **red color swatch** located in the first column, seventh row of the pop-up window.

8. Click the **OK** button to close the dialog box. The guide lines are now red.

Changing the Document Properties

Every document in Macromedia Flash has certain properties, such as Stage size, background color, and frame rate. (The frame rate is used when working with animations and specifies how many frames are to be displayed in one second. You will learn about using frames for animations in Tutorial 3.) The document properties are set at default values when you first open a new document in the program. For example, the Stage size has the default dimensions of 550 pixels wide by 400 pixels high. In addition to the default dimensions, the Stage background color is set to white, the frame rate is set to 12 frames per second and the ruler units are set to pixels. The ruler units determine what unit of measurement is displayed on the rulers. A document's default properties can be changed by accessing the Document Properties dialog box. To open the Document Properties dialog box, you select the Document command on the Modify menu. You can also open the Document Properties dialog box by clicking the Size button in the document Property inspector. Changes you make in the dialog box are reflected on the Stage.

Aly suggests you practice changing the Sample document's properties by changing its background color.

To change the Sample document's background color:

1. Click **Modify** on the menu bar, and then click **Document**. The Document Properties dialog box opens. See Figure 2-9.

Figure 2-9	DOCUMENT PROPERTIES DIALOG BOX

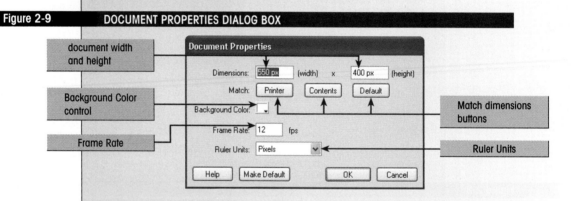

You can use the options in this dialog box to change the dimensions and background color of the document. These options are described in Figure 2-10.

Figure 2-10	OPTIONS IN THE DOCUMENT PROPERTIES DIALOG BOX

OPTION	DESCRIPTION
Dimensions (width and height)	Values for the size of the Stage are entered into the width and height text boxes
Match: Printer	Matches the size of the Stage to be the same as the maximum print area
Match: Contents	Matches the size of the Stage to that of the current contents; an equal amount of space is placed around all sides of the existing contents
Match: Default	Sets the size of the stage to the default values for width and height
Background Color	Opens a color palette to select a color for the Stage's background
Frame Rate	Determines how many frames of animation are displayed per second; a frame is one particular image in a series of images that create an animation
Ruler Units	Determines what unit of measurement is displayed on the rulers

2. Click the **Background Color** list arrow to open its color pop-up window. Using the eyedropper ✏ click the **light-gray** color swatch (first column, fifth row).

The default setting of 12 for the Frame Rate is appropriate, as is the Ruler Units at pixels. You can close the Document Properties dialog box.

3. Click the **OK** button to close the dialog box. The Stage now appears with the new background color.

Now that you have set the Stage and changed the document properties, you feel ready to begin drawing images. Aly decides to review some basic drawing terms and concepts that you will need to understand before you continue your work in Flash.

Drawing in Macromedia Flash

Recall from Tutorial 1 that the drawing and painting tools available with Macromedia Flash include the Line, Pen, Pencil, Oval, Rectangle, and Brush. These tools allow you to create the lines and shapes that make up the images in a Flash document. Before using these tools it is important to understand how the objects you draw behave and how you can change their basic characteristics, such as their color. In particular, you need to be aware of how shapes or lines you draw interact with existing shapes or lines.

Also, when drawing objects you can specify the colors for the lines and shapes before or after you draw them. Selecting the colors can be done through the toolbox color controls, the color controls in the Property inspector, or through the Color Mixer panel.

Strokes and Fills

When drawing objects in Flash you create strokes and fills. **Strokes** are the lines that you draw. These lines may be straight or curved and can either be individual line segments or they can connect together to form shapes. The drawing tools in Flash give you a great deal of flexibility and allow you to draw almost any type of line you need for your document. **Fills** are the areas you paint with color. These areas may or may not be enclosed by strokes.

Before you draw a shape, such as an oval or a rectangle, you can specify whether you want the shape to have a stroke, a fill, or both. For example, you can draw a circle that has both a fill and a stroke. You can draw one that has a painted fill but has no stroke. Or you can draw the circle with a stroke but no fill. See the examples in Figure 2-11.

Figure 2-11	SAMPLE SHAPES WITH FILLS AND STROKES

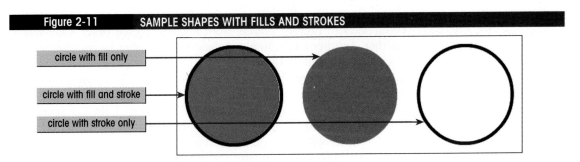

circle with fill only

circle with fill and stroke

circle with stroke only

You can also add a stroke or fill after you draw an object, and you can always modify its stroke or fill properties.

When drawing objects you need to be aware of how the various objects interact with each other and how you can control their interaction.

Grouping Objects

All objects drawn on the Stage are at the same level unless they reside on different layers. **Layers**, which are covered in more detail in a later tutorial, allow you to organize the various graphic objects that are part of a document and to keep these objects from changing each other when they overlap. Layers are displayed in the document's Timeline. By default, a Flash document starts with one layer, but you can add more layers as needed.

Objects on the same layer are not considered to be on top of or below one another. As a result, objects drawn or moved on top of other objects connect with or **segment** the existing objects. For example, when you draw a line through an existing shape such as a circle, the line is split into line segments at the points where it intersects the circle. The circle is also split into separate shapes. These line segments and split shapes can then be moved individually as shown in Figure 2-12.

Also, if you draw a fill on top of another fill of the same color the two fills connect and become one shape. If you draw a fill of one color on top of another fill of a different color, then the new fill cuts away at the existing fill as shown in Figure 2-12.

Figure 2-12	LINES AND SHAPES INTERSECTING EACH OTHER

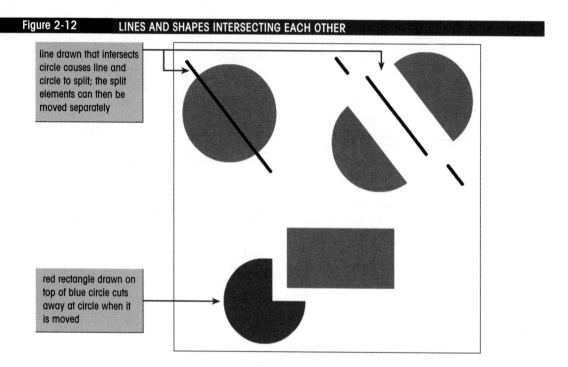

line drawn that intersects circle causes line and circle to split; the split elements can then be moved separately

red rectangle drawn on top of blue circle cuts away at circle when it is moved

There are several ways to prevent objects from impacting each other. One way is to group objects together. Another way is to place objects on different layers. Placing objects on different layers will be covered in Tutorial 3.

If you want to treat two or more objects such as a stroke and a fill as one entity, you can group them. To group the objects you first select them at the same time using the Arrow tool. Selecting objects is covered later in this tutorial. You then click the Group command on the Modify menu. A thin, blue rectangular outline appears around the grouped object when it is selected. Grouped objects are on top of nongrouped objects so they do not connect with or segment other objects. To modify a grouped object, you select the object, and then click the Edit Selected command under the Edit menu. You can also double-click the grouped object. You can then edit the individual objects within the group. When editing the objects within a group, the rest of the objects on the Stage are dimmed, indicating they are not accessible as shown in Figure 2-13. Once you are done modifying the individual objects you exit the group editing mode by clicking the Edit All command on the Edit menu or by double-clicking a blank area of the Stage away from the grouped object.

Figure 2-13	EDITING A GROUPED OBJECT

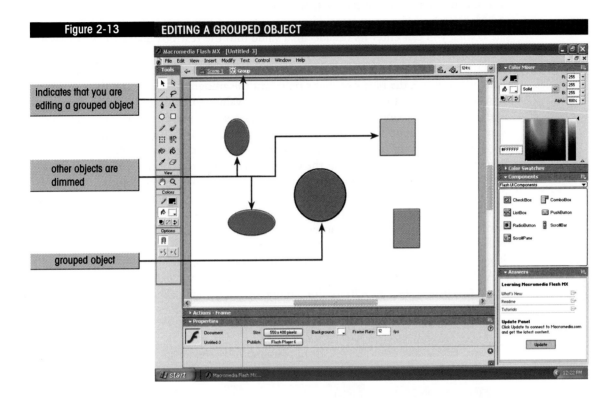

indicates that you are editing a grouped object

other objects are dimmed

grouped object

As you draw objects on the Stage you will want to control the colors of both the strokes and the fills. There are various ways to set the colors before and after you draw an object.

Color Controls and the Color Mixer

All strokes and fills can be drawn with different colors. You can specify the colors before you draw strokes and fills or you can change the colors of existing strokes and fills. Macromedia Flash provides several methods by which you can specify colors. The first method is by using the color controls found in the colors area of the toolbox. You use the Stroke Color control to specify the color for strokes and you use the Fill Color control to specify the color for fills. Each of these controls has a list arrow that you can click to open a color pop-up window. Figure 2-14 shows the color pop-up window for the Fill Color control.

Figure 2-14	COLOR POP-UP WINDOW FOR THE FILL COLOR CONTROL

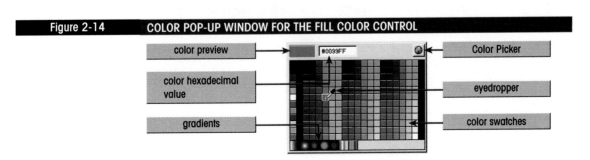

color preview

color hexadecimal value

gradients

Color Picker

eyedropper

color swatches

When the color pop-up window opens, the pointer changes to an eyedropper ✐. You use the eyedropper to select a particular color in the pop-up window. A color square in the pop-up window is referred to as a **swatch**. By default, the color swatches displayed in the color pop-up window are the 216 **Web-safe colors**. These are colors that are displayed the same on both Internet Explorer and Netscape Navigator browsers, as well as on both Windows and Macintosh operating systems. If you need to use a color that is not one of the 216 Web-safe colors, you can enter its hexadecimal value into the text box above the color swatches. The hexadecimal value (such as #000000 for black) is based on the three basic colors used on computer monitors, red, green, and blue, or RGB. The first two hexadecimal digits represent the amount of red, the next two digits represent the amount of green, and the last two digits represent the amount of blue. These three color values combine to form the desired color. The color pop-up window for fills also displays a set of preset gradients below the color swatches. A **gradient** is a blend of two or more colors. A **linear gradient** blends the colors from one point to another in a straight line. A **radial gradient** blends the colors in a circular pattern. Also from within the color pop-up window you can click the Color Picker button to open the Color dialog box which you use to create custom colors.

You can also select colors using the Property inspector. When you select a tool used to draw strokes or fills, color controls are displayed in the Property inspector. These controls work the same way as those you access using the Stroke Color and Fill Color controls in the toolbox. These controls are also displayed when you select an existing stroke or fill on the Stage, allowing you to change the color of the selected object.

A third way to select colors is by using the Color Mixer panel shown in Figure 2-15. Using this panel, you can select colors in one of several ways. You can use the panel's color controls to open the color pop-up window, you can enter a color's hexadecimal value, or you can create custom colors.

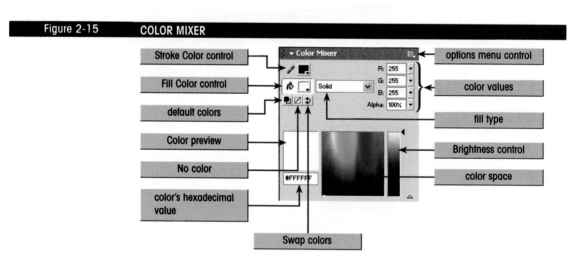

Figure 2-15   COLOR MIXER

Figure 2-16 gives a description of each of the main elements in the Color Mixer panel.

	Figure 2-16	COLOR MIXER ELEMENTS

OPTION	DESCRIPTION
Fill type	Lists the types of fills you can use: solid, gradient, or bitmap
Stroke Color control	Displays the color pop-up window to select colors for strokes
Fill Color control	Displays the color pop-up window to select colors for fills
Default colors	Sets the stroke color to black and the fill color to white
No color	Sets the stroke or fill to have no color
Swap colors	Swaps the stroke and fill color selections
Color preview	Previews the currently selected color
Color's hexadecimal value	Used to enter a color's hexadecimal value
Options menu control	Opens the panel's options menu
Color values	Used to enter specific values for red, green, and blue
Brightness control	Adjusts the brightness of the color being previewed
Color space	Shows the range of available colors

The Color Mixer allows you to create custom colors in several ways. You can use the RGB color mode, which is the default mode, and enter specific values for red, green, and blue. The RGB values combine to form a particular color. Or you can choose to work with the HSB color mode and enter values for hue, saturation, and brightness. You change modes by using the panel's options menu, which you open by clicking the options menu control located in the panel's title bar. As you enter or change the values, the color sample preview window displays the selected color. Any custom color you create can be added to the color pop-up window by clicking the Add Swatch command from the panel's options menu. This then makes the color available any time you access the color pop-up window for that document.

Now that you have an understanding of the individual elements—strokes, fills, and colors—of graphics created in Flash, you are ready to learn how to select these objects to enhance or modify them.

Selecting Objects

Once you draw a graphic object on the Stage, you can change its characteristics. However, to change an object's characteristics you first need to select the object using the selection tools. The selection tools include the Arrow, Subselection, and Lasso. With these tools you are able to select part of an object, the entire object, or several objects at one time. It is important to be familiar with these tools, especially the Arrow tool, as you will be using them frequently as you create graphics for Actions Web Design's clients.

Arrow Tool

The **Arrow** tool is used to select strokes or fills and can also be used to select a group of objects. You can also use the Arrow tool to move objects on the Stage or in the Work Area and to modify objects once they have been selected. You select objects by clicking them or by clicking and dragging the pointer to draw a rectangular selection marquee around the object, which is useful when you need to select more than one object at a time. When you select a graphic object, Flash will cover it with a pattern of dots to indicate it has been selected. Some selected objects, such as text blocks, display a rectangular outline around them instead of a pattern of dots. These objects have special characteristics you will learn about later. Once you have selected an object you are able to move or modify it. To move an object with the Arrow tool, you click and drag it to its new position. To modify an object with the Arrow tool, you move the pointer to one of the object's edges or corners. If you move the pointer to a corner of a rectangle, for example, the pointer changes to a corner pointer ⌐ as shown in Figure 2-17. You can then drag this pointer to change the shape of the object.

Figure 2-17	MODIFYING AN OBJECT USING THE ARROW TOOL

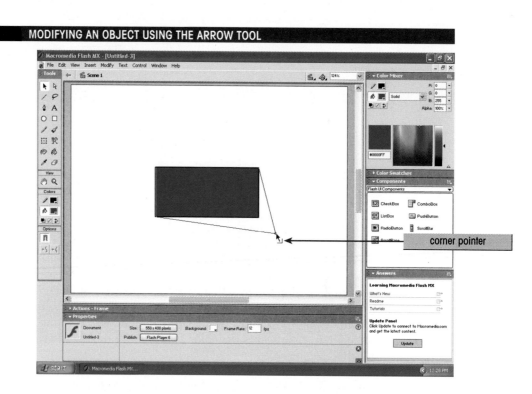

As you learned in Tutorial 1, many of the tools in the toolbox have modifiers that change the way they work. These modifiers display in the options area of the toolbox when the tool is selected. The Arrow tool includes the **Snap to Objects**, **Smooth**, and **Straighten** modifiers which are shown in Figure 2-18.

Figure 2-18	ARROW TOOL MODIFIERS

MODIFIER ICON	MODIFIER	DESCRIPTION
🧲	Snap to Objects	Snaps selected objects to other objects when they are moved close together
�	Smooth	Smooths the selected line or shape outline
↘	Straighten	Straightens the selected line or shape outline

To continue your training in Flash, Aly wants you to practice using the Arrow tool to select and modify objects. You can do this using the graphics in her sample document.

To select and modify objects with the Arrow tool:

1. Click the **Zoom** tool 🔍 in the toolbox, and then click the **Enlarge** modifier ⊕. Now, you will zoom in and enlarge the red circle.

2. Click the **red circle** to enlarge its view and to bring it to the center of the Stage window.

3. Click the **Arrow** tool ▸ in the toolbox to select it.

4. Click the center of the red circle and drag it to the right. Release it just before you get to the rectangle. The circle's fill is now separated from its stroke and has a pattern of dots showing it is still selected. See Figure 2-19.

Figure 2-19	CIRCLE'S FILL AND STROKE SEPARATED

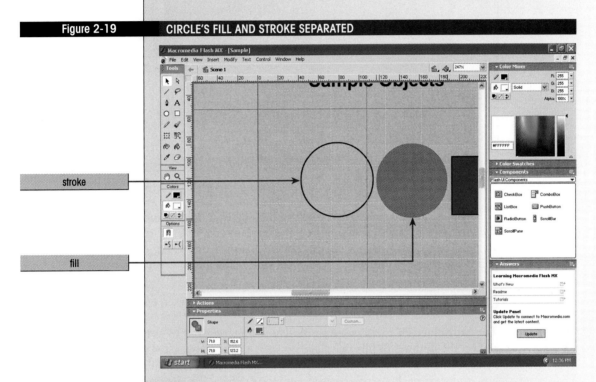

stroke

fill

Now you will restore the fill to its original location by undoing the previous step.

5. Click **Edit** on the menu bar, and click **Undo**, and then click a blank area of the Stage to deselect the circle's fill. You can also use the Arrow tool to select both the fill and the stroke of the circle simultaneously. You do this by double-clicking the image.

6. Double-click the **circle** to select both the fill and the stroke, and then drag the selected **circle** to the right. Both the stroke and the fill move together.

7. Click a blank area of the Stage to deselect the circle.

   You can also use the Arrow tool to modify a stroke or a fill. For example, you can use it to change the shape of the circle.

8. Move the pointer over the stroke of the circle until the pointer changes to ▸◡, then click and drag the stroke of the circle away from the center of the circle to change its shape as shown in Figure 2-20. When you release the mouse the fill expands to the new shape.

Figure 2-20   **CHANGING THE SHAPE OF THE CIRCLE**

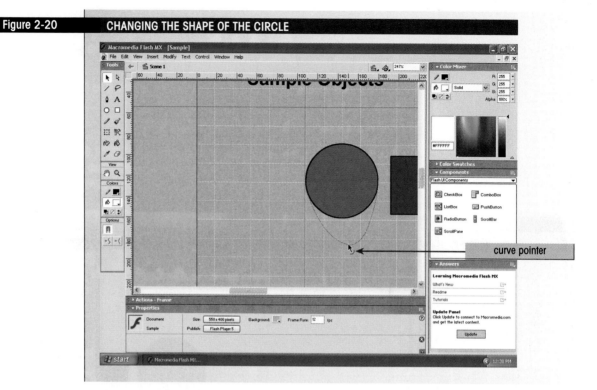

As you have seen, the Arrow tool can be used to modify a line or a shape. To more precisely modify an object, you use the Subselection tool. The Subselection tool reveals points on lines or shapes drawn with the Pencil, Brush, Line, Oval, or Rectangle tools. These points can then be adjusted to modify the lines or shapes.

Subselection Tool

The **Subselection** tool is used to display points, referred to as **anchor points**, on strokes and on the outlines of fills that have no stroke. The strokes and fills may then be modified by adjusting these points. To reveal anchor points, select the Subselection tool in the toolbox, and then click a stroke or the outline of a fill. This displays anchor points along the stroke or fill outline. If you click and drag an anchor point on a straight line segment, you can change the angle or the length of the line. If you click an anchor point on a curved line, **tangent handles** are displayed next to the selected point. See Figure 2-21. You can then change the curve by dragging the tangent handles.

Figure 2-21   **CHANGING A CURVE'S ANCHOR POINT**

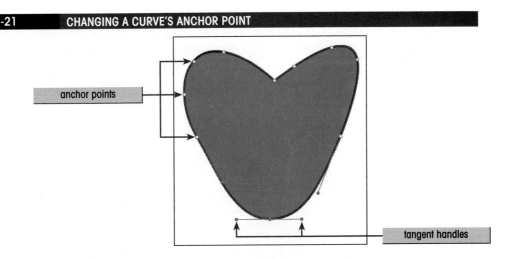

anchor points

tangent handles

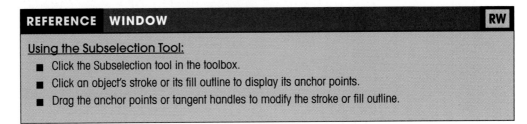

REFERENCE   WINDOW   **RW**

Using the Subselection Tool:
- Click the Subselection tool in the toolbox.
- Click an object's stroke or its fill outline to display its anchor points.
- Drag the anchor points or tangent handles to modify the stroke or fill outline.

Aly suggests you use the Sample.fla document to practice using the Subselection tool to select and modify objects.

To modify an object using the Subselection tool:

1. Click the **Hand** tool 🖑 in the toolbox to select it, and then use the 🖑 to drag the view of the Stage so that the blue rectangle is in the middle of the Stage window.

2. Click the **Subselection** tool ▷ in the toolbox to select it. Now use this tool to display the rectangle's stroke anchor points.

3. Click the stroke of the blue rectangle. A thin blue outline displays around the rectangle, and square anchor points are displayed on the rectangle's corners. To modify the stroke you can drag an anchor point.

4. Drag the anchor point for the upper-right corner away from the center of the rectangle as shown in Figure 2-22.

Figure 2-22   DRAGGING AN ANCHOR POINT TO CHANGE THE SHAPE

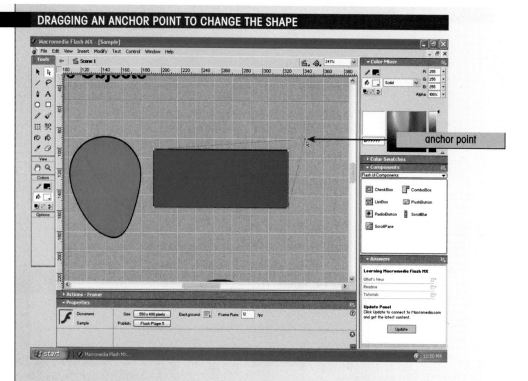

anchor point

When you release the pointer, the rectangle's fill expands to fill the new shape. Now you will use the Subselection tool to modify the green oval.

5. Use 🖐 to move the view of the Stage so that the green oval is in the center of the Stage window.

6. Click ▶, and then click the green oval's outline. Anchor points appear along the oval's outline.

7. Click the anchor point at the bottom of the oval's outline once. Because this is a curved outline, tangent handles display. Now you can modify the oval using a tangent handle.

8. Click and drag the tangent handle on the left side of the bottom anchor point to change the shape. The shape's fill expands to fit the new shape as shown In Figure 2-23.

Figure 2-23   MODIFIED OVAL WITH TANGENT HANDLES

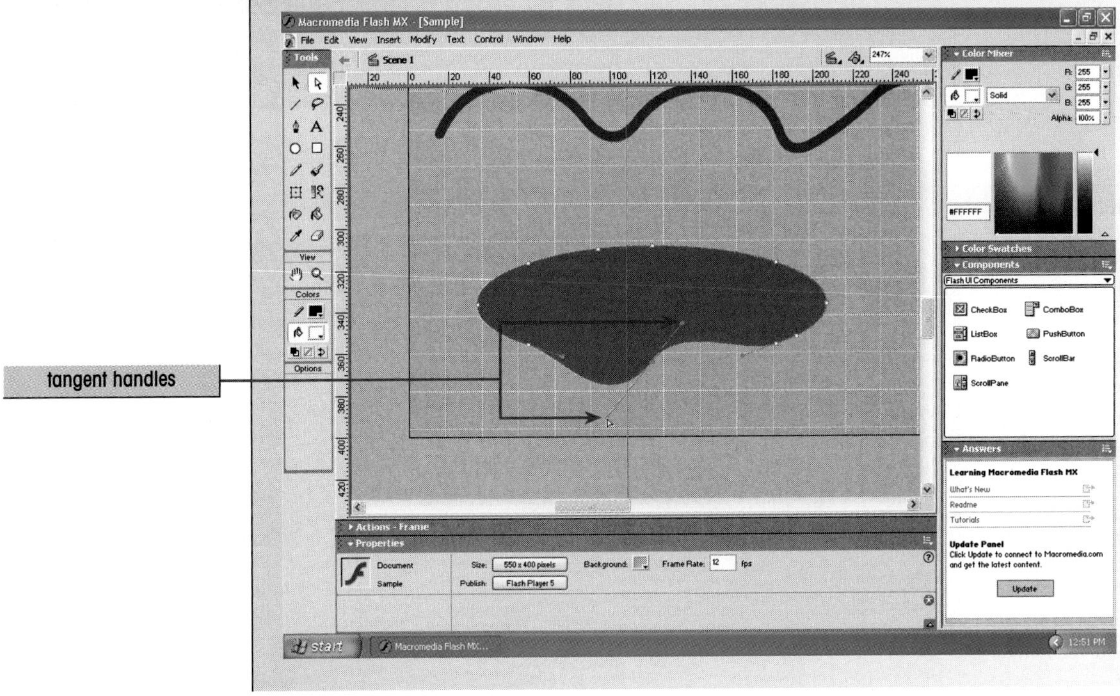

tangent handles

You have used the Arrow tool to select and modify objects, and you have used the Subselection tool to select a line's or fill outline's anchor points to modify them. Now you will see how the Lasso tool is used to select an object, several objects at one time, or just part of an object. The Lasso tool is especially useful if you need to select just part of a fill or a stroke, which you cannot do with the Arrow or Subselection tools.

Lasso Tool

The **Lasso** tool is used to select several objects at one time or to select an irregularly shaped area of an object by drawing a free-form selection marquee around the area. You select the Lasso tool in the toolbox and then click and drag the Lasso pointer ♀ on the Stage to draw a selection marquee around the area or objects you want selected. Once you have made the selection you can move the selection or apply other effects to it such as changing the color of all the selected fills at one time.

Aly suggests you practice using the Lasso tool with the objects on the Sample.fla document.

To select objects with the Lasso tool:

1. Double-click the **Hand** tool ⟨ᵐ⟩ to change the Stage view to make all of the Stage visible.

2. Click the **Lasso** tool ♀ in the toolbox to select it. The pointer changes to a lasso ♀ when moved over the Stage. You will use this tool to select multiple objects at once.

3. Click and drag the pointer to create a free-form selection marquee that includes part of the blue rectangle, part of the red heart, part of the brown S-shape, and part of the red vertical line. Figure 2-24 shows the marquee around the selected areas before the mouse button is released. After you release the mouse button all the selected areas appear with a dot pattern to indicate they have been selected.

| Figure 2-24 | FREE-FORM MARQUEE |

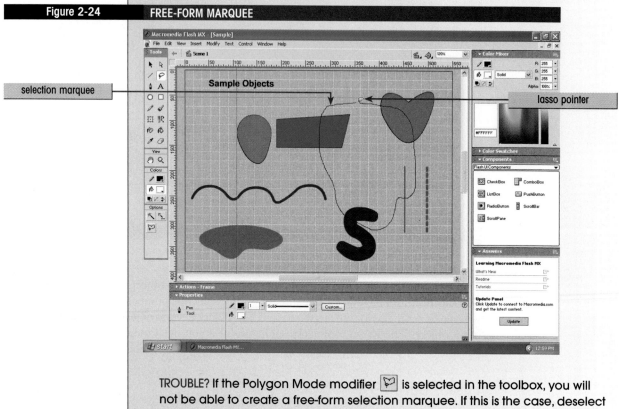

selection marquee

lasso pointer

TROUBLE? If the Polygon Mode modifier 🖾 is selected in the toolbox, you will not be able to create a free-form selection marquee. If this is the case, deselect the modifier, and then repeat Step 3.

Now you will change the color of the fills that have been selected.

4. Click the **Fill Color control list arrow** in the toolbox to open the color pop-up window. Click the **yellow** color swatch (first column, tenth row). The fill color of the areas in the rectangle, heart, and S-shape change to yellow. The line and strokes are not affected because they are not fills. See Figure 2-25.

| Figure 2-25 | NEW FILL COLOR FOR SELECTED AREAS |

yellow color on
selected fills

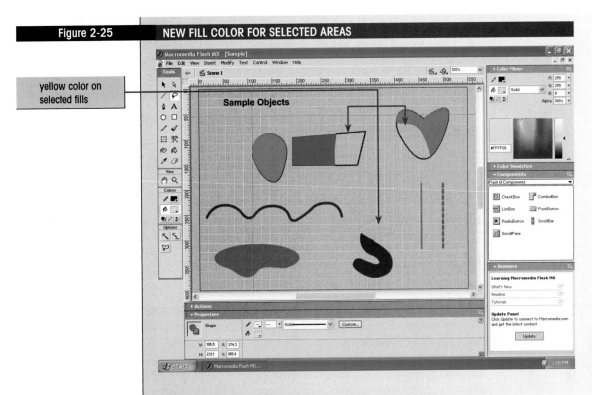

Save the Sample.fla document with all of the changes you have made so far using a new filename.

5. Use the Save As command on the File menu to save your document as **Mysample.fla**. Save it in the **Tutorial.02\Tutorial** folder on your Data Disk. Note that you do not need to type the .fla extension in the File name text box.

6. Close the file and exit Flash.

Aly is pleased with all that you have learned in this session. You have examined the various ways in which the view of the Stage can be modified to make your work with Macromedia Flash easier. You have also learned that when you draw objects they may contain strokes, fills, or both. And you also learned about how objects interact with each other when they are drawn or moved over each other on the Stage. You have learned about colors, and how to use the selection tools to select and modify objects or parts of objects. In the next session you will learn how to use the drawing tools to create the graphics for the banner in the Flounders Pet Shop Web site.

Session 2.1 QUICK CHECK

1. What are the default dimensions for a Macromedia Flash document?

2. Which area of the Flash program window do you use to create, import, and assemble all of the graphic objects for your document?

3. Describe two ways to access the magnification levels to change the view of the Stage.

4. The Grid displays lines on the Stage that become part of your document. True or False?

5. How do you get the rulers to display on the Stage window?

6. How do you create a horizontal guide?

7. What is the difference between strokes and fills?

8. If you draw a blue oval on top of an ungrouped red rectangle, the rectangle will not be modified. True or False?

9. Grouped objects cannot be edited. True or False?

10. By default, how many colors are shown on the color pop-up window for the Stroke Color control?

11. Which panel can be used to create custom colors?

12. What are two ways you can select both the stroke and the fill of an oval at the same time?

13. How can you select several objects at the same time using the Lasso tool?

SESSION 2.2

In this session you will learn how to use the main drawing tools in Macromedia Flash. You will use some of these tools to create graphic elements for the Flounders Pet Shop banner. You will learn how to draw lines, curves, ovals, rectangles, and paint brush strokes. In addition to the drawing tools, you will learn how to apply and change the colors of strokes and fills, and how to apply properties of one object to another object.

Drawing Lines and Shapes

Now that you have seen how to select and modify objects with the selection tools, you are ready to create graphic images from scratch. To draw lines and curves you use the Line, Pen, and Pencil tools. If you create an enclosed shape as you draw with these tools, the enclosed areas will be filled with the currently selected fill color (as shown in the Fill Color control in the toolbox.) To draw shapes you use the Rectangle, Oval, and Brush tools. These tools allow you to create shapes of various sizes and colors. The ovals and rectangles you draw can include strokes as well as fills or you can draw them with only a stroke or only a fill.

Refer to Figure 2-1 which shows the sketch of the banner you are to create. In this session you will use the Oval, Pencil, Paint Bucket, Eyedropper, and Pen tools to create the fish and plant graphics. You will also use the Rectangle tool to create a frame around the banner. You will use the Arrow tool to modify the shapes you draw, and you will display the grid which will be useful as you draw and align objects on the Stage.

Oval and Rectangle Tools

Drawing simple shapes is easy with the Oval and Rectangle tools. Both of these tools work in a similar manner. You simply select the tool in the toolbox, select colors for the stroke and fill using the Stroke and Fill Color controls, and then click and drag the pointer on the Stage. The size of the shape is determined by where you release the pointer. Each shape you draw may contain both a stroke and a fill or you can draw shapes that contain only a fill or only a stroke. If, for example, you select the no color option for the stroke, then the drawn shape contains a fill but no stroke. Once you draw a shape you can still change its stroke or fill color. Recall from Session 1 that you can also apply colors to existing strokes and fills using the Color Mixer panel, the Property inspector, or the Fill Color and Stroke Color controls in the toolbox.

You can also use the Oval and Rectangle tools to draw a perfect circle or a perfect square. You do this by first selecting the Snap to Objects command on the View menu. For example, as you draw with the Oval tool, a small solid ring appears next to the pointer to let you know when you have drawn a perfect circle. The same thing happens when you draw with the Rectangle tool to let you know you have drawn a perfect square.

When you select the Rectangle tool, the Round Rectangle Radius modifier becomes available in the options area of the toolbox. If you click this modifier, a dialog box opens in which you can enter a value for the number of points by which you want to round the corners of the rectangle. The higher the value, the more rounded the corners will be. See the rectangle examples in Figure 2-26.

Figure 2-26	RECTANGLES WITH ROUNDED CORNERS

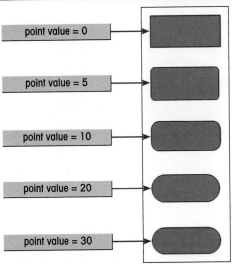

point value = 0
point value = 5
point value = 10
point value = 20
point value = 30

You are now ready to begin creating the banner for Flounders Pet Shop. You will first set the document properties and display the rulers. You will then save the banner file to your Data Disk.

To set the document properties, show the rulers, and save the document:

1. Start Macromedia Flash, and if necessary, click **File** on the menu bar, and then click **New** to create a new document.

2. Close the Timeline, and set the Stage view to **Show Frame**. Now you will set the document dimensions according to the banner sketch. These dimensions are 400 by 200 pixels.

3. Click **Modify** on the menu bar, and then click **Document**.

4. When the Document Properties dialog box opens, the value in the Width text box should be selected. If it is not, click the value in the Width text box, type **400** for the width value, and then double-click the value in the **Height** text box and type **200** for its value. Do not press Enter or click OK yet.

   You will now set the background color to blue as shown in the sketch.

5. Click the **Background Color** control list arrow to open the color pop-up window. Using the eyedropper ✐ click the **blue** color swatch in the first column, ninth row.

6. Leave the Frame Rate at 12 frames per second and the Ruler Units at pixels, and then click the **OK** button to close the dialog box. The Stage changes to match your document settings. Next, display the rulers.

7. Click **View** on the menu bar, and then click **Rulers**. The rulers display on the Stage window. Your Stage window should look like that shown in Figure 2-27.

| Figure 2-27 | STAGE WINDOW SHOWING NEW DOCUMENT PROPERTIES AND RULERS |

rulers

note blue background
and smaller Stage

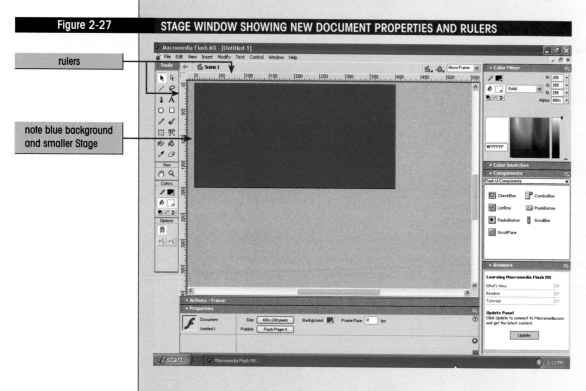

You will now save your document with these new settings.

8. Use the Save As command on the File menu to save your document as **Banner.fla**. Save it in the **Tutorial.02\Tutorial** folder on your Data Disk.

Now that you have the document ready, you will create the large fish in the center of the banner Aly sketched. Aly suggests that you use the Oval tool to draw a large oval for the body of the fish and a smaller oval that will become the fish's tail. You can create guide lines to guide you as you draw. You can then use the Arrow tool to modify the smaller oval to resemble the tail.

To draw the fish using the Oval tool and guide lines:

1. Double-click the **Hand** tool ✋ to make all of the Stage visible.

2. Click the **Arrow** tool ▸ in the toolbox to select it. First, you will create two horizontal guides.

3. Click the top horizontal ruler and drag a horizontal guide onto the Stage. Use the vertical ruler on the left to place the guide approximately 50 pixels from the top of the Stage. Drag another horizontal guide and place it approximately 110 pixels from the top of the Stage.

4. Click the vertical ruler and drag a vertical guide onto the Stage. Use the horizontal ruler to place the guide approximately 100 pixels from the left of the Stage. Drag another vertical guide and place it approximately 220 pixels from the left of the Stage. See Figure 2-28.

Figure 2-28   GUIDES

horizontal guides

vertical guides

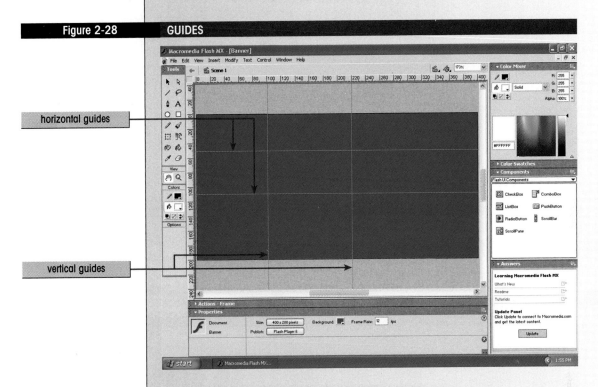

Next, using the guides to help you draw, you will use the Oval tool to create the fish body.

5. Click the **Oval** tool ○ in the toolbox. Before drawing the oval that will be the body of the fish, select the stroke and fill colors.

6. In the Property inspector, click the **Stroke Color** control list arrow to open its color pop-up window, and then click the **black** swatch in the first column, first row. Enter **2** in the Stroke height list box, and make sure the Stroke style is set to **solid**.

7. In the Property inspector, click the **Fill Color** control list arrow, and then click the **orange** swatch in the seventh row from the top, third column from the right. You will now draw the fish body.

8. Use the ＋ to draw an oval on the Stage starting at the upper-left corner of the rectangular area formed by the guides. Drag the pointer to the lower-right corner of the rectangular area formed by the guides. Release the mouse button at this lower-right corner to create the oval as shown in Figure 2-29.

Figure 2-29   OVAL

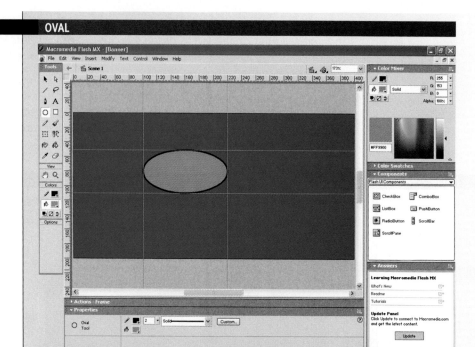

9. Draw another smaller oval that overlaps the left end of the first oval. Draw it so that it is centered on the left vertical guide as shown in Figure 2-30.

Figure 2-30   OVERLAPPING OVALS

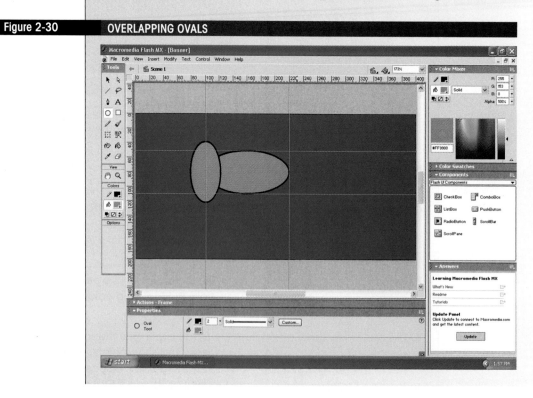

Now that you have drawn these two ovals, you will use the Arrow tool to modify them to more closely resemble the fish Aly sketched for you. For example, the stroke segment of the smaller oval that overlaps the larger oval can be removed. Then, the stroke segment on the left edge of the smaller oval needs to be modified to curve inward, toward the larger oval.

To modify the ovals using the Arrow tool:

1. Click the **Arrow** tool ▶ in the toolbox, and then click the part of the small oval's stroke that is inside the larger oval as shown in Figure 2-31. The stroke segment that is inside the larger oval is selected.

Figure 2-31	STROKE SEGMENT SELECTED

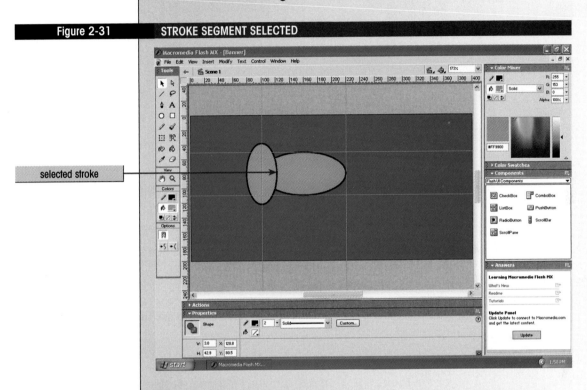

selected stroke

2. Press the **Delete** key to delete this stroke segment.

3. Move the pointer to the stroke on the left edge of the smaller oval until you see a curve pointer ▶ͻ. Drag the line to the right to about the center point of the small oval. The center point should be at the left vertical guide as shown in Figure 2-32.

Figure 2-32   **MODIFYING THE OVAL'S STROKE**

stroke moved with
Arrow tool

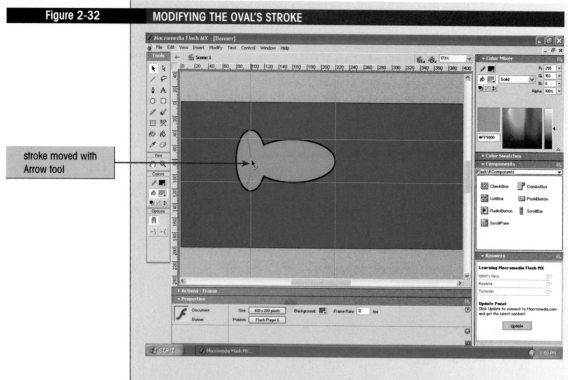

Now remove the guides; you will not use them anymore.

4. Using the **Arrow** tool ⬕, drag each of the horizontal guides to the top ruler, and then drag each of the vertical guides to the left ruler.

Now you are ready to draw the eye for the fish. You can use the Oval tool for this.

To use the Oval tool to draw the eye for the fish:

1. Click the **Zoom** tool 🔍, make sure the **Enlarge** modifier ⊕ is selected, and then click the right side of the fish shape once to zoom in.

2. Select the **Oval** tool ○ in the toolbox, and then in the Property inspector, set the stroke color to **No Color** and the fill color to **white**. Now you can draw the eye. Flash helps you draw a perfect circle if the Snap to Objects command is turned on. By default, the Snap to Objects command is turned on.

3. If necessary, click **View** on the menu bar, and then click **Snap to Objects** to select this option.

4. Use the ╋ to draw a small circle on the right end of the fish shape as shown in Figure 2-33.

Figure 2-33	FISH EYE

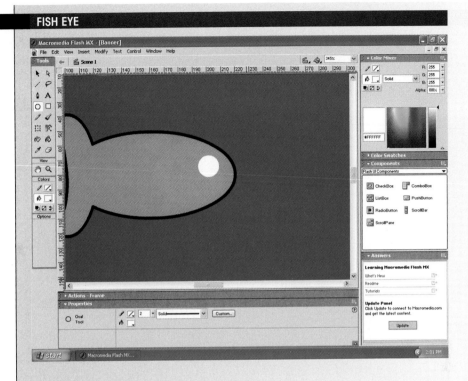

To make it easier to draw a small oval for the pupil, you will turn off the Snap to Objects command.

5. Click **View** on the menu bar, and then click **Snap to Objects** to remove the check mark and deselect this option.

6. With ⬭ still selected in the toolbox, use the Fill Color control in the toolbox to change the fill color to **black**.

7. Draw a smaller oval inside the eye to represent the eye's pupil.

TROUBLE? If you make a mistake and draw over the orange fill of the fish, click Edit on the menu bar, click Undo, and then draw the oval again.

Now you have completed the fish. As shown in the sketch of the banner, several bubbles need to be drawn coming from the fish's mouth. Again, you can use the Oval tool. Because you want these bubbles to appear as perfect circles, you need to select the Snap to Objects command to turn this feature on.

To draw bubbles using the Oval tool and the Snap to Objects command:

1. Make sure the Oval tool ⬭ is still selected in the toolbox, and then use the Fill Color control in the toolbox to change the fill color to **white**. Now ensure the ovals you draw will appear as perfect circles.

2. Click **View** on the menu bar, and then click the **Snap to Objects** command.

3. Draw four circles of varying sizes on the right side of the fish. These circles represent bubbles as shown in Figure 2-34.

Figure 2-34   FISH WITH BUBBLES

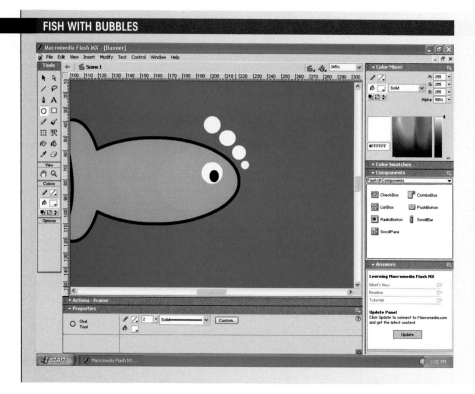

Next you will create a rectangle shape around the banner to provide a frame around all of the graphic elements. As indicated in Aly's sketch the rectangle will have a stroke and no fill and will have rounded corners.

To draw a rectangle to frame the banner:

1. Double-click the **Hand** tool 🖐 to make all of the Stage visible.

2. Click the **Rectangle** tool ☐ in the toolbox.

3. Click the **Stroke Color control** in the Property inspector. In the color pop-up window select the **light gray** color swatch located in the first column, fifth row. Set the stroke height to **2** and the stroke style to **Solid**.

4. Click the **Fill Color control** in the toolbox, and then click the **No Color** button ☑.

5. Click the **Round Rectangle Radius** modifier 🔲 in the options area of the toolbox. In the Rectangle Settings dialog box, enter **10** in the Corner Radius text box. Recall from the previous session that the point values entered for the Corner Radius determine how much to round the corners of the rectangle. Click the **OK** button to close the dialog box.

6. On the Stage draw a **rectangle** that forms a border just inside the Stage area as shown in Figure 2-35.

Figure 2-35	RECTANGLE DRAWN ON THE STAGE

rectangle with rounded corners

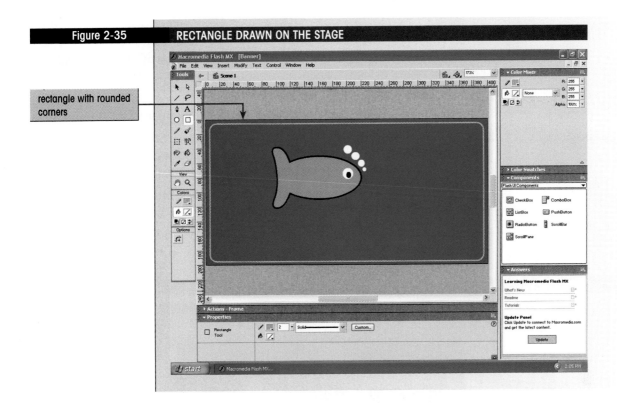

You show Aly the work you have completed thus far on the banner. She thinks everything looks great, but notices you forgot to draw the fish's mouth and fins. She suggests you use the Pencil tool to add these elements to the drawing.

Pencil Tool

The **Pencil** tool works in a similar way to the Line tool, however, you are not limited to drawing straight lines. The Pencil tool allows you to draw lines and shapes in a free-form manner as if you were using an actual pencil to draw on paper. As is the case with the Line tool, you can select a color, height, and style for the lines drawn with the Pencil tool. You make these selections using the Property inspector. When you select the Pencil tool, the pointer changes to a pencil 🖉 as you move it over the Stage. You click and drag the pointer to draw lines. The Pencil tool has the **Pencil Mode** modifier in the options area of the toolbox that you can use to control the way your lines appear as you draw them. Figure 2-36 summarizes the options for this modifier.

Figure 2-36	PENCIL MODE MODIFIER OPTIONS	
ICON	**OPTIONS**	**DESCRIPTION**
⌐	Straighten	The program helps straighten the lines you draw
S	Smooth	The program smooths out the lines and curves you draw
✎	Ink	The program provides minimal assistance as you draw

Now use the Pencil tool to add a mouth and fins to the fish. You will zoom in on the fish to make it easier to work with it.

To add the fins and the mouth to the fish using the Pencil tool:

1. Click the **Zoom** tool 🔍 in the toolbox, select the **Enlarge** modifier ⊕, and click the center of the fish once.

2. Click the **Pencil** tool ✏ in the toolbox to select it. You will select the Smooth option for the Pencil Mode modifier so that the lines you draw will be smooth.

3. Click the **Pencil Mode** modifier 🔖 in the options area of the toolbox, and then click the **Smooth** option 𝑆 from the list of pencil modes. Now use the Property inspector to set the stroke color, height, and style before drawing lines.

4. In the Property inspector make sure the stroke color is **black**, the height is **2**, and the style is **Solid**. Now you will draw the fins.

5. Draw a **fin** on the top side of the fish and another one on the bottom side as shown in Figure 2-37.

Figure 2-37	FINS ON THE FISH

fins drawn with Pencil tool

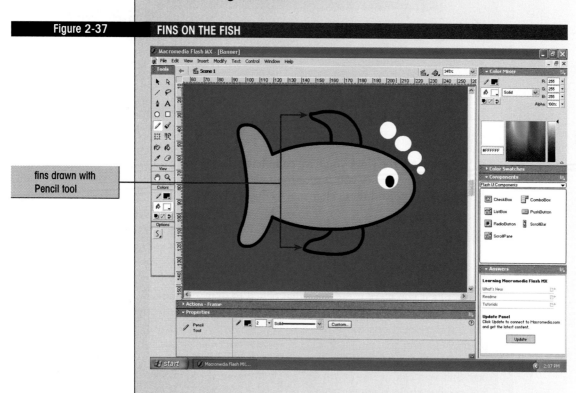

Next you will draw the mouth.

6. In the Property inspector, change the stroke height to **1**, and draw a small curved line for the fish's mouth starting right below the eye and ending on the stroke in the lower-right side of the fish. You will now create lines on the body of the fish.

7. Using the ✏, draw three pairs of lines in the middle of the fish starting on the top part of the stroke and ending on the bottom stroke. The fish should look similar to that in Figure 2-38.

Figure 2-38   **FISH WITH FINS, MOUTH, AND LINES**

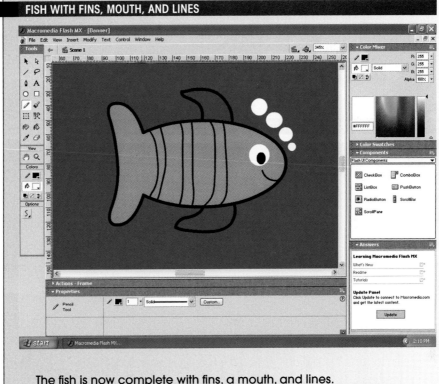

The fish is now complete with fins, a mouth, and lines.

In reviewing the sketch of the banner, you realize the lines on the fish should actually be bands of color. You can add the color to these parts of the fish using the tools in the toolbox that apply color to strokes and fills—the Paint Bucket tool, the Ink Bottle tool, and the Eyedropper tool. You will use the Paint Bucket and the Eyedropper tools on the banner.

Changing Strokes and Fills

Once you draw an object, you can still change its stroke and fill. You can change the stroke's color, height, or style and you can change a fill's color. You can even add a fill or a stroke to an object that does not have one or the other. The tools used for changing existing strokes and fills include the Paint Bucket, Ink Bottle, and Eyedropper tools. The **Paint Bucket tool** is used to modify an existing fill's color or to apply a fill to an enclosed area that does not have a fill. The **Ink Bottle tool** changes the attributes or properties of a stroke or it applies a stroke to an object that has no stroke. The **Eyedropper tool** copies the attributes of a stroke on one object to the stroke of another object. It also copies a fill's color from one object to another. In this tutorial we will discuss the Paint Bucket and Eyedropper tool in more detail as these tools will be used to complete the banner for the Flounders Pet Shop.

Paint Bucket Tool

The **Paint Bucket** tool can be used to change the color of a fill or to create a fill for an enclosed area. To use the Paint Bucket tool you simply select it from the toolbox, select a fill color using the Fill Color control in the toolbox, the Property inspector, or the Color Mixer panel, and then click an object's enclosed area using the Paint Bucket pointer ⬡. The Paint Bucket tool also has a Gap Size modifier and a Lock Fill modifier in the options area of the toolbox. The **Gap Size modifier** determines how the tool will paint areas that are not completely enclosed. The **Lock Fill modifier** affects gradient and bitmap fills. Gradients and bitmaps will be covered in Tutorial 5. The Paint Bucket modifiers and their options are described in Figure 2-39.

Figure 2-39	PAINT BUCKET TOOL MODIFIERS AND OPTIONS		
ICON	**MODIFIERS**	**OPTIONS**	**DESCRIPTION**
⊙	Gap Size	Don't Close Gaps option	Areas not completely enclosed are not painted
⊙	Gap Size	Close Small Gaps option	Areas not enclosed, but with small gaps, are painted
⊙	Gap Size	Close Medium Gaps option	Areas not enclosed, but with medium gaps, are painted
⊙	Gap Size	Close Large Gaps option	Areas not enclosed, but with large gaps, are painted
🔒	Lock Fill		Causes gradient or bitmap fills to extend across multiple objects

You will use the Paint Bucket tool to fill the bands on the fish with some bright colors.

To apply fills to the fish with the Paint Bucket tool:

1. Click the **Paint Bucket** tool ⬡ in the toolbox. Now select a fill color to apply to the fish.

2. Click the **Fill Color** control list arrow in the toolbox to open the Fill Color pop-up window. Select the **yellow** swatch (first column, tenth row) for the fill.

3. Using ⬡ click the area enclosed by the two lines on the far left as shown in Figure 2-40. The fish now has a yellow stripe.

   TROUBLE? A padlock icon next to the paint bucket pointer means the Lock Fill modifier is selected. This will not affect the way the tool works in these steps.

   TROUBLE? If the yellow color fills other areas of the fish, the lines may not be connected to the fish body outline. If so, make sure that Snap to Objects is turned on and redraw the lines so that they snap to the fish body outline.

Figure 2-40 APPLYING A FILL COLOR

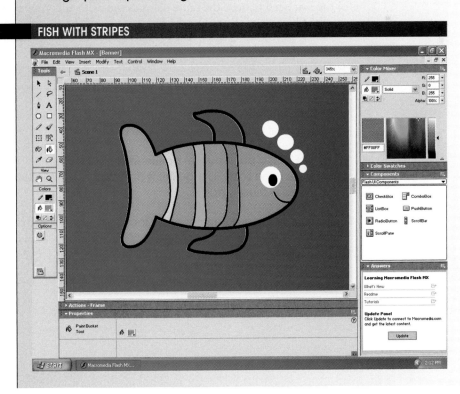

paint bucket pointer

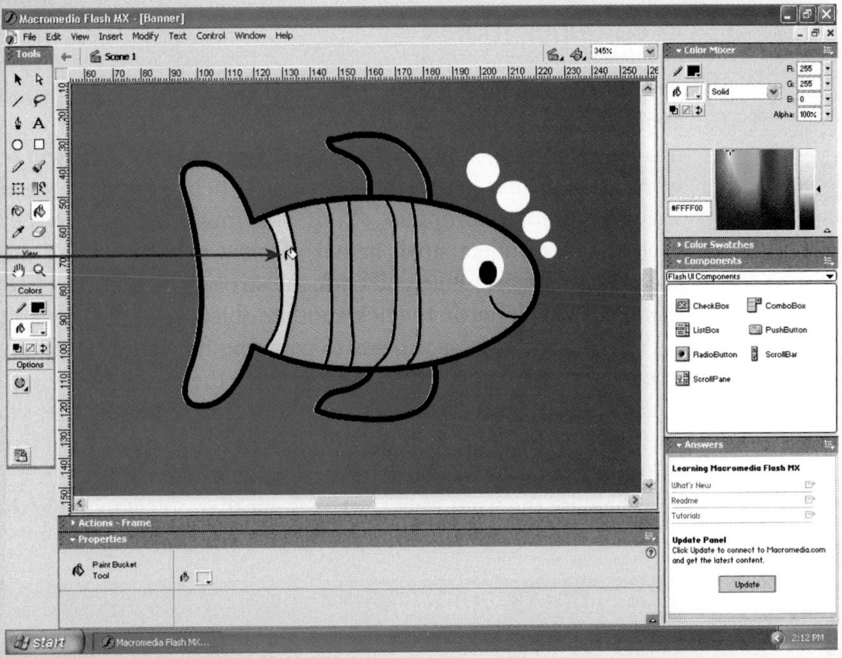

4. Click the **Fill Color** control list arrow in the toolbox to open its color pop-up window, click the **green** swatch (first column, eighth row), and then click the area enclosed by the middle two lines on the fish to make a green stripe.

5. Repeat Step 4 to apply the **pink** color (first column, twelfth row in the color pop-up window) to the area enclosed by the two lines on the far right to give the fish a bright pink stripe. See Figure 2-41.

Figure 2-41 FISH WITH STRIPES

Next, you will learn about the Eyedropper tool.

Eyedropper Tool

The **Eyedropper** tool is used to copy the fill or stroke properties of one object and then apply them to another object. You can also use the Eyedropper tool to copy the properties of a text block and apply them to another text block. You will learn more about creating and working with text in the next session. When you select the Eyedropper tool, the pointer changes to an eyedropper ✎. If you move the eyedropper over a stroke, the pointer changes to include a small pencil ✎ next to it indicating that you are about to copy the stroke's attributes. Once you click the stroke, the pointer changes to an ink bottle ✎. You then use the ink bottle to click another object to apply the copied stroke attributes.

You follow a similar process to copy the fill attributes of one object to another. First you select the Eyedropper tool, and then move the eyedropper over a fill. The pointer changes to include a small paintbrush ✎ next to it; this indicates that you are about to copy the fill's attributes. When you click the fill whose attributes you want to copy, the pointer changes to a paint bucket ✎. The pointer may include a padlock ✎ if the Lock Fill modifier is selected. You then use the paint bucket to click another object to apply the copied fill attributes.

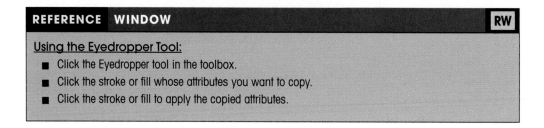

REFERENCE WINDOW   RW

Using the Eyedropper Tool:
- Click the Eyedropper tool in the toolbox.
- Click the stroke or fill whose attributes you want to copy.
- Click the stroke or fill to apply the copied attributes.

You compare the work you have completed thus far on the banner to Aly's sketch. The fins of the fish need to have the same color as the fish's tail. You can use the Eyedropper tool to copy the fill color of the tail to the fins.

To apply a color using the Eyedropper tool:

1. Click the **Eyedropper** tool ✎ in the toolbox.

2. Click the **orange** fill color on the tail of the fish. The pointer changes to ✎ to indicate that you can now apply the orange color to another part of the fish.

   TROUBLE? If the paint bucket pointer does not have a padlock icon next to it, that means the Lock Fill modifier is not selected. This will not affect the way the tool works in these steps.

3. Click the blank area enclosed by the top fin as shown in Figure 2-42. The top fin now has the same color as the rest of the fish.

Figure 2-42	APPLYING A COPIED COLOR

pointer changes to paint bucket to apply fill color

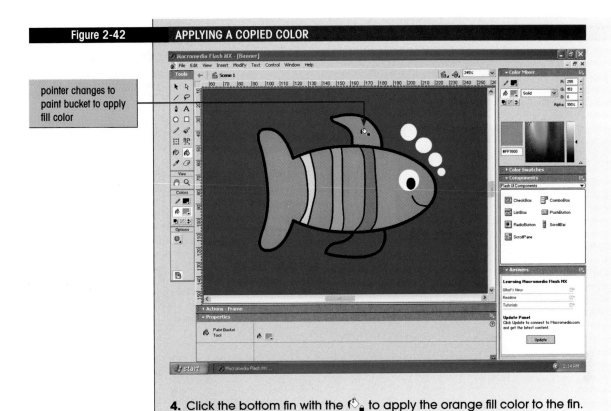

4. Click the bottom fin with the 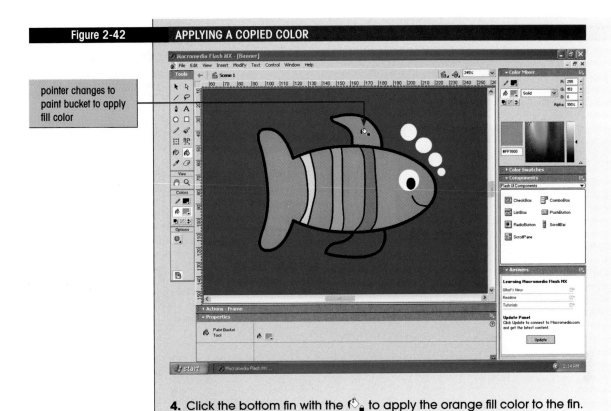 to apply the orange fill color to the fin.

You have completed drawing the fish by applying colors to the fins to match its body. To keep the various parts of the fish and the bubbles together you will group them so that they are treated as one object. This will allow you to modify the fish graphic as a whole or to create copies of the fish graphic without having to work with each of its individual elements.

To group the fish graphic and bubbles:

1. Using the Arrow tool draw a selection marquee around all of the fish and bubbles.

2. Click **Modify** on the menu bar, and then click **Group**. The graphic elements are now grouped and a thin rectangular blue line surrounds the grouped object to show it is selected. See Figure 2-43.

Figure 2-43   **GROUPED FISH GRAPHIC**

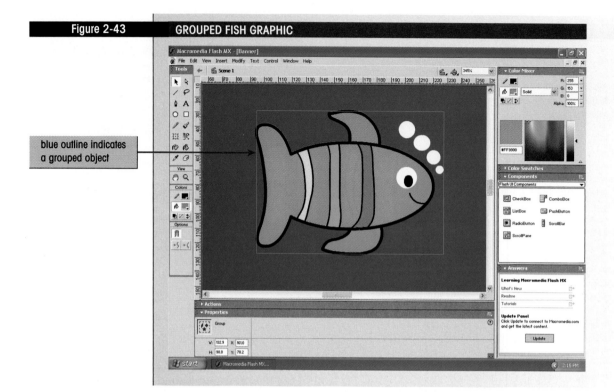

blue outline indicates a grouped object

You have completed the fish graphic and grouped it to make it easier to work with. In reviewing the sketch you see that plant leaves are still needed for the banner. Aly suggests that you use the Pen tool to draw the plant leaves because the Pen tool can be used to draw line segments that can then be modified to resemble leaves.

Pen Tool

The **Pen** tool can be used to draw shapes consisting of straight and curved lines connected by anchor points. Areas that are enclosed when you draw these lines are filled with the fill color currently selected in the Fill Color control in the toolbox. When you select the Pen tool, the pointer changes to a pen icon ♟ₓ with a small "x" next to it indicating that you are about to start a new line or curve. Clicking the Stage with the Pen tool pointer creates points that are then connected with straight lines. To draw curved lines you click and drag instead of just clicking points. As you drag the pointer, a curved line is drawn. Drawing curved lines can be tricky especially because you cannot always see the curve as you are drawing it. To make it easier to see what you are drawing, you can select the Show Pen Preview command, which is located on the Editing tab of the Preferences dialog box. To open the Preferences dialog box, you click Edit on the menu bar, and then click Preferences.

You will use the Pen tool to draw the plant leaves Aly sketched as part of the banner.

To draw with the Pen tool:

1. Double-click the **Hand** tool 🖑 to change the Stage view to make all of the Stage visible.

2. Click the **Arrow** tool ▶ and then click a blank area of the Stage to deselect the fish.

3. Click the **Pen** tool ♟ in the toolbox. Before using the Pen tool to draw the leaves, set the stroke and fill colors.

4. In the Property inspector, select **black** for the stroke color, and **dark green** (located in the fourth column, first row of the color pop-up window) for the fill color. Set the stroke height to **1** and the stroke style to **Solid**. Now you are ready to draw the object that will become the plant leaves.

5. On the left side of the Stage above the gray rectangle's bottom side, click to create the anchor points shown in Figure 2-44. Click the points in the shape of the letter M. Do not worry about the exact shape as you can modify the shape later. Your last click should be back on the beginning anchor point to complete the shape.

Figure 2-44	ANCHOR POINTS DRAWN WITH PEN TOOL

anchor points

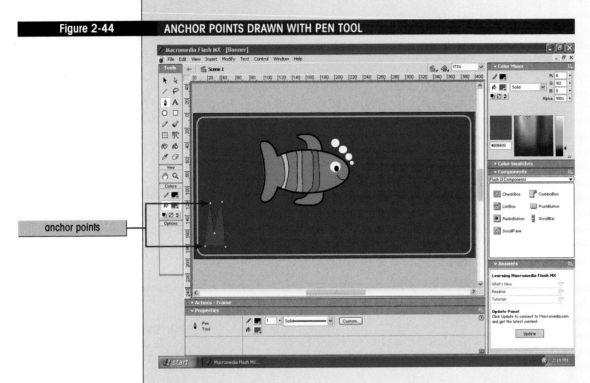

TROUBLE? If you want to adjust the anchor points, click the Subselection tool in the toolbox, click the anchor points, and then drag them to new positions.

Now you will use the Arrow tool to modify the lines you have drawn so they appear curved like plant leaves.

To modify the lines using the Arrow tool:

1. Click the **Arrow** tool in the toolbox.

2. Point to the left edge of the plant leaves shape. When the pointer changes to , drag the line slightly to the left to curve it as shown in Figure 2-45.

Figure 2-45   LINE MODIFIED WITH ARROW TOOL

line curved to the left

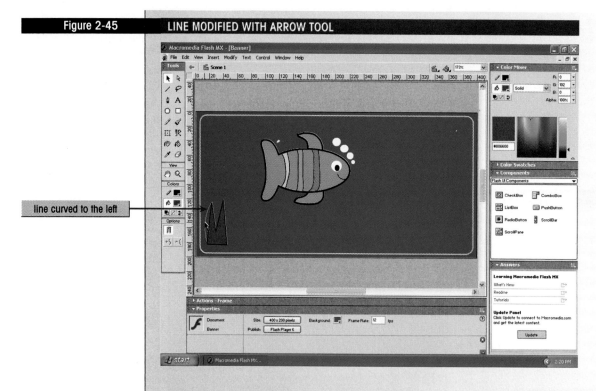

3. Repeat Step 2 to curve each of the other lines, except the bottom one, to make them look more like plant leaves. Now group the lines that make up the plant leaves.

4. With ▶ still selected, double-click the **plant leaves** to select all of its strokes and fills.

5. Click **Modify** on the menu bar, and then click **Group**. The leaves are now grouped together as one object.

Now you will make a copy of the plant leaves you created earlier and you will transform the copy by using the Flip Horizontal command on the Transform menu which is found on the Modify menu. You will then create a copy of the two sets of plant leaves and move the copy to the right side of the banner.

To create more plant leaves:

1. Click the **plant leaves** group with the Arrow tool ▶ to select it, if necessary. Click **Edit** on the menu bar, and click **Copy**. Click **Edit** again, and then click **Paste** to create the copy.

2. Drag the **copy** of the plant leaves to the right side of the original plant leaves. Now you will use the Transform command to flip the selected leaves horizontally.

3. Click **Modify** on the menu bar, point to **Transform**, and then click **Flip Horizontal**. See Figure 2-46.

Figure 2-46   PLANT LEAVES

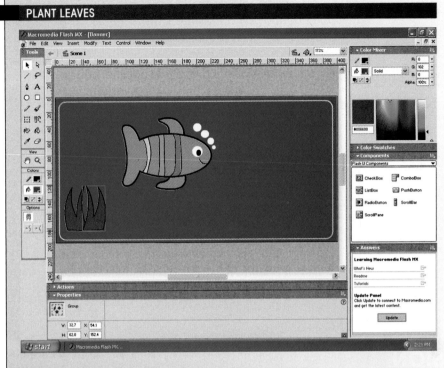

4. Draw a rectangular marquee around the two groups of plant leaves to select both of them at the same time. Make sure you do not select any other objects.

5. Click **Edit** on the menu bar, click **Copy**, click **Edit** on the menu bar again, and then click **Paste**. A copy of the set of plant leaves is placed on the center of the Stage.

6. Move the new set of plant leaves to the lower-right corner of the Stage as shown in Figure 2-47.

Figure 2-47   FINAL PLANT LEAVES

7. Save the **Banner.fla** file and exit Flash.

In this session you learned how to use the drawing tools, and to add colors to strokes and fills. You saw how you can change a fill's color and a stroke's color, height, and style. In the next session you will work with various tools used to modify objects and their properties.

Session 2.2 QUICK CHECK

1. When drawing a shape with the Oval tool, Macromedia Flash helps you draw a perfect circle when the Snap to Grid option is selected. True or False?

2. How can you draw a rectangle with rounded corners?

3. The _____ tool is used to draw line and curve segments by creating anchor points that connect them.

4. The _____ modifier helps straighten lines you draw with the Pencil tool.

5. Describe how to use the Eyedropper tool to copy a stroke's attributes to another object.

6. Which tool can you use to add a fill to an enclosed area that has no fill?

SESSION 2.3

In this session you will learn how to modify the objects you draw in Macromedia Flash. You learn how to transform objects by rotating, scaling, and distorting them. You will also learn how to use the Text tool to create different types of text boxes.

Modifying Strokes and Fills

Once you draw objects you may want to modify them in various ways other than just changing their color. Flash provides several tools to modify an object's strokes and fills. These include the Eraser, Free Transform, and Fill Transform tools. With these tools you can rotate an object, change its size, erase its strokes or fills, or even distort the object to achieve a special effect. In this tutorial, you will use the Free Transform tool to continue your work on the banner for Flounders Pet Shop. The Eraser and Fill Transform tools will be covered in more detail in later tutorials.

Free Transform Tool

One way to modify objects in Macromedia Flash is by using the **Free Transform** tool. This tool allows you to move, rotate, scale, skew, or even distort objects. You can transform a particular stroke or fill of an object or you can transform the entire object at one time. When you select an object with the Free Transform tool, a bounding box with selection handles surrounds the object as shown in Figure 2-48.

Figure 2-48	BOUNDING BOX ON AN OBJECT

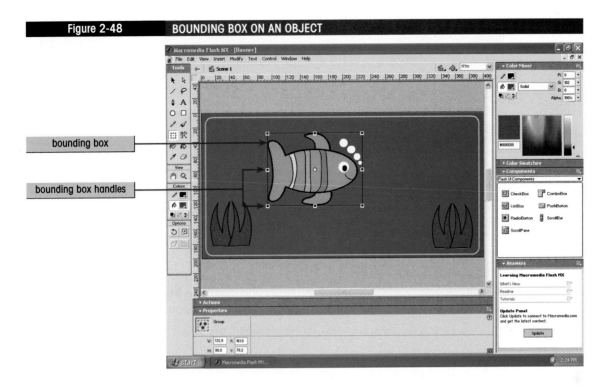

You drag the handles of the bounding box to transform the object. These selection handles are different from the anchor points you used with the Pen tool and Subselection tool. The anchor points are used to modify the curves, lines, or specific shapes. The selection handles on the bounding box affect the whole object at one time.

As you move the pointer near a handle, the pointer changes to indicate how the object will be modified when you drag the handle. For example, when you point just outside a corner handle, the pointer changes to a Rotate pointer, meaning you can rotate the object by dragging the corner. The Free Transform tool also has several modifiers in the options area of the toolbox. These include the **Rotate and Skew**, **Scale**, **Distort**, and **Envelope** modifiers, and they are described in Figure 2-49.

Figure 2-49	FREE TRANSFORM TOOL MODIFIERS	
ICON	**MODIFIER**	**DESCRIPTION**
↻	Rotate and Skew	Allows you to freely rotate an object by dragging a corner handle or to skew it at a different angle by dragging an edge handle
⊡	Scale	Allows you to change the size of an object by dragging on a corner or edge handle
◰	Distort	Allows you to reposition the corner or edge of an object by dragging its handle
▨	Envelope	Displays a bounding box with points and tangent handles; you can then adjust these points or tangent handles to warp or distort the object

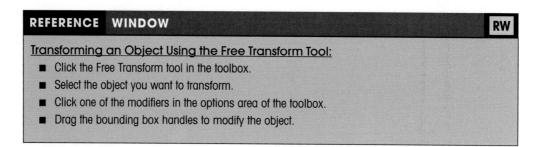

REFERENCE WINDOW **RW**

Transforming an Object Using the Free Transform Tool:
- Click the Free Transform tool in the toolbox.
- Select the object you want to transform.
- Click one of the modifiers in the options area of the toolbox.
- Drag the bounding box handles to modify the object.

The sketch for the banner shows another, smaller fish swimming next to the larger fish you already drew. Instead of drawing the smaller fish from scratch, you can simply copy the existing fish, and then use the Free Transform tool to resize the copied fish.

To make a copy of the fish:

1. If necessary, start Macromedia Flash and open the **Banner.fla** document located in the **Tutorial.02\Tutorial** folder on your Data Disk.

2. Close the Timeline panel, then double-click the **Hand** tool to change the Stage view to show all of the Stage.

3. To create a copy of the fish, click the **Arrow** tool , and then click the **fish** once to select it.

4. Click **Edit** on the menu bar, and then click **Copy**. Click **Edit** on the menu bar again, and then click **Paste**. A copy of the fish is placed in the center of the Stage.

5. Use to drag the copy and position it to the right of the original fish as shown in Figure 2-50.

Figure 2-50   COPY OF FISH

fish copy

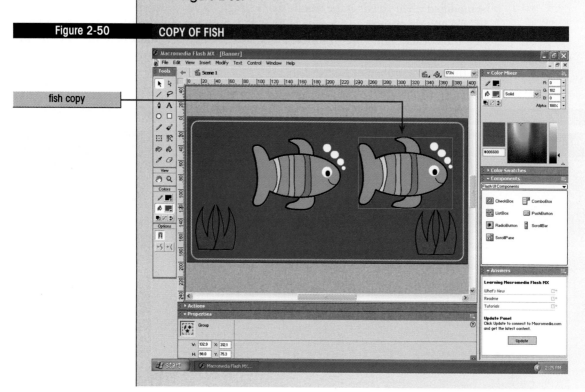

Now that you have a copy of the fish, you can use the Free Transform tool to modify it.

To modify the copied fish with the Free Transform tool:

1. Click the **Free Transform** tool ⊡ in the toolbox, and then click the **Scale** modifier ⊡ in the options area of the toolbox.

   A bounding box with selection handles appears around the fish. You can use this to reduce the size of the copied fish.

2. Drag a corner handle to reduce the size of the fish to about half the size of the original. Now you will rotate the fish.

3. Click the **Rotate and Skew** modifier ⟲ in the options area of the toolbox, click the copied fish, and drag the lower-right corner handle down to rotate the fish so that it appears to be swimming in a downward direction as shown in Figure 2-51.

Figure 2-51	ROTATING THE FISH

bounding box handles
used to rotate object

You decide to show Aly the work you have completed thus far on the banner. She is very pleased with the fish and the plants and suggests you now turn your attention to the text that is to appear at the top of the banner.

Adding Text

In Macromedia Flash, you add text to a document by creating either a static text block or a text field. A **static text block** is simply an object that contains text which can be edited, and does not change when you display your document as a movie. You use a **text field** when the text in the field is changeable. There are two types of text used in text fields, dynamic and input. **Dynamic text** is an advanced feature where the text is updated automatically with information from a Web server when the movie is displayed in a Web browser as part of a Web site. An example of this would be a text field that displays up-to-the-minute sports scores retrieved from a Web server. **Input text** allows the user to enter text in forms or surveys. You will only work with static text blocks in this tutorial.

You create a text block using the Text tool located in the toolbox. To set or change the properties of text such as the font size, color, alignment, and spacing between characters, you need to use the Property inspector. These properties will be displayed in the Property inspector when the Text tool or a text block is selected.

Text Tool

The **Text** tool is used to create text blocks for your documents. Text can be created in a **fixed-width** text block or in a **single-line** text block that extends as you type. If the width of the text block is fixed, the text wraps around to create new lines as needed. To create a fixed-width text block, you click the Text tool in the toolbox, and then you click and drag the text pointer on the Stage. The text block has a square handle in its upper-right corner indicating that the width of the text block will remain fixed. As you type, the words wrap around to the next line when you reach the right margin of the block. To create a single-line text block, click once on the Stage with the text pointer where you want the text to appear and begin typing. The text block has a round handle on the upper-right corner which indicates that the width of the text block extends as you type.

You can change a fixed-width text block to a single-line text block by double-clicking its square handle. The text block changes to one line and its handle becomes round. Similarly, if you drag the round handle of a single-line text block to adjust the width of the block, the handle becomes square indicating that the width of the block is now fixed.

Once you create a text block, you can move it on the Stage using the Arrow tool and you can also resize, rotate, and skew it using the Free Transform tool. The font, size, color, and other properties of the text are determined by the settings you specify in the Property inspector. You can set these properties before you type the text or you can select existing text and then change its properties. The Property inspector has many options. The main options you will work with are Font, Font Size, Text (fill) color, and text style. You choose the color for the text using the various Fill Color controls in the toolbox, the Color Mixer panel, or the Property inspector. The text options in the Property inspector are indentified in Figure 2-52.

Figure 2-52	PROPERTY INSPECTOR

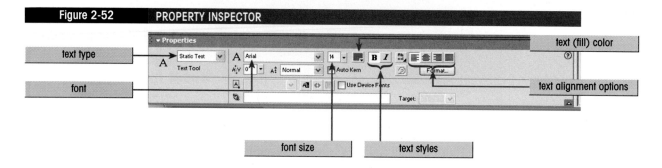

Use the Text tool to add two text blocks to the banner. You will set the Property inspector options before you create the text.

To add text to the banner:

1. Click the **Text** tool A in the toolbox. Now set the text properties.

2. Using the Property inspector, set the font to **Arial**, the font size to **22**, and the text (fill) color to **white**. Also, click the **Bold** button B to apply bold if necessary. Now you are ready to create the text block.

3. Click once in the top area of the Stage to create a single-line text box. Type **Flounders Pet Shop** as shown in Figure 2-53.

Figure 2-53   **TEXT BLOCK FOR BANNER**

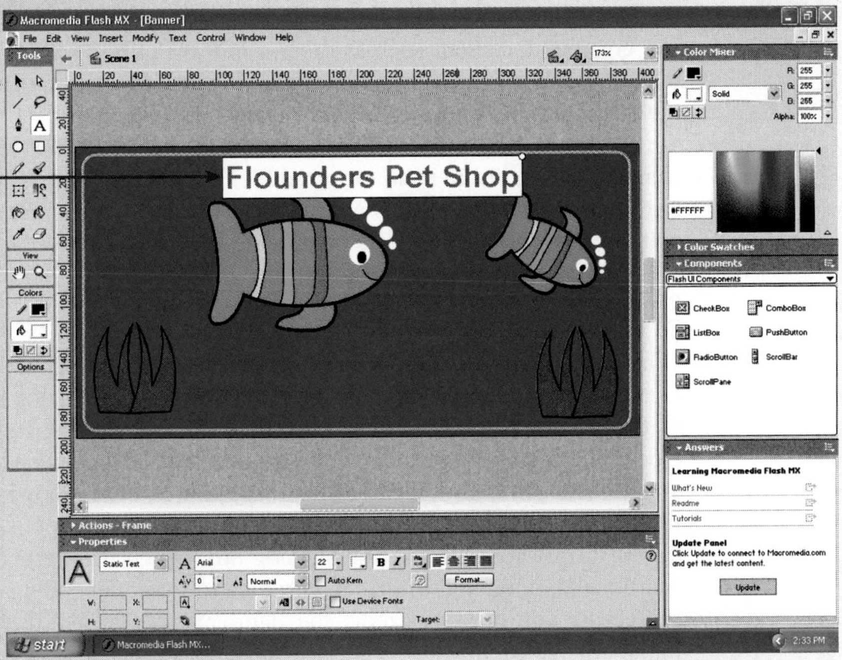

text block

4. Click the **Arrow** tool ⇡ in the toolbox, and then drag the **text block** to center it at the top of the Stage.

5. Click an empty area of the Stage to deselect the text block. Now you will create a second text block. First, change the text properties in the Property inspector for this text block.

6. Click the **Text** tool A. In the Property inspector, change the text font to another font of your choice, such as Times Roman, change the font size to **16**, and select **white** for the text color.

7. Now create a second text block by clicking once toward the bottom of the Stage. Type *Aquarium Tank and Fish Sale* in this text block.

8. If necessary, use the Arrow tool to center the text block. The banner is now complete, and matches the sketch Aly provided.

9. Click **File** on the menu bar, and then click **Save** to save the Banner.fla file.

You have completed the banner. Aly is very pleased with your work. She asks you to export the banner for use on the pet shop's Web site. Chris has recommended that the banner be exported in the GIF file format. Recall from Tutorial 1 that most Web pages use graphics that are in the GIF or JPG file format because these formats do not require a plug-in to display a Web page.

Exporting a Graphic for Use on the Web

A document you create in Macromedia Flash is saved in the FLA format. This format contains all of the different elements you create in Flash. When you need to revise the document you open the FLA file. When you are ready to place the image on a Web page, however, it needs to be published or exported. Publishing a movie will be covered in more detail in Tutorial 3 when you add animations to your documents. A published movie is in the SWF file format and requires the Flash Player plug-in to play in a Web browser. When you create a document such as the Flounders Pet Shop banner that does not have animation, you can export it instead of publishing it. **Exporting** means that the program converts the document into another file format such as GIF or JPG. Exporting also combines all of the individual elements of your document into one graphic. You cannot edit the individual elements of the image in an exported file. To edit the image's elements you need to go back to the corresponding FLA file. Once you export the document into a GIF or JPG file format, it can be placed in a Web page using HTML code.

Export Image Command

When you are ready to export a document you use the Export Image command on the File menu. When you select this command an Export Image dialog box opens in which you specify the location where the file will be saved, and the name of the exported file. You specify the type of file you want to export in the Save As type list box. The list box contains formats such as GIF and JPG, as well as formats specific to other drawing programs such as Adobe Illustrator. When you click the Save button, another dialog box may open, depending on the export format you selected. This dialog box, which is different for each export format, has additional options and settings from which to select depending on the particular file format.

Because you need to export the Banner.fla file to a GIF file format, you will use the Export Image command.

To export the banner to a GIF file format:

1. Make sure your Data Disk is in the appropriate drive.

2. Click **File** on the menu bar, and then click **Export Image** to open the Export Image dialog box.

3. In the Export Image dialog box, select the **Tutorial** folder in the **Tutorial.02** folder on your Data Disk. Enter **Banner** as the name of the file, and select **GIF Image** from the **Save As type** list box as shown in Figure 2-54. Click the **Save** button. An Export GIF dialog box opens.

| Figure 2-54 | EXPORT IMAGE DIALOG BOX |

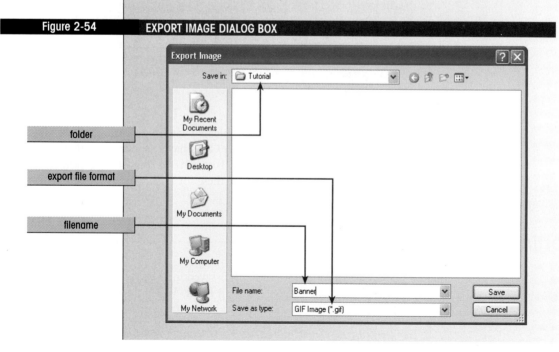

4. Accept the settings in the **Export GIF** dialog box by clicking the **OK** button. The banner is exported as a GIF file. Now you can close the FLA file.

5. Click **File** on the menu bar, and then click **Close** to close the file. If you are prompted to save your changes click the **Yes** button.

6. Click **File** on the menu bar, and then click **Exit** to exit Macromedia Flash.

You have exported the banner as a GIF file. Aly gave this GIF file to Chris, and had him place it in a Web page with the HTML needed to display the Banner.gif image. You can preview this Web page in your Web browser.

To preview the Banner.gif file in Internet Explorer:

1. Click the **Start** button ⊞ start on the taskbar. If you do not see Internet Explorer on the Start menu, then point to **All Programs** to display all the programs installed on your computer.

2. Click **Internet Explorer** on the Start menu or on the Programs menu. The Internet Explorer window opens, and displays the home page currently designated on your computer.

3. Click the URL that appears in the Address bar to select it. You will now enter the URL for the page stored on your Data Disk.

4. Type **A:\Tutorial.02\Tutorial\Flounder.htm** in the Address bar, and then press the **Enter** key.

5. When the Web page opens, the Banner.gif file displays as part of the page as shown in Figure 2-55.

Figure 2-55	WEB PAGE WITH EXPORTED BANNER

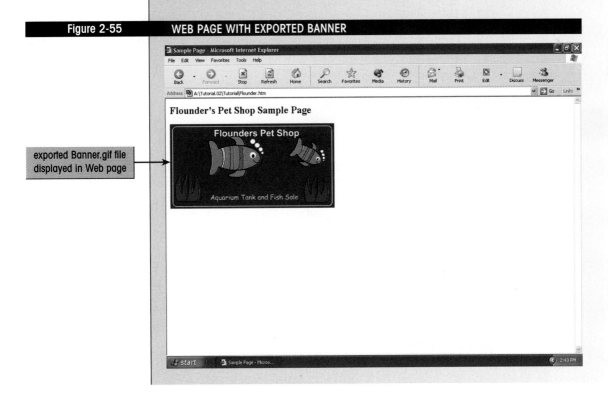

exported Banner.gif file displayed in Web page

TROUBLE? If the Banner.gif image is missing, you may have saved it in a different folder than that specified in the previous set of steps on exporting. Export it again into the Tutorial.02\Tutorial folder. Also, make sure the name of the exported file is Banner.gif, otherwise the browser will not display the banner.

6. Close Internet Explorer when you are done viewing the Web page with the banner.

In this session you learned how to use the tools to modify existing strokes and fills. You learned how to use the transformation tools to rotate, scale, and distort objects. You also learned how to create text blocks and how to set the properties for the text. You have used these tools to work on the banner for Flounders Pet Shop. Finally, you have exported the finished banner as a GIF file and previewed this file in a Web page.

Session 2.3 QUICK CHECK

1. The _____ tool changes a stroke's attributes such as its color. It also adds a stroke to a fill that has no stroke.

2. Which modifier can be used with the Free Transform tool to resize a selected object?

3. The Free Transform tool is used to modify an object's gradient fill. True or False?

4. What are the two types of text fields you can create with Macromedia Flash?

5. How do you create a fixed-width text block?

6. Which panel is used to set text attributes such as the font and size?

7. How can you change a single-line text block into a fixed-width text block?

8. If a text block displays a square handle in its upper-right corner, what type of text block is it?

REVIEW ASSIGNMENTS

Aly is very pleased with the progress you have made in learning the basic tools of Macromedia Flash. She is especially pleased with the banner you created for the Flounders Pet Shop's Web site. She asks you to modify the banner by changing the color of one fish, adding a third fish, modifying one of the plant leaves, and changing one of the text blocks. She also wants you to change the color and style of the rectangle and to draw several lines.

If necessary, start Macromedia Flash and insert your Data Disk in the appropriate disk drive, and then do the following:

1. Open the **Banner.fla** file which you created in the tutorial from the Tutorial.02\ Tutorial folder on your Data Disk, set the panels to their default layout, close the Timeline, and set the Stage magnification level to show the entire banner in the Stage window.

2. Move the larger fish so that it is centered on the Stage. Create a copy of this fish. Move the copy to the left side of the banner, reduce its size to about half the size of the original, and rotate it so that it appears to be swimming in an upward direction.

3. Use the Paint Bucket tool to change the orange color of the new fish to blue. (*Hint*: You need to double-click the fish first to get into group-edit mode to make the changes. Double-click an empty area of the Stage to exit group-edit mode.)

4. Use the Paint Bucket tool to change the orange color of the small fish on the right side of the banner to pink. Also, change the color of its stripes so that the left one is blue, the middle one is dark green, and the right one is yellow.

5. Select the second group of plant leaves on the left side of the banner. Reduce the size of the leaves to about one-third of the original size. Repeat this for the second group of plant leaves on the right side of the banner.

Explore 6. Select and then delete the bottom text block. Add three new text blocks with the same text properties as the text block you deleted. One text block should read **Fish**, the other should read **Aquarium Tanks**, and the third should read **On Sale Now!**. Place the first text block on the left side below the blue fish. Place the second text block on the right side below the pink fish, and place the third text block in the center below the larger fish.

7. Use the Pencil tool to draw horizontal lines under each of the three new text blocks. The lines should be yellow, have a height of 2, and appear as underlines for the text.

Explore 8. Use the Property inspector and the Text tool to change the text in the top text block so that Flounders Pet Shop is in italics and has a font size of 26. (*Hint*: Select the text first before you apply the italics style). Center the text block if necessary.

Explore 9. Use the Ink Bottle tool to change the color, height, and style of the rectangle's stroke. First, choose a bright-green color, set the stroke height to 3, and choose a stroke style other than Solid in the Property inspector.

10. Save your revised banner to the Tutorial.02\Review folder on your Data Disk. Name it **Banner2.fla**.

11. Close the Banner2.fla file, and exit Flash.

CASE PROBLEMS

Case 1. Creating a Banner for Sandy's Party Center Sandy's Party Center is a party supplies store that specializes in products for every type of celebration. They sell party decorations such as balloons, ribbons, and banners. They also sell greeting cards, party plates, and napkins, and will even assist customers in planning their party. The store has just opened and is preparing for its grand opening celebration and sale.

Sandy Rodriguez, owner of the store, recently hired John Rossini to develop a Web site promoting the store's products and services. Sandy has asked John to develop a new banner for the Web site to promote the grand opening celebration. She asks John to include graphics on the banner that depict a party and to add text about the grand opening. An example of the completed banner is shown in Figure 2-56, which you can refer to as you complete this case problem.

Figure 2-56   SANDY'S PARTY CENTER BANNER

If necessary, start Macromedia Flash, insert your Data Disk in the appropriate drive, and then complete the following:

1. Start with a new document. Change the document properties so that the width is 500 pixels and the height is 150 pixels. Change the background color to a light yellow (use #FFFF99).

2. Add a text block at the top of the Stage. Use a font such as Comic Sans MS, a font size of 40, and blue text. Bold and italicize the text. Type **Sandy's Party Center** in the text block.

3. Add a second text block with a smaller font size of 18 and black text. Type **Grand Opening this Saturday!**, and on a separate line in the same text block type **Come celebrate with us!**. Make sure this text is centered within the text block.

4. Draw three balloons on the left side of the Stage using the Oval tool with different colors for each balloon. Do not include a stroke for the balloons. Draw a string for each balloon using the Pencil tool with a light-gray color for the stroke. Draw three more balloons on the right side of the Stage with different colors.

5. Draw a party hat by first drawing a triangle shape with the Pen tool. Use a black stroke and a red fill. Once you have drawn the triangle shape, use the Arrow tool to curve the triangle's bottom line. Curve it slightly in a downward direction to make it look like a party hat, referring to Figure 2-56 if necessary.

6. Make several copies of the hat and change the fill color of each copy. When you copy the hat, make sure you select both its stroke and fill. Position the hats in different locations of the Stage.

Explore 7. Use the Brush tool to draw confetti on the Stage. Select a small brush size from the Brush Size modifier in the options area of the toolbox. Select a brush color using the Fill Color control in the toolbox. Then click dots with the tool on the banner to create the confetti. Create different colored dots throughout the Stage.

8. Create a rectangle as a border around all of the objects on the Stage. The rectangle should have slightly rounded corners, a pink stroke, no fill, a stroke height of 3, and a solid style. Draw the rectangle so that it is just inside the edges of the Stage.

9. Save the banner in the Tutorial.02\Cases folder on your Data Disk. Name the file **spcbanner**.

10. Use the Export Image command on the File menu to export the image to your Data Disk in GIF file format. Use the same name as the FLA file, and accept the default settings in the Export GIF dialog box. When you are done, close the FLA file and exit Flash.

Case 2. Creating a Banner for River City Music River City Music, established in 1990, is a musical instruments and supplies store that specializes in meeting the needs of local schools. The store provides many music-related services to its customers, including the sale of band instruments and sheet music for all age and skill levels. River City Music staff also work with private piano teachers by referring potential students to them and by allowing them to use the store's large presentation room for piano recitals.

Alex Smith was recently commissioned by Janet Meyers, store manager, to develop a new banner for the River City Music Web site. The new banner will be used to advertise an upcoming piano sale that will be held in conjunction with their anniversary sale. After meeting with Janet, Alex decides that the banner and its graphic elements can be developed using Macromedia Flash. The banner will contain text with the store's name and sale information as well as graphic elements depicting piano keys and musical notes. An example of the completed banner is shown in Figure 2-57, which you can refer to as you complete this case problem.

Figure 2-57	RIVER CITY MUSIC BANNER

If necessary, start Macromedia Flash, insert your Data Disk in the appropriate drive, and then complete the following:

1. Open the **music** document, located in the Tutorial.02\Cases folder on your Data Disk. This document is a partially completed banner. Save the document as **rcmbanner** in the Cases folder on your Data Disk.

2. Change the document properties so that the width is 300 pixels and the height is 200 pixels. Change the background color to a light blue by entering #0099FF in the color pop-up window's hexadecimal text box.

3. Use the rectangles contained in the document to create the piano keys graphic. The rectangles are grouped so that their strokes and fills can be copied and moved together as one object. Start by creating two copies of the larger white rectangle.

4. Display the rulers and drag a horizontal guide line and place it about 50 pixels from the top of the Stage. Drag a vertical guide line about 80 pixels from the left of the Stage. Make sure Snap to Guides is turned on. Move the three white rectangles to the middle of the Stage below and to the right of the guide lines. As you move the rectangles drag them from their top edges so they will snap to the horizontal guide. The rectangles should be placed right next to each other without overlapping.

5. Create one copy of the smaller black rectangle. Place the copy of the black rectangle on top of the two white rectangles on the far left so that it equally overlaps both of them. As you move the black rectangle, drag it from its top edge so that it snaps to the horizontal guide.

6. Move the original black rectangle on top of the two white rectangles on the far right so that it equally overlaps them. Adjust its position so that it is lined up with the first black rectangle. If the black rectangle is behind the white rectangles, use the Arrange options on the Modify menu to bring it forward.

7. Select all of the objects on the Stage and group them together. Create two copies of this larger group and line up all of the objects so that they form the piano keys graphic.

Explore ▷

8. To draw the musical notes, use the Oval tool. On the lower-left side of the Stage, draw a small oval with a black stroke and white fill. Make the oval about 10 pixels high and 15 pixels wide. You may need to turn off Snap to Objects to keep the program from drawing a perfect circle. Then use the Line tool to draw a vertical line about 30 pixels high for the note's stem. Draw the line on the right side of the oval so that the note resembles the letter "d". Select the entire note and make it into a group. Make one copy of the note.

9. Draw another musical note as before but this time use a black fill. Group the elements that make up the note, and then create a copy.

10. Rotate one of the white-filled notes. The note should now resemble the letter "p". Do the same for one of the black-filled notes.

11. In the lower-right corner of the Stage, draw a horizontal line about 100 pixels in length. The line should be black, have a stroke height of 1, and a solid style. Create four copies of the line. Arrange the lines so that they are approximately 15 pixels apart. Then use the Align options under the Modify menu so that the lines are aligned on their left sides and that they are distributed equally.

12. Move the musical notes between the horizontal lines. Use Figure 2-57 as a guide.

13. Create a single-line text block for the name of the store. Place the text block on the top part of the Stage. Use a font such as Monotype Corsiva, a font height of 36, and make the text bold and italic. Type **River City Music** in the text block. Create a fixed-width text block on the lower-left side of the Stage. Use the same font as before, but with a font height of 22. Type **Piano Sale! Now through the end of the month!**.

14. Create a rectangle as a border around all of the objects on the Stage. The rectangle should have a dark-blue stroke, no fill, a stroke height of 3, and a dotted style. Draw the rectangle so that it is just inside the edges of the Stage.

15. Save this banner in the Tutorial.02\Cases folder on your Data Disk.

16. Use the Export Image command on the File menu to export the image to your Data Disk in GIF file format. Use the same name as the FLA file and accept the default settings in the Export GIF dialog box. When you are done, close the FLA file and exit Flash.

Case 3. Creating a Logo for Sonny's Auto Center Sonny's Auto Center is a used car dealership offering competitive prices and a friendly no-pressure atmosphere. Sonny Jackson, owner of the auto center, has been in business for 10 years and has gradually built his business from a small corner lot with a few dozen cars to a large commercial lot with hundreds of cars. Sonny attributes his success to his focus on customer service. Customers are able to look through the auto center's inventory in a relaxed environment. When they are ready to buy, they find friendly, competent sales personnel willing to help them through the whole purchasing process.

Amanda Lester was recently contracted by Sonny to update the company's Web site. As other car dealers have developed new Web sites, Sonny wants to make sure his company's Web site stays up to date and remains an effective marketing tool for his business. Amanda meets with Sonny and he requests that she first develop a new logo for his business. The logo should contain the business name, phone number, and an appropriate slogan, along with some graphics. Amanda decides that Macromedia Flash is an ideal program to use to develop the logo. An example of the completed banner is shown in Figure 2-58, which you can refer to as you complete this case problem.

Figure 2-58   **SONNY'S AUTO CENTER LOGO**

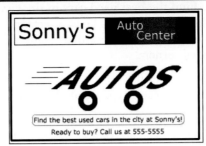

If necessary, start Macromedia Flash, insert your Data Disk in the appropriate drive, and then complete the following:

1. Start with a new document. Change the document properties so that the width is 300 pixels and the height is 200 pixels.

2. Start by creating a rectangle across the top of the Stage. Use a black stroke with a height of 1 and a solid style. Do not include a fill color. Make the rectangle about 280 pixels wide and about 50 pixels high. Place the rectangle about 10 pixels from the left of the Stage and 10 pixels from the top.

3. Create a text block inside the rectangle. Use Verdana or a similar font. Make the font size 30 and use black text. Type **Sonny's** in the text block. Position the text block on the left side of the rectangle.

4. Draw a straight vertical line inside the rectangle to the right of the text block. One end of the line should snap to the top of the rectangle and the other end should snap to the bottom of the rectangle. This line effectively splits the rectangle into two sections.

5. Apply a new fill to the right section of the rectangle. The fill should be a blue radial gradient. Use the fifth gradient from the left on the color palette.

6. Create a new text block on the inside of the rectangle over the gradient. The text should be white with a font size of 18. Type **Auto** in the text block. Position the text in the upper-left area of the rectangle.

7. Create another text block the same as in the previous step. Type **Center** in this text block. Position the text so that the "C" is right below the "o" in the "Auto" text block.

Explore

8. Create a text block in the center of the Stage with a font size of 46 and black text. Type **AUTOS** in this text block. Using the Free Transform tool skew the text block so that the letters are slanted to the right.

9. Add four straight horizontal lines of about 40 pixels in length each. Draw the lines to the left of the letter "A" in the center text block. Space the lines equally apart and place each one approximately the same distance from the letter "A".

10. On the bottom part of the Stage, draw a circle of about 30 pixels in diameter. The circle should have a black fill and no stroke.

11. Draw another circle of about 15 pixels in diameter. This circle should have a white fill and a black stroke. Group the stroke and fill for this second circle. Then move the smaller grouped circle into the middle of the larger circle to form the image of a car tire.

12. Select both of the circles that make up the tire and then make them into a group. Make a copy of this grouped object. Then move the two tire graphics right below the text block on the center of the Stage. Place one tire right below the "U" on the "AUTOS" text. Place the other one right below the "O".

13. Add a single-line text block below the tire graphics. Use a font size of 10 and black text. Type **Find the best used cars in the city at Sonny's!** into the text block. Center the text block on the Stage. Draw a rectangle around this text block. The rectangle should have a light-gray stroke with a height of 1 and no color for the fill. It should have rounded corners.

14. Below the previous text block create another text block with the same attributes as in the previous step. Type **Ready to buy? Call us at 555-5555** into the text block.

15. Add a rectangle to frame all of the graphic elements for the logo. Use a black stroke with a height of 3 and no color for the fill. Do not round the corners. Draw the rectangle so that is just inside the edges of the Stage.

16. Save the logo in the Tutorial.02\Cases folder on your Data Disk. Name the file **saclogo**.

17. Use the Export Image command on the File menu to export the image to your Data Disk in GIF file format. Use the same name as the FLA file and accept the default settings in the Export GIF dialog box. When you are done, close the FLA file and exit Flash.

Case 4. Creating a banner for LAL Financial Services LAL Financial Services, headquartered in San Antonio, Texas, is one of the state's largest commercial banking organizations and has been in business for more than 20 years. The company operates through an extensive distribution network in many of the major cities in Texas. LAL's primary businesses include deposit, credit, trust, and investment services. Through various subsidiaries the company also provides credit cards, mortgage banking, and insurance.

Christopher Perez, head of Marketing, is heading a new effort to improve the company's Web site. After meeting with Webmaster Elizabeth Danehill, they decide to start by developing a new banner to be used on the company's home page. Elizabeth assigns the task to the graphics designer, Mia Jones. The new banner is to portray the financial strength of the company and will include the company's name, as well as keywords highlighting their services. Mia decides to use Macromedia Flash to develop the banner. An example of the completed banner is shown in Figure 2-59, to which you can refer as you complete this case problem.

Figure 2-59   LAL FINANCIAL SERVICES BANNER

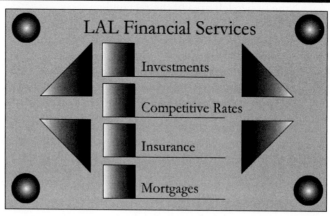

If necessary, start Macromedia Flash, insert your Data Disk in the appropriate drive, and then complete the following:

1. Start with a new document. Change the document properties so that the width is 500 pixels and the height is 300 pixels. Change the background color to a light gray.

2. Create a circle in the upper-left corner of the Stage. Use the gray radial gradient fill found in the color pop-up window. Do not use a color for the stroke. Make the circle about 45 pixels in diameter.

3. Create three copies of the circle and place each in a separate corner of the Stage.

Explore

4. Create a square of about 90 pixels on each side. Use the gray linear gradient fill found in the color pop-up window and use a thin black stroke. Convert this square into a triangle by moving one of its corner anchor points to the center of the square until the two lines adjacent to the corner point merge.

Explore

5. Group the elements of the triangle and create three copies of the triangle group. Place each copy in a separate quadrant of the Stage. Use the Transform submenu located on the Modify menu to rotate and arrange the four triangles as shown in Figure 2-59.

6. Create a square in the middle of the Stage. Use the same gray linear gradient as before and a stroke of 1. Make the square approximately 50 pixels on each side. Group the square's stroke and fill together. Create three more copies of the grouped square and line all four squares vertically.

7. Draw a straight horizontal line from the lower-right corner of the first square to extend to the right about 140 pixels. Copy this line three times and snap each copy to the lower-right corners of each of the copied squares.

8. Create a text block at the top of the Stage. Use a font such as Garamond, with a font size of 30, and black text. Type **LAL Financial Services** in the text block. Center the text block within the Stage.

9. Create another text block right above the top horizontal line, to the right of the square. Use the same font as in the previous step but reduce the font size to 22. Type **Investments** in this text block. Create three more text blocks in the same way. Type **Competitive Rates** in one, **Insurance** in the next, and **Mortgages** in the third. Position each block so that it is about 10 pixels from its respective square.

10. Save the banner in the Tutorial.02\Cases folder on your Data Disk. Name the file **lfsbanner.**

11. Use the Export Image command on the File menu to export the image to your Data Disk in GIF file format. Use the same name as the FLA file, and accept the default settings in the Export GIF dialog box. When you are done, close the FLA file and exit Flash.

QUICK **C**HECK ANSWERS

Session 2.1

1. The default dimensions for a Macromedia Flash document are 550 pixels in width and 400 pixels in height.

2. You create, import, and assemble all of the graphic objects for your document on the Stage.

3. To access the magnification levels to change the view of the Stage you can click View on the menu bar, point to Magnification, and select one of the levels. Or you can access the levels from the Zoom control list arrow in the upper-right corner of the Stage window.

4. False. The grid lines do not become part of your document.

5. To display the rulers, click View on the menu bar, and then click Rulers.

6. To create a horizontal guide, drag your pointer from the top ruler down to the Stage window.

7. Strokes refer to lines and outlines, while fills refer to the areas enclosed by lines and outlines.

8. False. The blue oval cuts away at the ungrouped red rectangle.

9. False. Grouped objects can be edited in group-edit mode.

10. By default, 216 Web-safe colors are shown in the color pop-up window.

11. The Color Mixer panel is used to create custom colors.

12. You can select both the stroke and the fill of an oval at the same time by double-clicking on either the stroke or fill. Or you can draw a rectangular marquee around the oval with the Arrow tool.

13. To select several objects at the same time using the Lasso tool, drag a marquee around the objects.

Session 2.2

1. False. When drawing a shape with the Oval tool, Flash helps you draw a perfect circle when the Snap to Objects options is selected.

2. To draw a rectangle with rounded corners, click the Round Rectangle Radius button, and enter a point value in the Rectangle Settings dialog box.

3. The Pen tool is used to draw line and curve segments by creating anchor points that connect them.

4. The Pencil Mode modifier helps straighten lines you draw with the Pencil tool.

5. Click an object's stroke with the Eyedropper tool. The pointer turns into an ink bottle. Then click the other object to apply the stroke's attributes.

6. You can use the Paint Bucket tool to add a fill to an enclosed area that has no fill.

Session 2.3

1. The Ink Bottle tool changes a stroke's attributes such as its color. It also adds a stroke to a fill that has no stroke.

2. The Scale modifier can be used with the Free Transform tool to resize a selected object.

3. False: You use the Fill Transform tool to modify an object's gradient fill.

4. The two types of text fields are dynamic and input.

5. To create a fixed-width text block, click and drag the Stage to set the desired width.

6. You use the Properties panel to set the text attributes such as the font and size.

7. You can change a single-line text block into a fixed-width text block by dragging its round corner handle.

8. A text block that displays a square handle in its upper-right corner is a fixed-width text block.

In this tutorial you will:

- Learn the different elements of animation

- Create frames and layers

- Organize frames and layers using the Timeline

- Create symbols and instances of symbols

- Organize symbols in the Library panel

- Edit symbols and instances of symbols

- Create frame-by-frame animations

- Create tweened animations

- Animate text blocks

CREATING ANIMATIONS

Developing Animations for Action Web Design Clients

CASE

Actions Web Design

At the regular staff planning meeting for Actions Web Design, Aly Garcia, graphics designer, reports that she has been very pleased with the progress you have made learning Macromedia Flash. She is especially pleased with the Flounders Pet Shop banner you created using the program's drawing and painting tools, which she shows to the rest of the staff. Gloria Adamson, co-owner of Actions Web Design, asks Aly to meet with Joe Flounders, owner of Flounders Pet Shop, to show him the banner. She also mentions that in a previous conversation with Joe he expressed an interest in having animation added to the banner. He has recently seen some Web sites that use animated graphics and thinks that animation could attract more attention to the sale the banner will be promoting. Aly meets with Joe to show him the banner and to discuss what type of animation he had in mind. After this meeting Aly revises the banner you previously created for Flounders Pet Shop and uses it to put together a partially completed banner which will be the basis for the new animated banner. In a meeting with Aly it is decided that the banner will be revised so that there will be two animated fish swimming in the tank. The plant will also be animated by making the leaves move slightly back and forth. The text blocks with the store's name and the sale promotion will also be animated. Aly gives you a printout of the partially completed banner with instructions on what needs to be done to complete it. Figure 3-1 shows a printout of the preliminary banner with instructions on what needs to be done to complete it.

Figure 3-1	FLOUNDERS PET SHOP PARTIALLY COMPLETED BANNER

animate fish to swim from one side of the aquarium to the other; create copy of fish; change this copy to have different colors than original fish; make it smaller and animate it to swim in opposite direction of original fish

add text block; animate it to move in from side; use yellow text color

add text block; animate it to move in from side; use yellow text color

Flounders Pet Shop

Aquarium

Tank

and
Fish Sale!

animate plant graphic and add two more copies next to it; make one copy larger and flip another one horizontally

add text blocks; make "and" appear after "Aquarium" and "Tank" are in place; animate "Fish Sale!" to appear last, and size; use yellow text color

You will continue your training in Flash by learning how to create animations and by adding the fish, plant, and text animations to the Flounders Pet Shop banner.

Aly has also been working on a banner for another of Actions clients, Jackson's Sports. She has added some animations to this banner. To familiarize yourself with Flash animations, she suggests you study what she has done.

In this tutorial you will learn how to create frame-by-frame, motion tweened, and shape tweened animations. You will learn how to coordinate these animations in the Timeline using frames and layers. You will also learn how to use the Library panel to organize and edit symbols used in animations.

SESSION 3.1

In this session you will learn about the different elements that make up a Macromedia Flash animation. You will also explore the Timeline, work with layers, frames, and explore the Library panel. You will also create and edit symbols and instances of symbols.

Elements of Animation

Recall one of the most powerful features of Macromedia Flash is its ability to create animation. Animation is achieved by changing the content of an object from one moment in time to the next. In order to create an animation you need to review some basic elements of a Flash document. A document is made up of scenes, layers, frames, and the graphic objects, such as symbols, that display on the Stage as shown in Figure 3-2.

Figure 3-2 ELEMENTS OF A FLASH DOCUMENT

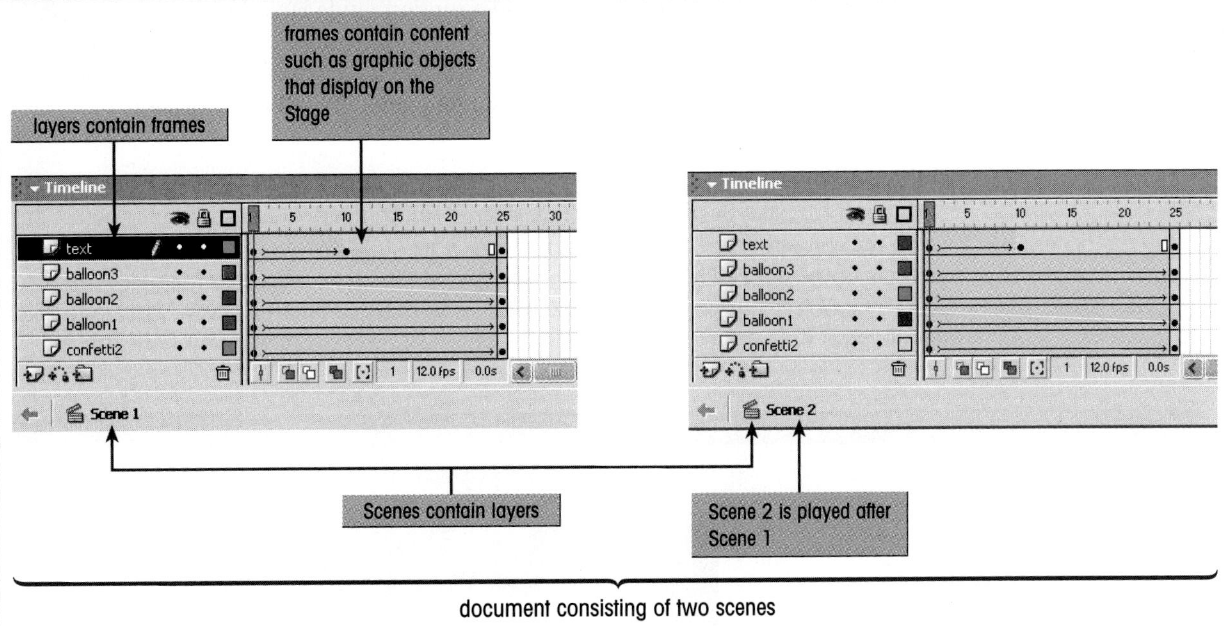

frames contain content such as graphic objects that display on the Stage

layers contain frames

Scenes contain layers

Scene 2 is played after Scene 1

document consisting of two scenes

Scenes provide a way to break up a large movie into smaller movies that are more manageable. A Flash document may be divided into scenes similar to a motion picture. Just like the scenes in a motion picture are played in order, the scenes in a Flash movie are also played one after the other. Every Flash document starts with one scene. In this and the other tutorials you will work with only one scene in each document. This tutorial focuses on the other three components of animation. The Timeline is the tool you use in Flash to create, organize, and modify the layers and frames for each scene in your document. The Library panel is the tool you use to work with symbols.

Layers

Layers are used to organize the content of your document. A Flash document starts with one layer. You can add more layers as you add more graphic objects to a document and then place these objects on the different layers to keep them from interacting with each other. Recall from Tutorial 2 that objects you draw or move on top of other objects will split or merge with those objects. Placing objects on separate layers prevents this and allows you to overlap the objects on the Stage. Objects on different layers can also be moved in front or in back of each other by changing the order in which the layers are organized. Layers are especially useful when animating more than one object at the same time. An object on one layer can be animated to move in one direction while an object on another layer can be animated to move in a different direction. Both animations can occur at the same time, but do not impact one another in any way. In certain types of animations, which will be covered later in this tutorial, an object that is animated must reside on its own layer.

Guide Layers

A **guide layer** is a special type of layer that may be used to align objects on other layers to the objects on the guide layer. The contents of the guide layer do not appear in the published movie. For example, if you draw a rectangle on a guide layer you can use the rectangle to guide you as you draw all the objects of the document. The rectangle appears on the Stage in your document but does not show in the published movie. Any layer can be converted to a guide layer by selecting Guide in the Layer Properties dialog box.

A guide layer may also be used to provide a path for an animated object to follow. This is called a **motion guide layer**. You can add a motion guide layer by clicking Motion Guide on the Insert menu or by clicking the Add Motion Guide icon at the bottom of the Timeline. The layer below a motion guide layer is called a **guided layer**. You will be creating a guide layer for the animated banner for Flounders Pet Shop in Session 3.2.

Mask Layers

Another special type of layer is a mask layer. A **mask layer** contains a graphic object through which the content of the **masked layer** shows. The masked layer is below the mask layer. The contents of the masked layer are hidden except for the area covered by the object on the mask layer. The object can be a filled shape such as an oval, or it can be text. The content of the masked layer only shows through when the object is over it as shown in Figure 3-3.

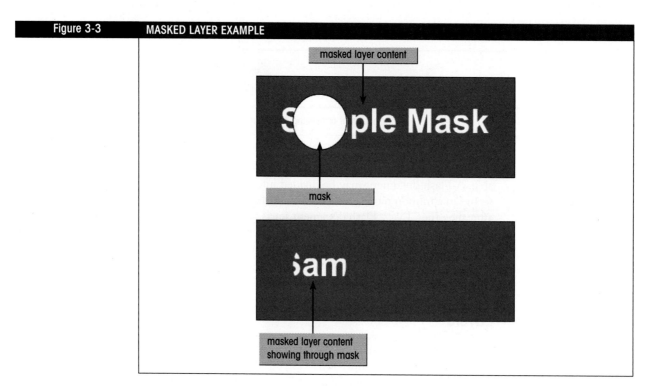

| Figure 3-3 | MASKED LAYER EXAMPLE |

You can convert a layer into a mask layer by selecting Mask from the Layer Properties dialog box for that layer. You will view mask layers in Session 3.3.

Frames

Frames contain the content for an animation and represent a particular instant in time. For example, at the default frame rate of 12 frames per second, one frame is displayed for 1/12 of a second during the animation. Placing different content on each frame or slightly modifying the content from one frame to the next creates the perception of movement. This movement is what makes up an animation. To create an animation you start by adding more frames to a layer. The frames you add are used to create new content or to change the content from previous frames. As you add more frames, you are extending the life of the animation. Initially, a document contains just one frame and that one frame is called a keyframe. A **keyframe** is a frame that represents a change in the content from the previous frame. If you add regular frames, the content remains the same in the new frames. If you want the content to change, then you add a keyframe. Adding frames is done using the Timeline.

The Timeline

The **Timeline**, which appears above the Stage in the Flash program window, is used to control and coordinate the timing of the animation by determining how and when the frames for each layer are displayed. The Timeline is also a means of creating, modifying, and organizing layers and frames. Figure 3-4 shows the Timeline for an animation Aly has created for Jackson's Sports. Figure 3-5 identifies and describes the components of the Timeline.

Figure 3-4	TIMELINE OF A SAMPLE DOCUMENT

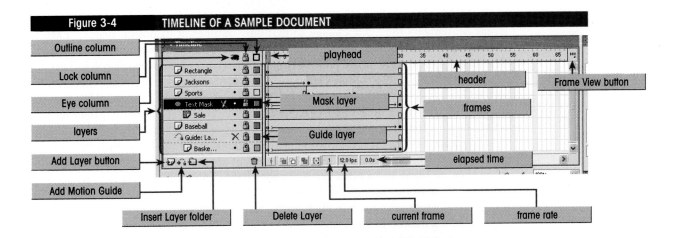

Figure 3-5	ELEMENTS OF THE TIMELINE

TIMELINE ELEMENT	PURPOSE
Layers	Used to organize the various graphic objects that are part of a document
Eye column	Hides or displays the content for all layers
Lock column	Locks or unlocks the content for all layers; you must unlock a layer before it can be edited
Outline column	Displays the content for all layers in Outline view or Normal view
Playhead	Indicates which frame is currently being displayed
Header	Displays the frame numbers; you can click a frame number in the header to select the frame
Frames	Contain content to be displayed for each instant in time
Frame View button	Displays the Frame View pop-up menu with options for controlling the way frames are displayed
Add Layer button	Adds a new layer above the current layer
Add Motion Guide	Inserts a motion guide layer above the current layer; the current layer becomes the guided layer
Insert Layer folder	Inserts a layer folder above the current layer
Delete Layer	Deletes the current layer
Current frame	Indicates the current frame being displayed on the Stage
Frame rate	Number of frames displayed in each second of time
Elapsed time	Shows how much time has elapsed since the start of the animation

The layer controls are displayed in the area on the left side of the Timeline. Each row within this column represents one layer. Above the list of layers there are three icons. The icon in the first column is the Show/Hide icon. When you click the dot in this column for a layer a red x is displayed in place of the dot and the layer's content is temporarily hidden. You click the red x to display the content again. The icon in the next column represents the Lock column. When you click the dot in this column a padlock icon replaces it to indicate the layer is locked and cannot be edited. It is a good idea to lock a layer once you finish editing its content. You click the layer's padlock icon again to unlock the layer. The icon in the third column represents the Outline column. When you click the colored square in this column, the layer's content is displayed in Outline view. When you select Outline view, the layer's contents on the Stage change so that only outlines of its objects display. Each layer has its own outline color to distinguish its contents on the Stage when it is in Outline view. The color of the outline is the same as the Outline view control square's color. This is useful when working with a complex animation and you want to see how the objects from the various layers overlap each other. You click a layer's square in the Outline column to return to Normal view where the contents are not in outline form. Each of these properties may be set at one time for all of the layers by clicking the icons at the top of the columns.

The frames for a layer are shown in a row to the right of the layer. Regular frames that are empty are white. Those that have some content are gray. Keyframes contain a white dot when they are blank and a black dot when they have content. The layer icon to the left of a layer's name indicates the type of layer it is. For example, regular layers have a page icon, while a mask layer has a mask icon. A guide layer has a guide icon and a motion guide layer appears with a motion guide icon.

Another important element of the Timeline is the playhead. The **playhead** indicates which frame is currently being displayed. The playhead is represented on the Timeline header by a red rectangle with a red vertical line below it. When you play an animation the playhead moves along the Timeline header to display the different frames that make up the animation.

Aly wants you to explore the Timeline of the Jackson's Sports banner she has been developing.

To explore the Timeline of the sports banner:

1. Make sure that your computer is turned on, that the Windows desktop is displayed, and that your Data Disk is in the appropriate drive.

2. Start Flash, and then position the panels to their default positions by clicking **Window** on the menu bar, pointing to **Panel Sets**, and then clicking **Default Layout**. Now you can open Aly's document containing the sports banner.

3. Open the **sports.fla** file located in the Tutorial.03\Tutorial folder on your Data Disk.

4. Click **View** on the menu bar, point to **Magnification**, and click **Show All**. The view of the Stage changes to show all of the contents. See Figure 3-6.

Figure 3-6   **SPORTS BANNER**

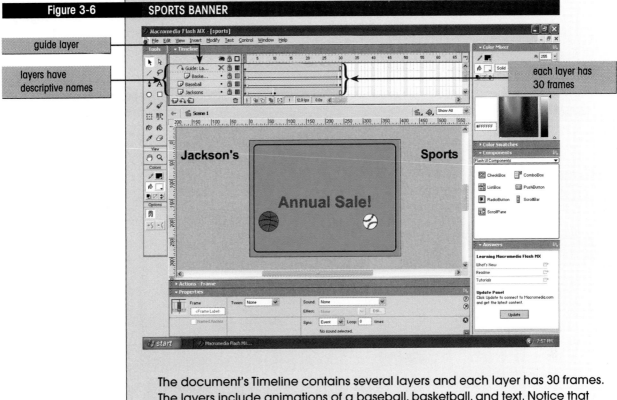

The document's Timeline contains several layers and each layer has 30 frames. The layers include animations of a baseball, basketball, and text. Notice that each layer has a name descriptive of its contents. You will see later in this session how to change the name of a layer. The Timeline also shows an example of a guide layer. Now play the animation and watch the Timeline as it displays the elements of the document.

5. Click **Control** on the menu bar, and then click **Play**. As the playhead moves from Frame 1 to Frame 30 in the Timeline, the baseball and basketball move in different directions on the Stage, the baseball decreases in size, and the text moves in from the sides of the Stage.

The Timeline displays useful information that you need to monitor as you view an animation. The Elapsed Time control displays the time that has elapsed from Frame 1 to the frame the playhead is currently on. The elapse time depends on the frame rate, which is also shown at the bottom of the Timeline. By default, the frame rate is 12 frames per second (fps), which means that an animation that spans 12 frames takes one second to play. The length of the Sports banner animation you just viewed can be determined by looking at the elapsed time when the playhead is in the last frame. In this case the length of the animation is 2.4 seconds.

As you can see from the sports banner animation, a movie can have a large number of frames, and the contents of the frames may look very similar from one frame to the next. As you work with content on the Stage it is important to always be aware of which frame is being displayed, because that is the frame whose content you are working with. Because the Stage and its contents may look very similar from one frame to the next, it is easy to get confused. If you are not careful you can change or create the content for the wrong frame. The Timeline makes it easy for you to determine which frame you are working with. Recall you can check the location of the playhead in the Timeline header. In Figure 3-7 the playhead in the Timeline header is on Frame 30, which means the contents of Frame 30 are currently displayed on the Stage. You can also see which frame is currently being displayed by looking at the Current frame indicator at the bottom of the Timeline window. This changes as the playhead moves to a different frame.

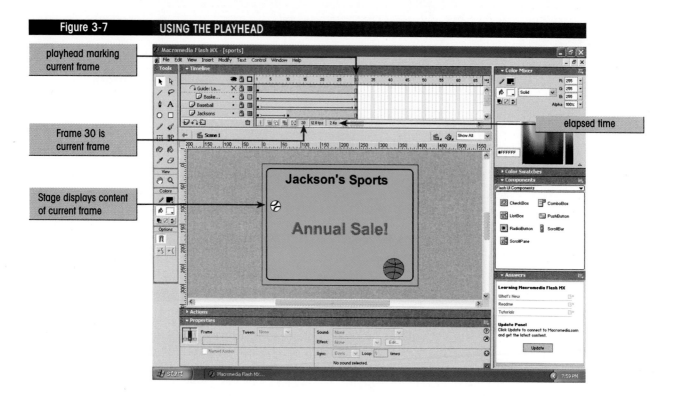

Figure 3-7   **USING THE PLAYHEAD**

playhead marking current frame

Frame 30 is current frame

Stage displays content of current frame

elapsed time

As you develop your animation, the number of frames can grow very rapidly, as well as the number of layers. So there may come a time when you need to change the view of the Timeline in order to work more efficiently with the elements of your animation.

Changing the View of the Timeline

The Timeline can be modified in several ways. For example, you can extend the Timeline to show more frames by closing the panels on the right side of the Flash program window. Recall that to close a panel you click its options menu control to display the options menu, and you then click Close Panel. You can also temporarily hide the panels by pressing the Tab key on your keyboard. You press the Tab key again to redisplay the panels.

Another way to modify the view of the Timeline is by selecting one of the options on the Timeline's Frame View pop-up menu as shown in Figure 3-8.

Figure 3-8	TIMELINE'S FRAME VIEW POP-UP MENU

Frame View pop-up menu

select a width for the frame

reduce height of layers   displays frames' tints   Preview frame content

The first set of options, **Tiny**, **Small**, **Normal**, **Medium**, and **Large** change the width of the frames. Tiny and Small allow you to see more frames within the Timeline window. Medium and Large can be used when you need to see more of the frame's contents. An example of this is when you are working with sounds. (Sounds will be covered in Tutorial 4.) A sound's waveform, which is a representation of the sound, is displayed in a frame when you add it to a document. Making the frames wider makes it easier to see more of the waveform. The **Short** option reduces the height of the layers. This can be useful when you have many layers and you need to fit more of them into the Timeline window. If you deselect the **Tinted Frames** option, the color tints on the frames are removed. By default, the frames are tinted different colors depending on the type of content they contain. For example, the frames of a motion tweened animation are tinted blue. You will learn about motion tweened animations later in this tutorial. Finally, if you use the **Preview** or **Preview in Context** options, the frames in the Timeline will show thumbnail previews of their content. The Preview command shows a thumbnail of the frame's content that is scaled to fit the Timeline's frame. The Preview in Context command shows a preview of the entire frame's contents including white or empty space. The thumbnails for this command are generally smaller than for the Preview command.

Because you will be working extensively with the Timeline, you will practice changing the view of its frames and layers. You will continue to practice with the sports banner created by Aly.

To change the view of the Timeline:

1. To make more room for the Timeline, press the **Tab** key on your keyboard. The panels to the right of the Timeline close and the Timeline and Stage window expand across the width of the program window. Now resize the Timeline window so that all the layers for the sports banner are visible.

2. Position the pointer on the bottom border of the Timeline until the pointer changes to ÷, then drag the bottom border until the Rectangle layer is visible, as shown in Figure 3-9. Next you want to increase the size of the frames.

Figure 3-9	RESIZING THE TIMELINE WINDOW

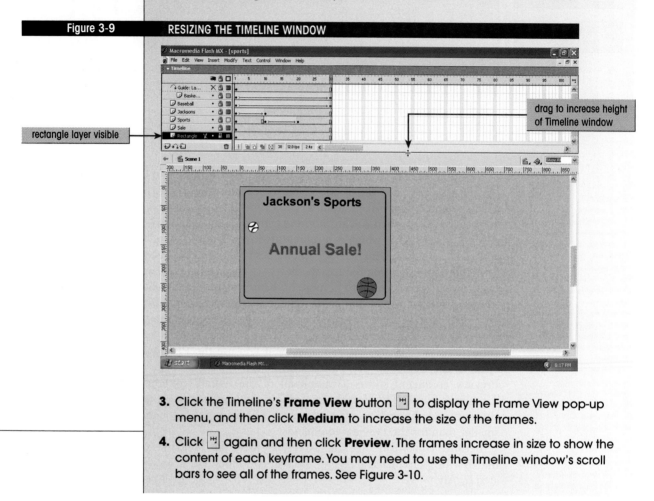

rectangle layer visible

drag to increase height of Timeline window

3. Click the Timeline's **Frame View** button to display the Frame View pop-up menu, and then click **Medium** to increase the size of the frames.

4. Click again and then click **Preview**. The frames increase in size to show the content of each keyframe. You may need to use the Timeline window's scroll bars to see all of the frames. See Figure 3-10.

| Figure 3-10 | FRAMES IN PREVIEW VIEW |

Preview of frame's content

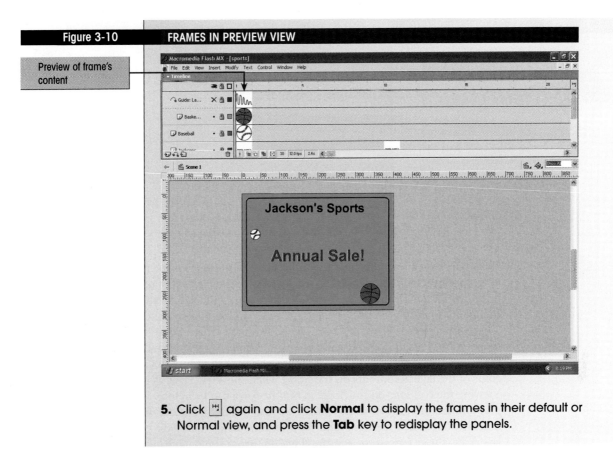

5. Click ⊞ again and click **Normal** to display the frames in their default or Normal view, and press the **Tab** key to redisplay the panels.

When working with a complex document, the number of layers can become difficult to manage. The Timeline is a useful tool in managing and organizing multiple layers in an animation.

Organizing Layers Using the Timeline

Recall that when you open a new document in Macromedia Flash, it contains one layer and one frame within that layer. As you create your animation, you add more layers to the document. In a particularly lengthy or complex animation, you could have a large number of layers. Therefore, you need to know how to use the Timeline to work with the different layers in your document most efficiently.

To select a layer you click it. The layer is then highlighted and a pencil icon is displayed to the right of the layer's name. To delete a layer, you select it and then click the Delete Layer button at the bottom of the Timeline. You can also drag the layer to the Delete Layer button or right-click the layer to display a context menu. You can then click Delete Layer from the context menu.

To add more layers to a document you can use the Layer command on the Insert menu or you can click the Add Layer button in the lower-left corner of the Timeline. As you add more layers to the Timeline it is a good idea to name each one according to the content it contains. This helps you keep the content organized as the complexity of the animation increases. To change the name of a layer, you double-click its name in the Timeline and type a new name. You can also select the layer by clicking it, and then open the Layer Properties dialog box by clicking Layer on the Modify menu. You can also open this dialog box by double-clicking the Layer icon to the left of a layer's name. In the Layer Properties dialog box as shown in Figure 3-11, you can type a new name for the layer as well as change some of its other properties such as whether the layer is hidden or locked.

Figure 3-11   LAYER PROPERTIES DIALOG BOX

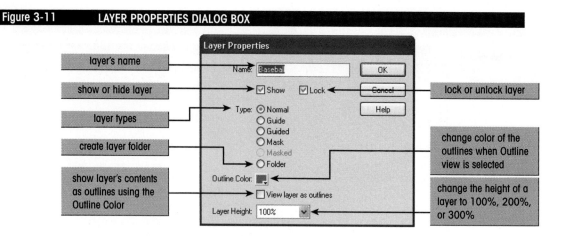

As your document gets more complex and the number of layers increases, you may want to temporarily hide some layers as you work with the content of other layers. Also, once you finish working with the content of one layer, you can lock it so that you do not accidentally change it. You can also change the layer type, the outline color, and the height of the layer. There are different types of layers, as mentioned earlier. There are guide layers and mask layers, as well as guided and masked layers. You can select each of these layer types within the Layer Properties dialog box. Another option is the Outline Color. This determines the color of the layer's contents on the Stage when the View layer as outlines option is selected. Viewing the contents on the Stage in outline form can be helpful when working with a complex animation and you want to see how the different objects on the Stage relate to each other throughout the animation. Also in this dialog box, you can increase an individual layer's height as represented in the Timeline from the default of 100% to 200% or 300%. This only affects the individual layer and is useful when you need to see more of the layer's contents in Preview or Preview in Context mode.

Another element of a Flash document is symbols, which are graphical elements that appear in frames. Where layers and frames are organized and displayed in the Timeline, you create, manage, and store symbols for your document using the Library panel.

Symbols

Symbols are elements such as graphics and buttons that can be used more than once in your document. You can create a symbol from an existing object by selecting the object on the Stage and then using the Convert to Symbol command on the Insert menu. You can also create a new symbol by using the New Symbol command on the Insert menu. You can also use symbols from other Flash documents in your current document.

The symbols in your document are characterized as having one of three types of behavior. These include movie clip, graphic, and button. **Movie clips**, the default behavior, contain their own Timeline and operate independently of the Timeline of the movie in which they appear. For example, a movie clip may contain an animation sequence that spans 10 frames within its own Timeline. When the movie clip is used in the document, its 10 frames do not occupy 10 frames in the document's Timeline. Instead, the movie clip occupies only one frame within the document's Timeline and yet it still plays its own 10-frame animation. Most of the symbols you create can be movie clips. **Graphic** symbols can be static images or animated images. They operate in sync with the Timeline of the movie in which they appear. A graphic symbol with a 10-frame animation sequence occupies 10 frames in the document's Timeline. **Button** symbols have their own four-frame Timeline. You will learn more about buttons in Tutorial 4. Most of the time, you can select the default behavior of Movie Clip for the symbols you create. When you need to have a symbol's animation synchronized with the rest of the document's Timeline, then you choose Graphic. And when you want to make a symbol into an interactive button, you choose Button. You can easily change a symbol's behavior at any time.

Symbols are stored in the document's library and are accessible from the Library panel.

The Library

The **Library** stores symbols you create for a document. You view, organize, and edit symbols stored in the library from the Library panel. When you create a symbol for a document, you assign a name to it, and you specify certain properties based on the behavior of the symbol. These properties of the symbol are stored with the symbol in the library. Symbols created within a document are saved with that document. However, you can share symbols with other documents by making them part of a shared library. Shared libraries are an advanced topic and are not covered in this tutorial. You can modify a symbol's properties using the Library panel. The Library panel, as shown in Figure 3-12, displays a list with the names of all the symbols in the library for the sports document.

Figure 3-12	LIBRARY PANEL

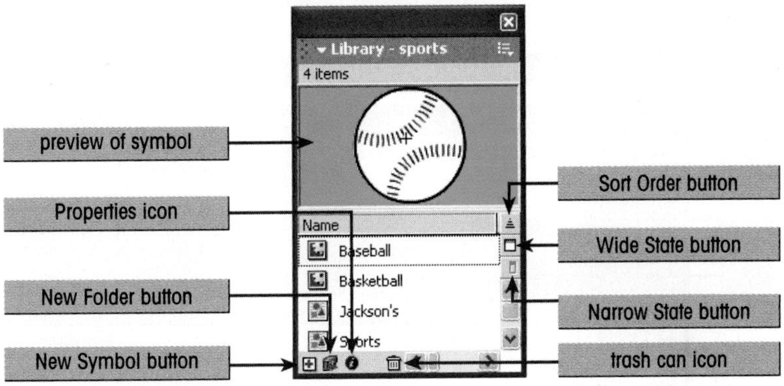

To view the Library panel, click the Library command on the Window menu. Each symbol in the Library panel has an icon to the left of its name to show what type of symbol it is. A symbol's type is the same as its behavior. You can click the name of a symbol to see a thumbnail preview of the symbol at the top of the Library panel. Within the Library panel, you can also organize the symbols into folders.

The options available from the Library panel are described in Figure 3-13.

Figure 3-13		LIBRARY PANEL OPTIONS
ICON	**NAME**	**DESCRIPTION**
⊞	New Symbol	Click to create a new symbol; opens the Create New Symbol dialog box in which you enter the symbol's name and behavior type; it then takes you into symbol-editing mode to create the symbol
🗀	New Folder	Click to create a new folder; a folder can be used to organize related symbols
🗑	Trash can	Click to delete a symbol; be careful when deleting symbols because you cannot undo this action
ⓘ	Properties	Click to view and edit a symbol's properties in the Symbol Properties dialog box; the Symbol Properties dialog box allows you to change the symbol's name and behavior type (movie clip, graphic, or button)
≛	Sort Order	Click to change the order in which the symbols are listed; toggle between A–Z and Z–A order based on the symbol names
▫	Wide State	Click to expand the view of the Library panel to show more details about each symbol, such as the date it was last modified
▫	Narrow State	Click to contract the view of the Library panel to show only the Name column; this is the default view

The Library panel can also be expanded to show several columns of information about each symbol. Figure 3-14 shows the Library panel in wide view. To switch to wide view, you click the Wide State button identified in Figure 3-12.

Figure 3-14	WIDE VIEW OF THE LIBRARY PANEL

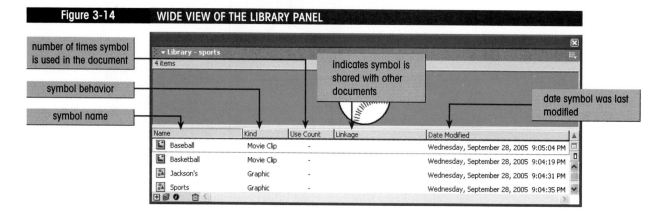

This view displays additional columns listing the symbol's behavior (Kind column), the number of times the symbol is used in the document (the Use Count column), whether the symbol is shared with other documents (Linkage column), and the date it was last modified (Date Modified column). You can also sort the symbols according to a column by clicking the column's header. For example, if you wanted to sort the symbols by date, you would click the Date Modified header to sort the symbols. The order of the dates would be from most recent to oldest. This order can be reversed by clicking the Sort Order button. To get back to the default view of the Library panel, click the Narrow State button.

Additional Library panel options can be accessed using the Library panel's options menu. This menu includes options to create new symbols, rename, edit, or delete symbols, as well as to create duplicates of a symbol.

To become familiar with the Library panel, you will explore the sports document's library to see how symbols are stored, and you will change the behavior of one of the symbols using the Library panel.

To open and explore the sports document's library:

1. Click **Window** on the menu bar, and then click **Library** to open the sports document's library. The Library panel displays the symbols for this document.

2. Click the **Basketball** symbol in the Name column of the Library panel. A preview of the basketball is displayed in the preview window. Next change the view of the Library panel.

3. Click the **Wide State** button □ to expand the view of the Library panel. You may need to reposition the Library panel to see all of it. See Figure 3-15. Now sort the symbols by behavior.

Figure 3-15	SPORTS BANNER LIBRARY PANEL

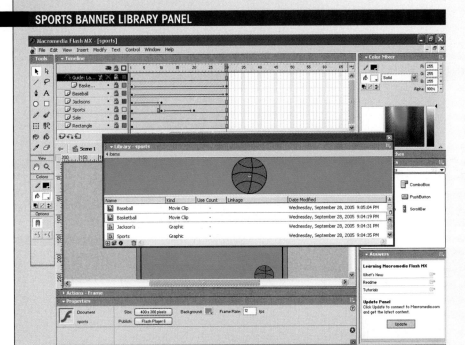

4. Click the **Kind** column header. The symbols are listed according to their behavior: buttons, graphics, and movie clips. To view the properties of a symbol, you use the Properties icon.

5. Click the **Properties** icon 🅘. The Symbol Properties dialog box opens for the Basketball symbol. Try changing this symbol's behavior.

6. Click the **Graphic** option button under Behavior, and then click the **OK** button to close the Properties dialog box. The basketball symbol's icon and Kind reflect the new behavior, as shown in Figure 3-16. Return the Library to its default view.

Figure 3-16   SYMBOLS IN LIBRARY PANEL

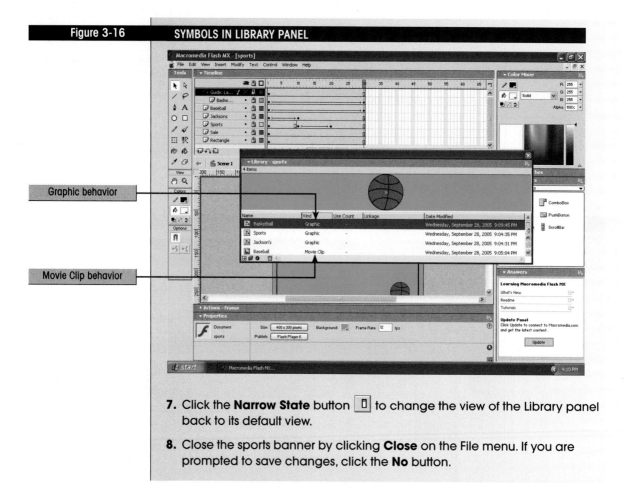

Graphic behavior

Movie Clip behavior

7. Click the **Narrow State** button [ ] to change the view of the Library panel back to its default view.

8. Close the sports banner by clicking **Close** on the File menu. If you are prompted to save changes, click the **No** button.

Now that you understand what symbols are, and how to use the Library panel to view and work with symbols, you are ready to create symbols to be used in the animation you will be creating for the Flounders Pet Shop banner.

Creating Symbols for the Flounders Pet Shop Banner

Aly wants you to open the partially completed banner for the Flounders Pet Shop Web site that she has created. Recall that you have been assigned to complete this banner by developing the various animation effects. Refer to Figure 3-1 that shows the document with a fish, a plant, a text block, and some lines around the perimeter of the Stage that resemble the outline of an aquarium tank. You will use these graphics as you complete the banner. You will start by converting the fish and the plant into symbols so that multiple copies of the symbol may be used. You will then create a copy of the fish and change its color.

Creating a Symbol
- Select an existing graphic, click Insert on the menu bar, and then click Convert to Symbol.
- In the Convert to Symbol dialog box, enter a symbol name in the Name text box, select a behavior by clicking the appropriate behavior option button, and click the OK button.

or

- Click Insert on the menu bar, and then click New Symbol.
- In the New Symbol dialog box, enter a symbol name in the Name text box, select a behavior by clicking the appropriate behavior option button, and then click the OK button to enter into symbol-editing mode.
- Create the graphic(s) for the symbol.
- Click Insert on the menu bar, and then click Edit Document.

To create symbols for the banner and view them in the Library panel:

1. Open the **banner.fla** file located in the Tutorial.03\Tutorial folder on your Data Disk. Now save the file with a new name, in case you want to work through these steps again at another time.

2. Click **File** on the menu bar, and then click **Save As**. In the Save As dialog box, enter **Floundersbanner.fla** as the new filename, and save the file in the **Tutorial.03\Tutorial** folder on your Data Disk.

3. Double-click the **Hand tool** in the toolbox to make all of the Stage visible. To make the fish graphic a symbol, you first must select it.

4. Click the **Arrow** tool in the toolbox, and then draw a marquee around the fish, making sure to enclose the whole fish. You will convert the selected fish into a symbol.

5. Click **Insert** on the menu bar, and then click **Convert to Symbol**. The Convert to Symbol dialog box opens. In this dialog box, you can specify a name for the symbol and select a behavior.

6. In the Convert to Symbol dialog box, type **Fish1** in the Name text box, and click the **Movie Clip** option button, if it is not already selected. You will use this behavior for most of the symbols you create in Flash unless you specifically need to create a graphic or button symbol. See Figure 3-17.

| Figure 3-17 | CONVERT TO SYMBOL DIALOG BOX |

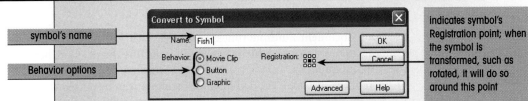

symbol's name

Behavior options

indicates symbol's Registration point; when the symbol is transformed, such as rotated, it will do so around this point

7. Click the **OK** button to close the dialog box. Now the symbol has been created and added to the library of symbols for this document. View the symbol in the Library panel.

8. Click **Window** on the menu bar, and then click **Library**. The Library panel opens. Click the **Fish1** symbol to see its preview. If necessary, reposition the Library panel so that you can see all of the Stage.

TROUBLE? The Library panel may open in Wide State. If this is the case, click the Narrow State button to change to the default view.

Now convert the plant to a symbol.

9. Select the plant with ↖, click **Insert** on the menu bar, and then click **Convert to Symbol**. In the Convert to Symbol dialog box, type **Plant** in the Name text box, and make sure the **Movie Clip** option button is selected. Click the **OK** button to close the dialog box.

Once a symbol is added to a document's library, you can create a duplicate of it. The duplicate symbol must have a different name. You can create a duplicate of a symbol by clicking the Duplicate command on the Library panel's option menu or by right-clicking the symbol in the Library panel to display its context menu, and then clicking the Duplicate command from the context menu.

Recall from Aly's planning sketch that there will be more than one fish animated in the Flounders Pet Shop banner, and these fish will differ. So you need to create a duplicate symbol of the Fish1 symbol that you can then edit, thereby creating a second, different fish symbol.

To create a duplicate of a symbol:

1. Select the **Fish1** symbol in the Library panel.

2. Click the Library panel's **options menu** icon 📋 to open the options menu, and then click **Duplicate**. The Duplicate Symbol dialog box opens.

3. In the Duplicate Symbol dialog box, enter **Fish2** in the Name text box, and then click the **OK** button.

Instances of Symbols

Once you create a symbol it is automatically stored in the document's library. To use the symbols in your document, you create instances. An **instance** is a copy of a symbol. To create an instance of a symbol, you drag it from the Library panel to the Stage. You can either drag the thumbnail from the preview window or drag the symbol's name from the list of symbols. Each time you drag the symbol onto the Stage you are creating an instance of the symbol in your document. The symbol, however, is stored only once in your document regardless of how many instances you have created. So if you have a graphic that will be used in a document multiple times, convert it into a symbol. Then insert instances of the symbol wherever that graphic is needed in your document. This helps keep the size of the file to a minimum.

Each of the instances created in your document can be edited without changing the original symbol stored in the document's library. For example, if you have several instances of a symbol in the same document, you can make one instance smaller than the others. Or you can rotate each instance to appear at a different angle. You can also change the color tint or brightness of one instance without affecting the other instances or the original symbol. If you modify the original symbol, however, then all the instances of that symbol are also changed.

You will create instances of the fish and plant symbols in the next session. Before you do that, Aly suggests you edit the Fish2 symbol in the document's library so that it has a unique appearance from the Fish1 symbol.

Editing a Symbol

Once you create a symbol you may still need to modify it. You can do this in one of several ways. If an instance of the symbol is on the Stage, you can select it and use the Edit in Place command on the Edit menu. You can also double-click the instance of the symbol on the Stage to edit it in place. Even though you double-click the instance, you are actually editing the symbol. When you do this, the other objects on the Stage will be dimmed and the Address bar at the top of the Stage window will show the symbol's name after a link called Scene 1, as shown in Figure 3-18.

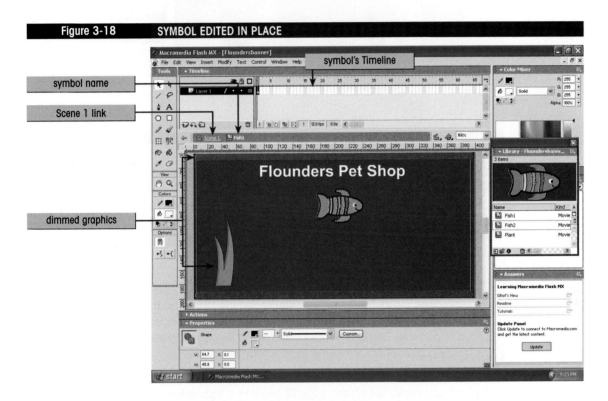

Figure 3-18   SYMBOL EDITED IN PLACE

You can also edit a symbol by right-clicking an instance of it on the Stage and selecting Edit, Edit in Place, or Edit in New Window from the context menu. **Edit** places the symbol in symbol-editing mode. **Edit in Place** dims all other objects on the Stage while you edit the symbol, and **Edit in a New Window** places the symbol in a separate window for editing. You have to close this window when you finish editing the symbol. After you edit the symbol, you can return to the document by clicking the Edit Document command on the Edit menu or by clicking the Scene 1 link on the Address bar. The Scene 1 link identifies the current scene. Recall that Flash documents may be divided into multiple scenes and that every document has at least one scene. The Scene 1 link takes you back to the document. You can also double-click an empty area of the Stage to get back to editing the document.

Another way to edit a symbol is to select the symbol in the Library panel and then double-click the symbol's icon. This will place the symbol in symbol-editing mode so that it can be edited as shown in Figure 3-19.

Figure 3-19	SYMBOL-EDITING MODE

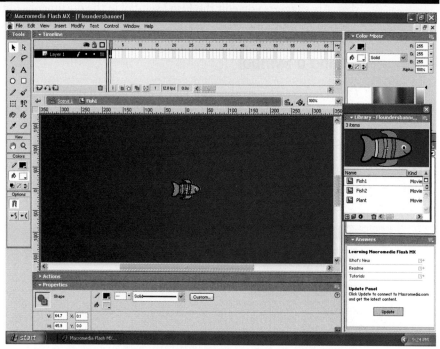

Once you are done editing the symbol, you can click the Scene 1 link to return to the document or you can click the Edit Document command on the Edit menu.

Now that you have two fish symbols in the Library you will change one of the symbols so that it has a different color and is smaller in size. This will distinguish the two fish symbols when they are used in the banner.

To edit a symbol in the document's library:

1. Make sure the **Fish2** symbol is selected in the Library panel. Click the Library panel's **options menu** icon, and then click **Edit** to open the symbol in symbol-editing mode. Click an empty area of the Stage to deselect it. Next, you will apply a different color to the fish2 symbol.

2. Click the **Paint Bucket** tool in the toolbox. Using the Fill color control in the Property inspector, change the fill color to a **light-blue** color (sixth row, seventh column in the color pop-up window).

3. Click each of the orange areas of the fish to change them to light blue. Now select the fish graphic so you can make it smaller.

4. Click **Edit** on the menu bar, and then click **Select All**. All of the fish should be selected.

5. Click **Window** on the menu bar, and then click **Transform** to open the Transform panel. In the Transform panel, make sure that **Constrain** is selected, and then change the **width** value to **75%**. Constrain keeps the width and height proportional when either one is changed. Press the **Enter** key to accept the new value, and then close the Transform panel. The fish has become smaller, as shown in Figure 3-20. Now that you are done editing the Fish2 symbol, exit the symbol-editing mode.

Figure 3-20   REVISED FISH2 SYMBOL

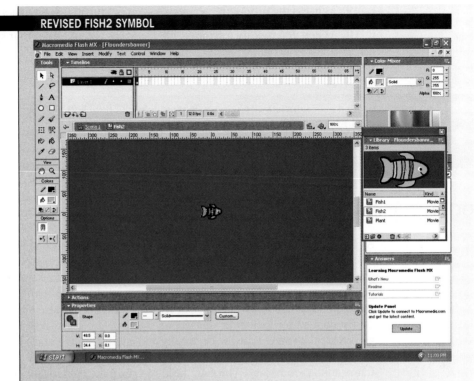

6. Click **Edit** on the menu bar, and then click **Edit Document** to exit the symbol-editing window.

7. Click **File** on the menu bar, and then click **Save** to save the changes you have made. You can either exit Flash, or leave the program open for the next session.

In this session you have learned about the basic elements of Macromedia Flash that are used in creating animations. You have learned how animations are based on a series of frames that contain graphics. Finally, you have learned about symbols and how to use the Library panel to work with the symbols in your document's library. In the next session, you will learn how to create multiple instances of these symbols in your document and create animations with them.

Session 3.1 QUICK | CHECK

1. What is the purpose of the Timeline?

2. How can you tell which is the current frame in the Timeline?

3. What is the default frame rate for a Flash document?

4. What is the difference between frames and layers?

5. List two ways to insert a new layer.

6. What is the purpose of the Library panel?

7. How do you delete a symbol from the Library panel?

8. What two buttons can change the view of the Library panel?

9. What is the difference between a symbol and an instance of a symbol?

10. When you modify a symbol, the instances created from that symbol are not affected. True or False?

SESSION 3.2

In this session you will learn how to create animations in Macromedia Flash. You will learn the difference between a frame-by-frame animation and a tweened animation. You will also learn about the different types of tweened animation, which are motion tweening and shape tweening. Finally, you will learn about the different ways to test an animation.

Creating Animation

As you learned in the previous session, animation is accomplished by displaying the content of different frames one after another. Each frame contains some graphic element that is displayed for a short instant in time. As the content of each frame is displayed in succession, the graphic elements appear to be moving. There are basically two types of animation you can create in Macromedia Flash. You can create a **frame-by-frame animation** in which you create the content for each individual frame. You can also create a **tweened animation** in which you create the content for the beginning and ending frames, and Flash creates the content for the in-between frames. A tweened animation is easier and quicker to create than a frame-by-frame animation because you only need to create the content for two frames, the one at the beginning of the animation and the one at the end. Each of these two frames is a keyframe. Frame-by-frame animations take more time to create because you need to create all of the content for all the frames in the animation. Frame-by-frame animations are usually used to build more detailed animations where you need to control the content of each step in the animation. Frame-by-frame animations also tend to produce larger-sized files than tweened animations. You will learn how to create these two types of animation in this session.

Recall from Aly's sketch, shown in Figure 3-1, the plant leaves for the Flounders Pet Shop banner will be animated so that the leaves' tips appear to be moving. This will be done with a frame-by-frame animation because you need to specify the positions of the leaves at different moments in time. The fish in the banner will be animated using tweened animations because you will only have to specify where the fish starts and where it ends. You can let Flash fill in the position of the fish in the in-between frames. You will start by exploring frame-by-frame animation.

Frame-by-Frame Animation

To create a frame-by-frame animation you need to create the graphic elements for the animation in each of its individual frames. If, for example, your animation is to have 15 frames, then you need to create the content for each of the 15 frames. Some of the content can be the same from one frame to the next, but other content can be slightly modified. As the frames are displayed one after the other the perception of movement is achieved. To create a frame-by-frame animation you start with a graphic object in the initial frame. Then for each place in the animation where you need the object to change, you add a keyframe. Recall that a frame that has different content from the previous frame is called a keyframe. Depending on the animation, every frame may be a keyframe or you may have intervening frames where the graphic object does not change. As you add keyframes, you change the position of the graphic object. Once you have all of the keyframes created you test the animation. Figure 3-21 shows the Timeline for a sample frame-by-frame animation. Notice the keyframes where the content changes throughout the animation.

Figure 3-21   **SAMPLE FRAME-BY-FRAME ANIMATION**

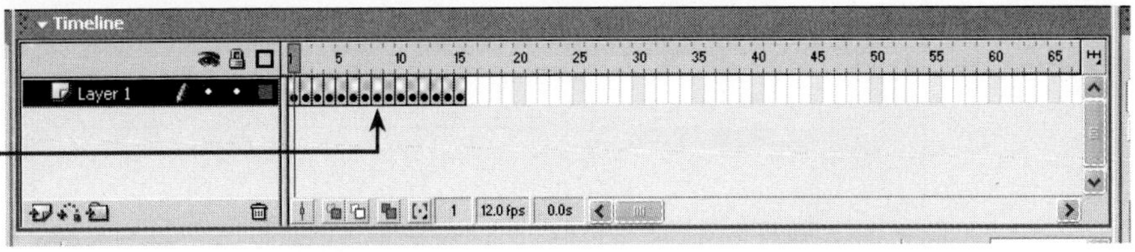

keyframes indicate content changes in each frame

Adding Animation to the Flounders Pet Shop Banner

The banner for the Flounders Pet Shop Web site contains a graphic element that looks like a plant. In the previous session, you converted this plant graphic into a symbol with a movie clip behavior, and now you will animate the plant's leaves so that they appear to be moving inside the aquarium tank. You will do this by creating a frame-by-frame animation. The plant's leaves will be animated within the Timeline of the plant symbol and not in the main Timeline of the document. Recall from the previous session that a movie clip symbol has its own Timeline which is independent of the document's Timeline. By adding the animation in the symbol's Timeline, every instance of the symbol automatically includes the animation. This means that each plant instance you create on the document's Stage will have the same animation built-in as part of the instance.

To create the animation of the plant leaves, Aly suggests you add keyframes to every other frame of the plant leaves layer from Frame 1 through Frame 9. She states that this will be sufficient to create the movement of the leaves. She further suggests that in each keyframe you move the tips of the leaves slightly, first in one direction and then in the opposite direction.

To create a frame-by-frame animation for the Plant symbol in the Flounders Pet Shop banner:

1. If necessary, start Flash and open the **Floundersbanner.fla** file stored in the Tutorial.03\Tutorial folder on your Data Disk. You need to first open the Library panel because you will be working with a symbol.

2. If necessary, open the Library panel, and then position the Library panel so that it does not overlap the Stage. You will select the Plant symbol so that it can be edited. You will create an animation within the Plant symbol's Timeline.

3. Click the **Plant** symbol in the Library panel. Double-click the **plant** icon in the Library panel to open the symbol in symbol-editing mode.

   The plant graphic is displayed in the center of the Stage. The symbol is now in symbol-editing mode where you can modify it as needed. You can tell you are in symbol-editing mode by the Address bar above the Stage that shows Scene 1 followed by the name of the symbol you are editing. You will add a keyframe to start creating the animation.

4. In the symbol's Timeline, click **Frame 3**, as shown in Figure 3-22. You will add a keyframe at Frame 3.

Figure 3-22   SELECTING A FRAME

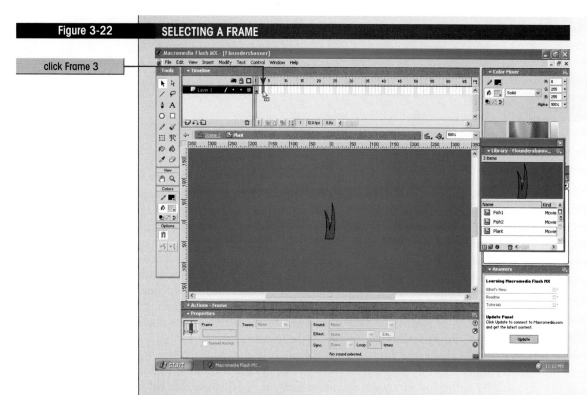

click Frame 3

5. Click **Insert** on the menu bar, and then click **Keyframe**. A keyframe is inserted in Frame 3 and a regular frame is added in Frame 2. When you add any kind of frame to a layer, Flash will add intervening frames. So when you added a keyframe in Frame 3, Flash automatically added a regular frame, not a keyframe, in Frame 2. The plant graphic is also automatically copied to all of the new frames. See Figure 3-23.

Figure 3-23   KEYFRAME ADDED TO PLANT SYMBOL TIMELINE

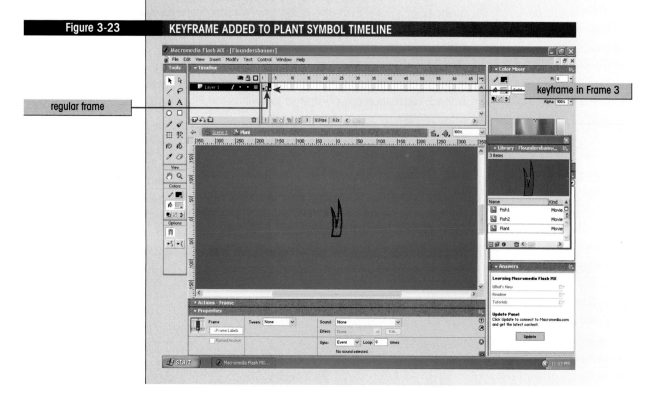

keyframe in Frame 3

regular frame

In this frame, move the tips of the leaves slightly to the right.

6. Using the **Arrow** tool ➤ deselect the plant by clicking an empty area of the Stage. Position the mouse pointer over the tip of one of the leaves until you see the corner pointer ➤. Once you see the ➤, click and drag the tip of the leaf slightly to the right. Repeat this for the other leaf's tip to reposition it slightly to the right. See Figure 3-24.

Figure 3-24	MODIFYING THE PLANT LEAVES

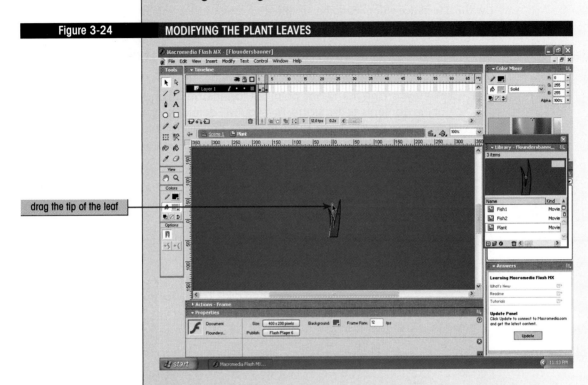

drag the tip of the leaf

You will now add keyframes in every other frame.

7. Now click **Frame 5** and insert a keyframe. Repeat Step 6 to reposition both of the leaves' tips slightly more to the right.

8. Click **Frame 7** and insert a keyframe. Repeat Step 6, but this time, reposition the leaves' tips back slightly to the left. Now you will finish the animation with another keyframe moving the leaves' tips to their starting position.

9. Click **Frame 9** and insert another keyframe. This time move the leaves' tips slightly more to the left to almost the same position where they started in Frame 1.

10. Drag the playhead back and forth through these frames to get a sense of what the animation looks like. You are done creating this frame-by-frame animation. You can exit symbol-editing mode.

11. To exit the symbol-editing mode, click **Edit** on the menu bar, and then click **Edit Document**.

You have created a frame-by-frame animation within the Plant symbol. Because the animation was created within the symbol's Timeline, each instance of the symbol has the same animation. You can, therefore, place several instances of the plant symbol in the document and all of the instances will be animated.

Recall from Aly's instructions, that the banner should have three animated plants in the lower-left corner of the tank. You will therefore add three instances of the animated plant symbol. The second instance will need to be modified to make it larger than the first, and the third instance will need to be modified such that its leaves point to the right of the tank.

To create instances of the animated plant symbol and then modify them:

1. Click **View** on the menu bar, point to **Magnification**, and click **Show All** to see all of the contents of the Stage. First you will delete the instances of the plant and fish from the first layer. These were the original graphic objects. When you created symbols using these objects, they became instances of the symbols. You will be placing instances of these symbols into separate layers.

2. Click the plant instance on the Stage, and press the **Delete** key to remove it. You are only deleting one instance of the symbol. The symbol itself is still in the document's library. Next delete the fish instance.

3. Click the fish instance on the Stage, and press the **Delete** key. Before you insert the plant instances into the document, create a new layer for the plant instances.

4. Click **Insert** on the menu bar, and then click **Layer**. To change the name of the new layer, double-click **Layer 2** in the Timeline, type **Plant** as the new name for this layer, and press the **Enter** key.

5. Make sure the Plant layer is the current layer, and drag an instance of the Plant symbol from the Library panel to the lower-left corner of the Stage.

6. Drag another instance of the Plant symbol from the Library panel and place it to the right of the first, as shown in Figure 3-25.

Figure 3-25 PLANT ARRANGEMENT

plant instances

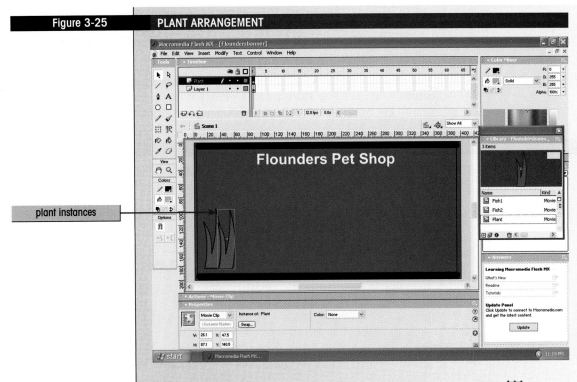

7. With this instance still selected, click the **Free Transform** tool in the toolbox, and then click the **Scale** modifier button in the options area of the toolbox. Drag one of the corners of the bounding box around the plant to make this plant instance slightly larger than the first. See Figure 3-26. If necessary, reposition the instance to align it with the bottom edge of the other plant instance.

Figure 3-26 ENLARGING THE PLANT INSTANCE

drag corner to enlarge instance

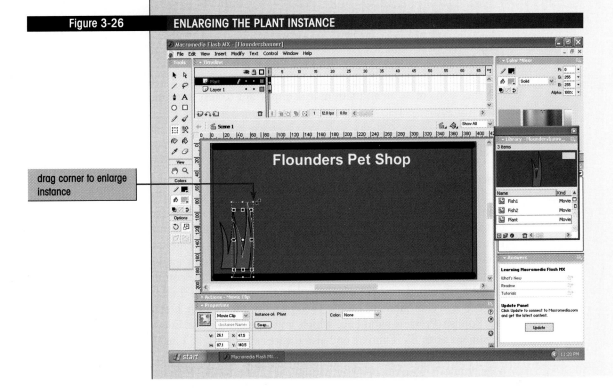

8. Click the **Arrow** tool ⬉ in the toolbox, then drag one more instance of the Plant symbol from the Library panel, and place it to the right of the other two. Next you will flip the horizontal position of the third instance.

9. With this instance still selected, click **Modify** on the menu bar, point to **Transform**, and click **Flip Horizontal**. Be sure to line up the bottoms of the plants with the bottom part of the tank outline. See Figure 3-27.

Figure 3-27	INSTANCES OF THE PLANT SYMBOL

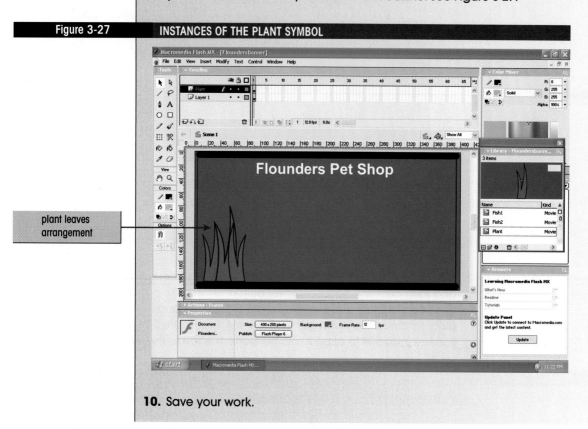

plant leaves
arrangement

10. Save your work.

Once you create an animation, it is important to test it, to make sure it works correctly when the movie plays.

Testing a Document's Animation

Once you create a document with animation, you need to test it to make sure it works correctly. To test your document's animation, you click the Play command on the Control menu or press the Enter key on the keyboard. This plays the animation on the Stage. You can also test the animation by dragging the playhead with the mouse pointer back and forth through the frames. This is known as **scrubbing** and is useful when you need to test a short animation sequence. Another way to test your document's animation is to click the Test Movie command on the Control menu. When you use this command, Flash actually creates an SWF file called a movie and then plays the movie using the Flash Player plug-in. Finally, you can test your animation on a Web page by clicking the Default (HTML) command on the Publish Preview submenu, which you open from the File menu. Flash publishes the document as an SWF movie and also creates a Web page. The Web page with the movie is then displayed in your computer's default browser. After viewing the movie in the Web page, you can close the browser window to return to the document.

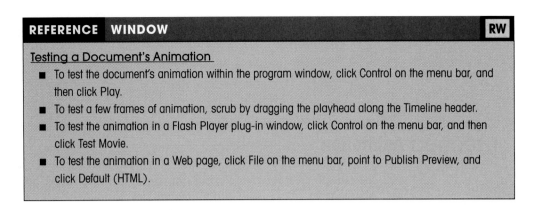

REFERENCE   WINDOW   **RW**

Testing a Document's Animation
- To test the document's animation within the program window, click Control on the menu bar, and then click Play.
- To test a few frames of animation, scrub by dragging the playhead along the Timeline header.
- To test the animation in a Flash Player plug-in window, click Control on the menu bar, and then click Test Movie.
- To test the animation in a Web page, click File on the menu bar, point to Publish Preview, and click Default (HTML).

Because the plant symbol's animation is within its own Timeline, you need to test the animation as an SWF file. If you test the animation within the Flash program window, the plant symbol's animation will not play. You will use the Test Movie command on the Control menu to test the document's animation.

To test the document's animation:

1. Click **Control** on the menu bar, and then click **Test Movie**. The movie plays in a Flash Player window as shown in Figure 3-28. The animation repeats until you close the window.

Figure 3-28   **FLASH PLAYER WINDOW**

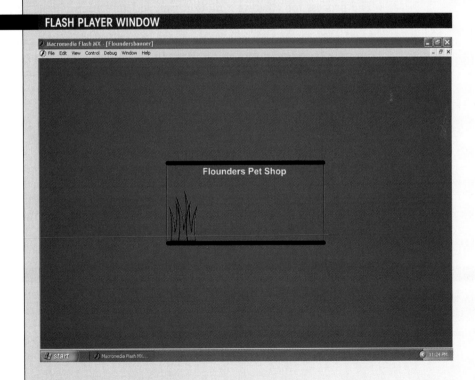

2. Click **File** on the menu bar, and then click **Close** to close the Flash Player window. Now test the animation on a Web page.

3. Click **File** on the menu bar, point to **Publish Preview**, and then click **Default (HTML)**. Your computer's default browser opens and the animation plays in a Web page.

4. Close the browser window when you are finished viewing the animation.

Tweened Animation

Instead of creating the content for each frame to build an animation, you can let Macromedia Flash build the animation for you. Recall this type of animation, called tweened animation, is where you create the content of the beginning frame and then change that content on the ending frame. The program then creates the in-between frames, varying the content evenly in each frame to achieve the animation. The beginning frame and the ending frame for a tweened animation must be keyframes.

There are two types of tweened animations. These are motion tweening and shape tweening. **Motion tweening** can be used to create an animation where an object changes its position, rotates, scales in size, or even changes in color. You can also make an object fade in or out. **Shape tweening** is used to change a shape into another shape over time. For example, you can create an animation where a circle shape is changed into a square shape.

Motion Tweening

The process for creating a motion tweened animation is relatively simple. You create an object in the beginning frame of the animation and convert the object to a symbol. In order for an object to be animated using motion tweening, the object must be a symbol. Also, you can only have one object in the layer in which you create the motion tween. If you have more than one object, Flash groups them and tries to animate them together. If an object is not to be part of a motion tween, then it should be placed on a separate layer. Once the object to be animated is a symbol, you create a keyframe in the frame where the animation will end. In this keyframe you move the object to a different position or you change its properties such as its color tint or color brightness. You create the animation in the first frame by selecting the Create Motion Tween command located on the Insert menu. Flash then creates the tweened frames varying the content in each frame to change the object's position or properties slightly from one frame to the next. You can also create the motion tween by using the Property inspector. Once you click the first frame where the animation is to begin, the Property inspector displays the Tween list box. You then select Motion from the list, and additional options are displayed as shown in Figure 3-29.

Figure 3-29	PROPERTY INSPECTOR WITH MOTION TWEEN OPTIONS

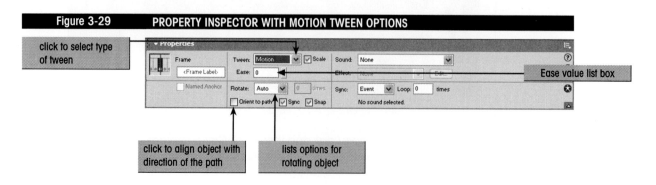

Two of these options are the Ease value list box and the Rotate list box. The **Ease** value makes an object accelerate or decelerate to create a more natural appearance of movement. With the default value of 0, the rate of change between the tweened frames remains constant. A negative value between –1 and –100 causes the object to begin slowly and accelerate toward the end of the animation. A positive value between 1 and 100 causes the object to begin rapidly and decelerate toward the end of the animation. The **Rotate** list box allows you to specify whether the object should also rotate during the motion tween. Selecting CW causes the object to rotate in a clockwise direction. Selecting CCW rotates the object in a counterclockwise direction. You then specify how many times to rotate the object throughout the motion tween in the times text box.

Once you create a motion tween, the frames in the Timeline will have a light-blue background and there will be a solid line across the frames. If there is a dashed line that means that the tween is broken or incomplete such as when there is no ending keyframe. Remember a motion tween starts at a keyframe and ends at a keyframe. If the ending keyframe is missing, the animation does not work and a dashed line appears in the Timeline. Also, if the object to be animated is not a symbol, you see a dashed line displayed.

Creating a Motion Tweened Animation

You will now continue your work with the Flounders Pet Shop banner by adding a motion tweened animation of the fish graphic. The fish will swim from one side of the tank, turn around, and swim back. In a discussion with Aly, she suggests making the animation approximately four seconds in length. At the frame rate of 12 frames per second this will take 48 frames. You will have the fish swim to the side of the tank and back in 48 frames. So you decide that the fish should arrive at the side of the tank at Frame 24 so that it can turn around and return to the other side during the second half of the animation.

To create a motion tween with the fish graphic:

1. Select the **Plant** layer in the Timeline. Now add a new layer for the motion tweened fish.

2. Click **Insert** on the menu bar, and then click **Layer**. A new layer is added to the Timeline above the Plant layer. Double-click the layer's name to select it, and change the name to **Fish1**. You will add an instance of the fish to this layer.

3. Make sure that the Fish1 layer is selected. Drag the **Fish1** symbol from the Library panel to the left side of the Stage, just inside the tank outline. This will create an instance of the Fish1 symbol. See Figure 3-30.

Figure 3-30

FISH1 INSTANCE CREATED ON THE STAGE

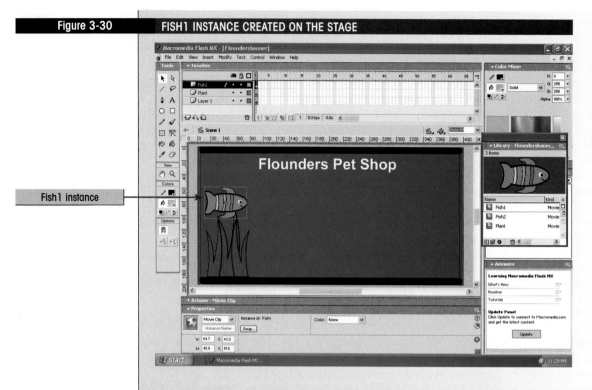

Fish1 instance

4. Click **Layer 1**, and then if necessary, use the Timeline horizontal scroll bar to make Frame 48 visible. Click **Frame 48** of Layer 1. Click **Insert** on the menu bar, and then click **Frame**. A regular frame is added at Frame 48. Regular frames are also automatically added between frames 1 and 48. The Layer 1 graphics from Frame 1 are copied to Frame 48.

   Notice the fish and the plant disappeared when you added the frame in Frame 48. This is because these graphics do not exist in Frame 48 yet. They only exist in Frame 1. In order for the plant and fish to exist through Frame 48 you need to add frames to their respective layers.

5. Click **Frame 48** of the Plant layer. Click **Insert** on the menu bar, and then click **Frame** to extend the layer through Frame 48. You will add a keyframe where the fish will arrive at the right side of the tank.

6. Click **Frame 24** of the Fish1 layer. Click **Insert** on the menu bar, and then click **Keyframe**. A keyframe is added at Frame 24 and regular frames are automatically added between frames 1 and 24. The Fish1 graphic is copied to Frame 24.

7. While still in Frame 24, drag the **Fish1** instance from the left side of the Stage to the right side. Be sure to stay within the tank outline as shown in Figure 3-31.

| Figure 3-31 | FISH1 INSTANCE REPOSITIONED FOR FRAME 24 |

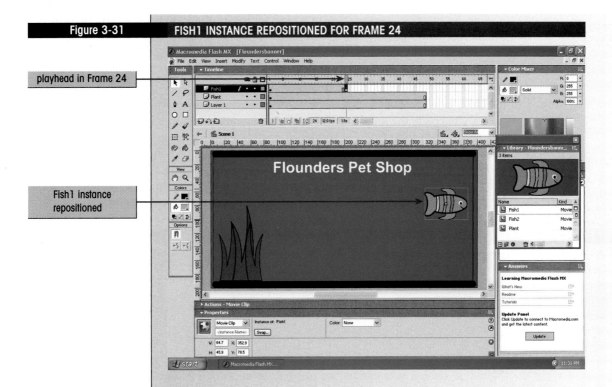

playhead in Frame 24

Fish1 instance repositioned

Now add a keyframe where the fish will turn around.

8. Click **Frame 25** and insert a keyframe. In this frame you will move the fish so that it faces in the opposite direction.

9. Click **Modify** on the menu bar, point to **Transform**, and then click **Flip Horizontal**. Next you need to add a keyframe at the end of the animation for the Fish1 layer.

10. Click **Frame 48** of the Fish1 layer, and insert another keyframe. In this keyframe, drag the **Fish1** instance so that it is back to its original starting position on the left side of the Stage. Now you can create a motion tween.

11. Click **Frame 1** of the Fish1 layer, click **Insert** on the menu bar, and then click **Create Motion Tween**. A motion tween is created as evidenced by the line and light-blue background on Frames 1 through 24 in the Timeline. Now you need to create another motion tween.

12. Click **Frame 25** of the Fish1 layer, click the **Tween** list arrow in the Property inspector, and then click **Motion**. This has the same result as selecting Create Motion Tween from the Insert menu.

Now that you have created the motion tweens, you should test them.

To test the motion tweened animations:

1. Click **Control** on the menu bar, and then click **Rewind**. The playhead moves to Frame 1.

2. Click **Control** again and click **Play**. The fish moves from the left of the Stage to the right and then back again to the left.

3. Click **File** on the menu bar, and then click **Save** to save your work.

You can create a shape tween in a way similar to the method used to create a motion tweened animation.

Shape Tweening

Recall a shape tween takes one shape and transforms it into another shape. To create a shape tween, you create the graphic content in the beginning and ending frames of the animation and Flash creates the tweened frames to complete the animation. The object you use in a shape tween must not be a symbol, and must not be a grouped object. This is different from a motion tween where you first have to convert an object into a symbol. A shape tween is indicated in the Timeline by a line and a light-green color for the frames, as shown in Figure 3-32. The Flounders Pet Shop banner does not require a shape tween.

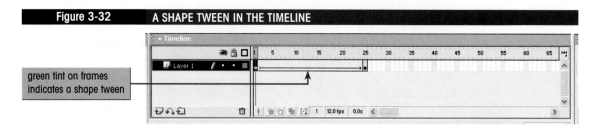

Figure 3-32   **A SHAPE TWEEN IN THE TIMELINE**

green tint on frames indicates a shape tween

In this session you created animations using two different methods. These methods include frame-by-frame animations and tweened animations. You also learned how to create motion tweens and shape tweens. In the next session you will create more advanced animation effects using specific types of layers, and you will animate text blocks.

Session 3.2 QUICK CHECK

1. Briefly describe the difference between a frame-by-frame animation and a tweened animation.

2. How many objects can you have on a layer with a motion tween?

3. How can you animate a movie clip symbol so that each of its instances automatically contains the animation?

4. What type of tweened animation would you create to have an object move from one side of the Stage to the other?

5. To create a shape tween, the object being animated must first be converted to a symbol. True or False?

SESSION 3.3

In this session you will learn how to create animations using motion guide layers and mask layers. Each of these layers can be used to create special animation effects. You will also see how you can animate text blocks.

Special Layers and Animation

As you learned previously in this tutorial, there are two special types of layers you can create in Macromedia Flash. These are guide layers and mask layers. A **guide layer** contains graphic elements that serve as a guide when creating content on other layers. A **mask layer** masks the contents of the layer below it which is called the **masked layer**. Both of these types of layers can also be used with animations. For example, you can create a guide layer which contains a path for an object on another layer to follow. You also can create an animation in a mask layer to show different areas of a masked layer throughout the animation. Both types of layers can be used with frame-by-frame and tweened animations.

Animation Using a Motion Guide Layer

When a guide layer is used together with a motion tween it is called a **motion guide** layer. A motion guide layer provides a path for an object in another layer to follow throughout the motion tween. To create a motion guide layer for a motion tweened animation you first create the motion tween in one layer. You then select the layer and insert a motion guide layer above it by selecting the Motion Guide command located on the Insert menu. You can also click the Add Motion Guide icon at the bottom of the Timeline. The layer with the motion tween will be indented and the motion guide layer will have a motion guide icon to the left of its name. You then use a tool such as the Pencil, Pen, Line, Oval, Rectangle, or Brush tool to draw a path in the motion guide layer. This is the path the object in the guided layer will follow. Once you draw the path, then you select the first frame of the motion tweened layer and move the object to the beginning of the path. In the last frame of the animation, you move the object to the end of the path. In each case you need to make sure the center of the object snaps to the path. You can do this by first making sure that the Snap to Objects option on the View menu is selected. You then drag the object from its center to the endpoint of the path.

Adding a Motion Guide Layer to the Flounders Pet Shop Banner

You have been revising the banner for the Flounders Pet Shop Web site by adding swimming fish and moving plant leaves. You show Aly the work you have completed on the banner, and she wants you to add another animated fish to the banner using the Fish2 symbol from the document's library. She wants the fish to swim from the right side of the tank to the lower left. She suggests you create this animation using a special type of guide layer called a motion layer. Recall a motion guide layer is used to specify a specific path for an animated object to follow. You decide to add a motion guide layer that will guide the fish along a path that you will draw.

To create a motion guide layer:

1. If necessary, start Flash and open the **Floundersbanner.fla** file from the Tutorial.03\Tutorial folder on your Data Disk.

2. Select the **Fish1** layer in the Timeline. Click **Insert** on the menu bar, and then click **Layer**. A new layer is inserted. To change the name of the new layer, double-click **Layer 4** in the Timeline, type **Fish2** as its new name, and then press the **Enter** key. Now create an instance of the Fish2 symbol in the Fish2 layer.

3. Click **Frame 1** of the Fish2 layer, and drag an instance of the **Fish2** symbol from the Library panel to the lower-right side of the Stage. See Figure 3-33. If the fish is to swim to the left side of the tank, it needs to be facing the other direction.

Figure 3-33 FISH2 INSTANCE

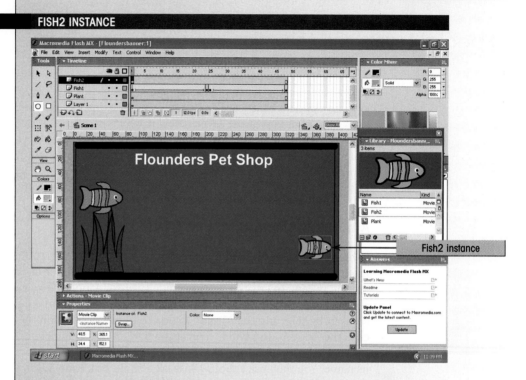

4. Click **Modify** on the menu bar, point to **Transform**, and then click **Flip Horizontal**. The fish now faces to the left. Now you will add a keyframe for the last frame in the layer.

5. Click **Frame 48** of the Fish2 layer. Insert a keyframe at Frame 48. Drag the **fish** to the left side of the Stage. Do not worry about the other fish because it is in a separate layer and will not be affected by the placement of this fish. Now, create a motion tween that causes the fish to move from the right side of the Stage to the left side.

6. Click **Frame 1** of the Fish2 layer. Click **Insert** on the menu bar, and click **Create Motion Tween**. A motion tween is created from Frame 1 through Frame 48. Now you will add a motion guide layer for the path the fish should swim.

7. Click **Insert** on the menu bar, and then click **Motion Guide** to insert a motion guide layer above the Fish2 layer. You will use the Pencil tool to draw the path the fish will follow.

8. Click **Frame 1** of the Guide layer, and then click the **Pencil** tool ✏ in the toolbox. Click the **Pencil Mode modifier** in the Options area of the toolbox, then click **Smooth**. In the Property inspector, select **black** for the stroke color, **1** for the stroke height, and **Solid** for the style.

9. Draw a line from the fish on the right side of the Stage curving up and then back down to the plants on the left side of the Stage. See Figure 3-34. The Fish2 instance attaches itself to the beginning of the line. Now attach the fish to the end of the line.

Figure 3-34   LINE DRAWN WITH PENCIL TOOL

path for fish to follow

fish snaps to end of line

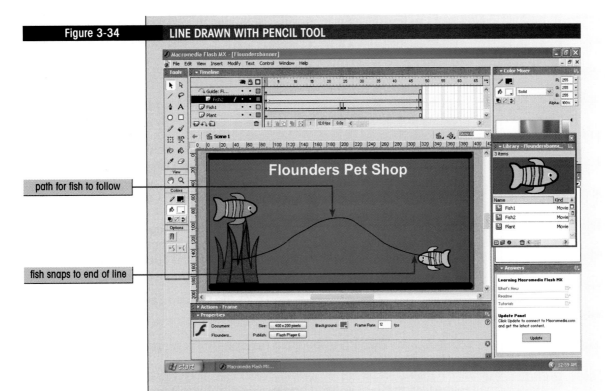

10. Click **Frame 48** of the Fish2 layer. Click the **Arrow** tool in the toolbox. Drag the small blue fish so that it snaps to the far-left endpoint of the line, as shown in Figure 3-35.

Figure 3-35   CENTER POINT OF FISH SNAPS TO ENDPOINT OF LINE

fish snaps to endpoint

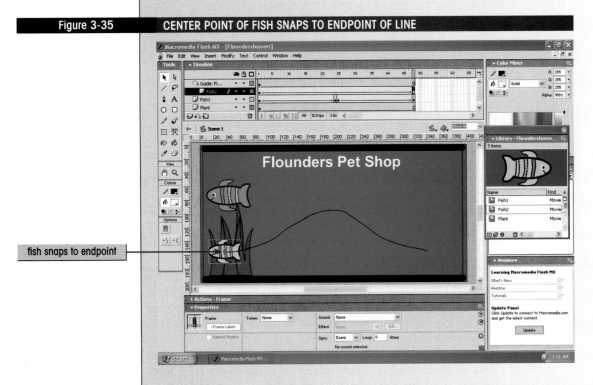

TROUBLE? If you move the endpoint of the line by mistake, just click Edit on the menu bar and click Undo, and then try moving the fish again.

Now you can test the animation with the motion guide layer, and make any necessary modifications.

To test the motion guide layer and make changes to it:

1. Press the **Enter** key to test the motion guide tween. The fish follows the path you drew in the guide layer.

   TROUBLE? If the fish does not follow the path, then its center point may not be snapped to the endpoints of the line. Check Frame 1 and also Frame 48 of the Fish2 layer to make sure the center point of the fish is snapped to the endpoints of the line. If necessary, move the fish again to snap it to the endpoints.

   Notice that as the fish moves along the line, it stays in a horizontal position. You should change it so it moves in a more natural way. You can do this by selecting the Orient to path option in the Property inspector. This causes the object to align itself with the direction of the path and gives the animation a more natural look.

2. Click **Frame 1** of the Fish2 layer, and click the **Orient to path** check box in the Property inspector.

   TROUBLE? If the Property inspector is not open, click Window on the menu bar, and then click Properties.

   Before testing the animation again, hide the Guide layer so that the path is hidden.

3. Click the dot in the **Guide: Fish2** layer in the Eye column to hide its contents.

4. Press the **Enter** key to test the animation again. This time the fish orients itself to the direction of the motion guide.

5. Click **File** on the menu bar, and then click **Save** to save your work.

Recall that another special type of layer is a mask layer. You can also create animations that incorporate a mask layer to create special effects.

Animation Using a Mask Layer

To create an animation using a mask layer, you first create the object or objects that will be masked in one layer. This is called the masked layer. You then create a new layer above this layer that contains the mask. The mask object can be a filled shape such as an oval or rectangle. It can also be text or an instance of an object. To change this layer to a mask layer, you click the Layer command on the Modify menu to open the Layer Properties dialog box, and then select Mask. You then select the other layer, open its Layer Properties dialog box, and change it to Masked. The objects in the masked layer are then masked by the object in the mask layer. To create the animation effect, you add a motion tween using the object in the mask layer. For example, you can have the object move from one side of the Stage to the other. You then add regular frames to the masked layer to extend the life of the layer throughout the animation. In order to see the masking effect on the Stage, lock each of the layers.

Aly suggests you explore the mask layer animation in a different version of the Jackson's Sports banner she has been working on to see how a mask layer animation works. You will create a mask layer animation yourself in Case Problem 3.

To explore the mask layer animation in the sports banner:

1. Open the **sports2.fla** file from the Tutorial.03\Tutorial folder on your Data Disk.

2. If necessary, expand the height of the Timeline window so that the Text Mask and Sale layers are visible. Before you can view the mask layer's contents, you first need to unlock it.

3. If the Text Mask layer has a padlock icon 🔒, click it to unlock the layer. Unlocking the layer displays the contents of the Text Mask layer as shown in Figure 3-36. When a mask layer is locked, the masking effect is visible in the Flash program window.

Figure 3-36	MASK LAYER ANIMATION

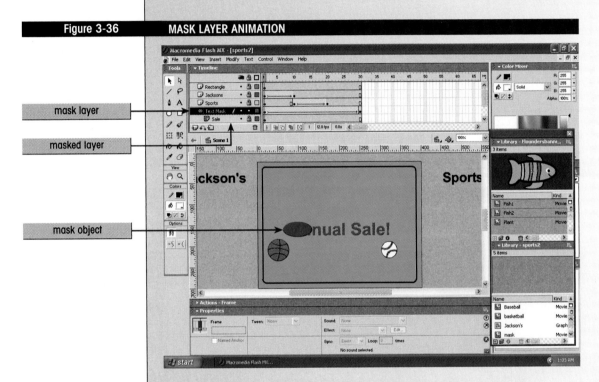

mask layer

masked layer

mask object

Notice that the content of the Text Mask layer is just a motion tween of an oval shape. The color of the shape is not significant because its color is not displayed. What is significant is its shape. This shape determines what part of the underlying Sale layer content is visible. As the oval moves from left to right, different parts of the underlying Annual Sale text become visible. Now test the animation. To do so, you must first lock the mask layer to test the mask effect.

4. Click the **dot** in the Lock column of the Text Mask layer to lock it.

5. Press the **Enter** key to test the animation. Notice how the part of the text that is under the oval is displayed as the oval moves across the Stage.

6. Close the sports2.fla file. When prompted to save changes to the file, click the **No** button.

Animating Text Blocks

Text blocks can also be animated using frame-by-frame or tweened animations. For example, you can have a text block move from one side of the Stage to the other. Using a motion tween you can animate a text block so that it rotates as the movie is played, or you can even have the text block change in size. To create a motion tween with a text block, you need to first convert the text block to a symbol. You then create the keyframes for the beginning and the ending of the animation and move the text block to its starting position in the first frame and to its ending position in the last frame. You then create the motion tween. This process is the same as you follow to create motion tweens for other symbols.

You can also apply a shape tween to text. To do so, however, you first need to convert the text to fills by using the Break Apart command on the Modify menu. When you apply this command to a text block, each of the letters in the text block becomes an individual text blocks. You can then apply the command again to the individual letters to convert them to fills. Once converted to fills, you can apply a shape tween to them. For example, you can make the letters change into an oval shape as shown in Figure 3-37. Note that once you convert the text to fills you can no longer edit the fills as text. You will have the opportunity to apply a shape tween to text in Case Problem 4.

Figure 3-37	SAMPLE SHAPE TWEEN

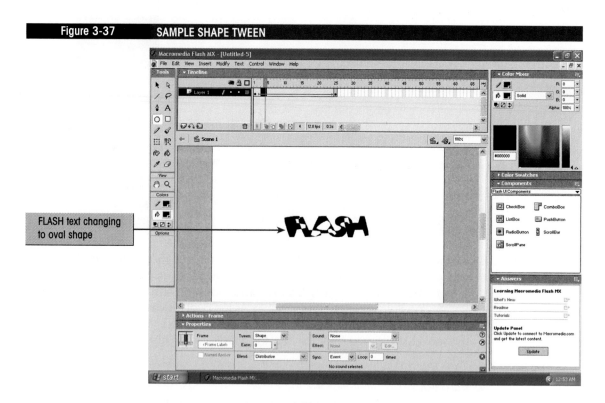

FLASH text changing to oval shape

Adding Animated Text to the Flounders Pet Shop Banner

After reviewing the banner printout with instructions from Aly, as shown in Figure 3-1, you see that you still need to add several text blocks to complete the banner. There are four text blocks. The Aquarium text block and the Tank text block will move off the sides of the Stage to the center of the Stage. One text block, the And text block, will not be animated but will only appear halfway through the animation. The fourth text block, Fish Sale, will also appear halfway through the animation but will increase in size throughout the second half of the animation. Each text block will be in its own layer so you can animate them individually. You will start by adding four new layers, one for each text block, to the document.

To add a text block to the banner and use motion tweening to animate it:

1. Select the **Guide: Fish2** layer in the Timeline, and insert a new layer named **Aquarium**. Insert three more layers above the Aquarium layer, and name them **Tank**, **And**, and **Fish Sale**, respectively.

2. Click the **Zoom** control list arrow and click **100%** to change the view of the Stage. If necessary, display the rulers by clicking **View** on the menu bar, and then **Rulers**. You will want to have the work area visible to create the text blocks, and have the rulers for aligning the text blocks. Set the text properties next.

3. Select **Frame 1** of the **Aquarium** layer. Click the **Text** tool A in the toolbox. In the Property inspector, select **Arial** as the font, **26** for the font size, and **yellow** for the font color. Click the **Bold** button $\boxed{B}$, and then click the **Italic** button $\boxed{I}$ to apply bold and italic formatting. Now you are ready to create the first block.

4. Create a text block to the left of the Stage as shown in Figure 3-38. Type **Aquarium** for the text. Before you can create a motion tween of this text block, it needs to be converted to a symbol.

Figure 3-38	AQUARIUM TEXT BLOCK

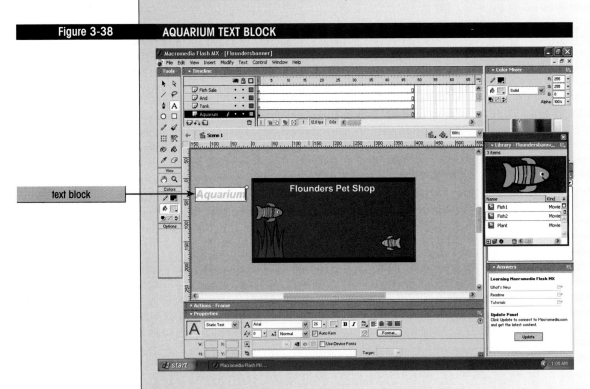

text block

5. Click the **Arrow** tool ⬉ in the toolbox. With the text block still selected, click **Insert** on the menu bar, and then click **Convert to Symbol**. In the Convert to Symbol dialog box, type **Aquarium text** in the Name textbox and make sure the **Movie Clip** option button is selected. Recall movie clip is the behavior you will use for most of your symbols. Click the **OK** button to close the Convert to Symbol dialog box.

6. Click **Frame 10** of the **Aquarium** layer. Insert a **keyframe** at Frame 10. Move the Aquarium text block to the center of the Stage. Place it about 100 pixels from the left of the Stage and 100 pixels from the top as shown in Figure 3-39.

Figure 3-39	END POSITION FOR TEXT

playhead on Frame 10

text block

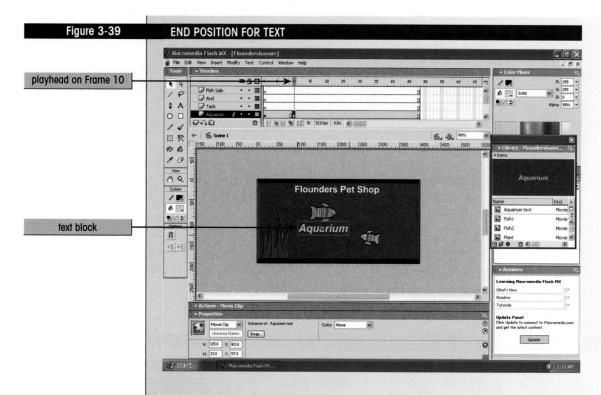

Now, create the motion tween for the text block.

7. Click **Frame 1** of the Aquarium layer. Click the **Tween** list arrow in the Property inspector, and then click **Motion**. A motion tween is created so that the text moves from the left of the Stage to the center of the Stage.

You have added a text block and then used a motion tween to animate it. Now you will repeat similar steps to add additional text blocks. You will use the other layers you created for these text blocks. You will start by creating a keyframe for the start of the Tank text.

To create more text animations:

1. Click **Frame 10** of the **Tank** layer. Insert a keyframe.

2. Click the **Text** tool A in the toolbox. In the Property inspector, select **Arial** as the font, **26** for the font size, and **yellow** for the font color. Click the **Bold** button B , and then click the **Italic** button I to apply bold and italic formatting.

3. Create a new text block to the right of the Stage with the word **Tank** as shown in Figure 3-40.

Figure 3-40 TANK TEXT BLOCK

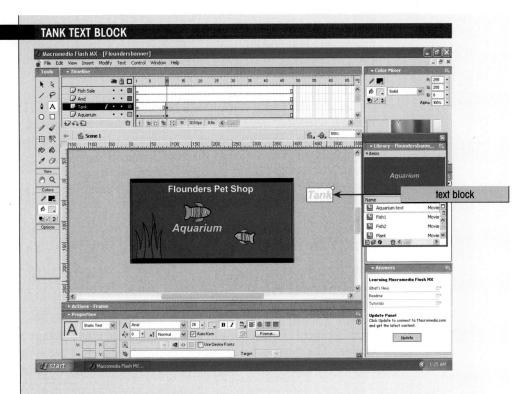

4. Select the text block and convert it to a symbol. Name the symbol **Tank text**, and make sure the **Movie Clip** option button is selected.

5. Click **Frame 20** of the Tank layer. Insert a keyframe. Move the Tank text block to the right of the Aquarium text block. Line up the text horizontally with the Aquarium text. See Figure 3-41. Now create a motion tween.

Figure 3-41 TANK TEXT ALIGNED WITH THE AQUARIUM TEXT

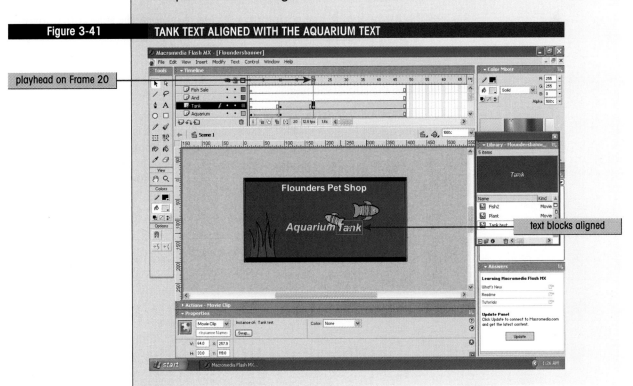

6. Click **Frame 10** of the Tank layer. Click the **Tween** list arrow in the Property inspector, and then click **Motion**. A motion tween is created so that the text moves from the right of the Stage to the right of the Aquarium text.

You will now repeat similar steps to add another text block. However, this text block will not have a motion tween because it will not be animated. Instead, it will only appear starting with Frame 25. That means that from Frame 1 to Frame 24 the text is not displayed. It is only displayed from Frame 25 through Frame 48.

To add a new text block:

1. Click **Frame 25** of the **And** layer. Insert a keyframe.

2. Create another text block below the Aquarium and Tank text blocks.

3. Type the word **And** in this text block.

Now you need to create one more text block. This text block will be animated with a motion tween. However, it will not move; instead it will change in size throughout the animation. The text block will not be visible until Frame 25 at which point the motion tween will start.

To create a text block that increases in size:

1. Click **Frame 25** of the Fish Sale layer. Insert a keyframe. Click the **Text** tool A in the toolbox, and in the Property inspector change the font size to **12**.

2. Create a text block below the And text block. Type **Fish Sale!** in this text block.

3. Click the **Arrow** tool in the toolbox. With the text block still selected, convert this to a symbol named **Fish Sale text** with the behavior of Movie Clip. Now you will add a keyframe for the end of the animation.

4. Click **Frame 35** of the **Fish Sale** layer. Insert a keyframe. In this frame you want to increase the size of the text.

5. Click **Window** on the menu bar, and then click **Transform** to open the Transform panel. Make sure that the Fish Sale text block is still selected. In the Transform panel, make sure that the **Constrain** checkbox is selected, and enter **300%** in the width box, as shown in Figure 3-42. Be sure to press the **Enter** key after you type 300. Close the Transform panel. Now create a motion tween.

Figure 3-42   TRANSFORM PANEL

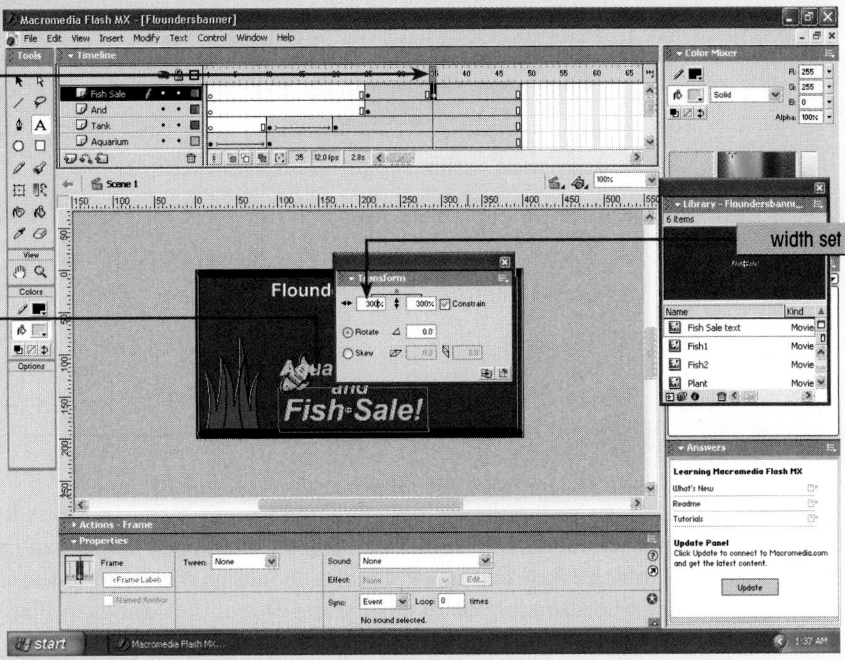

playhead on Frame 35

width set to 300%

text should increase in size

6. Click **Frame 25** of the **Fish Sale** layer. Click the **Tween** list arrow in the Property inspector, and then click **Motion**. A motion tween is created so that the text increases in size throughout the animation.

7. Move the **playhead** to Frame 1, and then press the **Enter** key to test the animation.

8. Save the changes you have made to the document, and exit Flash.

Aly is very pleased with the animated banner you created for the Flounders Pet Shop Web site. She will meet with Joe Flounders to show him the banner and get his approval. Once he has approved the banner, she can forward it to Chris Johnson, the site designer, to incorporate the banner into the Flounders Pet Shop Web site.

In this session you learned how to create animations using special layers. You learned how to create animations with motion guide layers and mask layers. You also learned how to animate text blocks.

Session 3.3 QUICK CHECK

1. List two ways to insert a motion guide layer.

2. Name two tools you can use to create a path in a motion guide layer.

3. How can you see the effect that a mask layer has on a masked layer when testing an animation within the program window?

4. A text block can be animated using a shape tween. True or False?

5. A text block, like any other object, must be converted to a _____ before it can be animated using a motion tween.

REVIEW ASSIGNMENTS

After reviewing the revised animated banner with Mr. Flounders, Aly asks you to add another animated fish that swims from the upper-left side of the banner down to just below the And text block. It then should continue up to the upper-right side of the banner. She also asks you to change the title of the banner so that it fades in throughout the animation.

If necessary, start Macromedia Flash, insert your Data Disk in the appropriate disk drive, and then do the following:

1. Open the **Floundersbanner.fla** file which you created in the tutorial from the Tutorial.03\Tutorial folder on your Data Disk, set the panels to their default layout, and set the Stage magnification level to show the entire banner in the Stage window.

2. Open the Library panel and make a duplicate of the Fish2 symbol. Name this duplicate **Fish3**. Edit the Fish3 symbol by changing each of the blue colored fills to light green. Be sure to exit the symbol-editing mode when you are finished making these changes.

3. In the document's Timeline, insert a new layer and name it **Fish3**. In this layer, drag an instance of the fish3 symbol to the upper-left corner of the banner. Then insert a keyframe in Frame 48. In Frame 48, move the fish3 instance to the upper-right corner of the banner. Now create a motion tween in Frame 1.

4. To make the fish follow a path, insert a motion guide layer. It should be above the Fish3 layer, and the Fish3 layer should be indented under the motion guide layer.

5. In the Guide layer, use the Pencil tool to draw a smooth curved line starting at the upper-left side, curving down to the lower-middle part of the banner, and then up to the upper-right side of the banner. This will be the path the fish follows.

6. In Frame 1 of the Fish3 layer, make sure that the Fish3 instance snaps to the beginning of the line. Also, check the Orient to Path option in the Property inspector. In Frame 48, make sure the fish snaps to the end of the line. Hide the motion guide layer so that the line is not visible on the Stage. Test the animation to make sure the fish follows the path you drew in the motion guide layer.

7. In Layer 1, select the top text block, and convert it to a symbol. Name the symbol **Title**. Then delete the text block from this layer.

8. Insert a new layer and name it **Title**. Drag an instance of the Title symbol to the top center of the banner. Insert a keyframe in Frame 30 and create a motion tween in Frame 1.

Explore

9. Select the title instance to display its instance properties in the Property inspector. Select Alpha under the Color Styles drop-down list. Set the Alpha amount to 0%. The text should become transparent. Test the animation. The text should fade in as the animation plays.

10. Save the revised banner as **Floundersbanner2.fla** in the Review folder of the Tutorial.03 folder of your Data Disk, and then close the file and exit Flash.

CASE PROBLEMS

Case 1. Creating an Animated Banner for Sandy's Party Center Planning is well underway at Sandy's Party Center for their grand opening celebration. Sandy Rodriguez, store owner, is expecting a good turnout for their celebration. Sandy meets with John Rossini to discuss the development of the banner for their new Web site. Sandy asks John to make the banner more festive by adding animation to it.

John has started developing the revised banner shown in Figure 3-43 and wants you to help him complete the task by adding animations for a text block, balloon graphics, and confetti graphics. The balloons will float up as the confetti comes down. The text block will move in from above the banner to the bottom of the banner.

Figure 3-43	INITIAL VERSION OF THE REVISED SANDY'S PARTY BANNER

duplicate confetti and animate the copies to fall from the top to the bottom

animate the text block to come down from above the banner

create different colored copies of the balloon, and animate them to float up

create several copies of the hat and place them throughout the banner

If necessary, start Macromedia Flash, insert your Data Disk in the appropriate drive, and then do the following:

1. Open the **partybanner.fla** file from the Cases folder of the Tutorial.03 folder on your Data Disk. The document contains some of the graphic elements that will be used to create the animated banner. Save the banner in the Cases folder of the Tutorial.03 folder on your data disk. Name the banner **partybanner2.fla**.

2. Select the confetti on the Stage, and convert it to a symbol. Make sure you select all of the confetti graphic at one time. Name the symbol **confetti**, and keep the default behavior type of Movie Clip.

3. Select and convert the party hat to a symbol. Make sure you select both the fill and the stroke that make up the graphic. Name the symbol **party hat**. The behavior type should also be Movie Clip.

4. Convert the balloon into a symbol, with the name of **balloon1** and behavior of Movie Clip.

5. Select the bottom text block and convert it to a symbol named **text**.

6. Delete the confetti, party hat, and balloon graphics, as well as the bottom text block from the Stage. Do not delete the top text block nor the rectangle around the banner.

7. Change the name of **Layer 1** to **background** and add regular frames to extend this layer through Frame 30.

8. Insert a new layer. Name this layer **confetti1**. Drag an instance of the confetti symbol to the upper-left corner of the banner. Create a motion tween so that the confetti instance moves from the upper left to the lower left of the banner. The motion tween should span frames 1 through 30.

9. Insert another layer and name it **confetti2**. Drag another instance of the confetti symbol, but this time place it on the upper-right side of the banner. Create a motion tween so that the confetti instance moves from the upper right to the lower right of the banner.

10. Open the Library panel. Create a duplicate of the balloon1 symbol. Name this symbol **balloon2**. Edit the balloon2 symbol to change the color of the balloon to red. Create another copy of the balloon1 symbol and name it **balloon3**. Edit the balloon3 symbol to change its color to pink.

11. Insert a new layer and name it **balloon1**. In this layer, drag an instance of the balloon1 symbol to the lower-left side of the Stage. Create a motion tween so that the balloon moves up to the top of the banner.

12. Insert a new layer and name it **balloon2**. In this layer, drag an instance of the balloon2 symbol to the middle of the Stage. Create a motion tween so that the balloon moves up to the top of the banner.

13. Insert a new layer and name it **balloon3**. In this layer, drag an instance of the balloon3 symbol to the lower-right side of the Stage. Create a motion tween so that the balloon moves up to the top of the banner.

14. Insert a new layer and name it **text**. In this layer, drag an instance of the text symbol and place it above the center of the banner, outside the Stage. Create a motion tween so that the text block moves from above the banner to the bottom center of the banner. This tween should span Frames 1 through 10 and the text should remain visible through Frame 30.

15. Add several instances of the hat symbol to the Background layer. Make sure you add them to the first frame.

16. Test your animation.

17. Save and close the file and exit Flash.

Case 2. Creating an Animated Banner for River City Music River City Music is getting ready for their upcoming anniversary sale and store manager, Janet Meyers, has met with Alex Smith to review the banner that Alex has developed. They agree to make the banner more interesting by adding animation to it.

Alex has started developing the revised banner as shown in Figure 3-44 and wants you to help him complete the task by adding two text blocks that will be animated and by animating the musical notes.

Figure 3-44 **INITIAL VERSION OF THE REVISED RIVER CITY MUSIC BANNER**

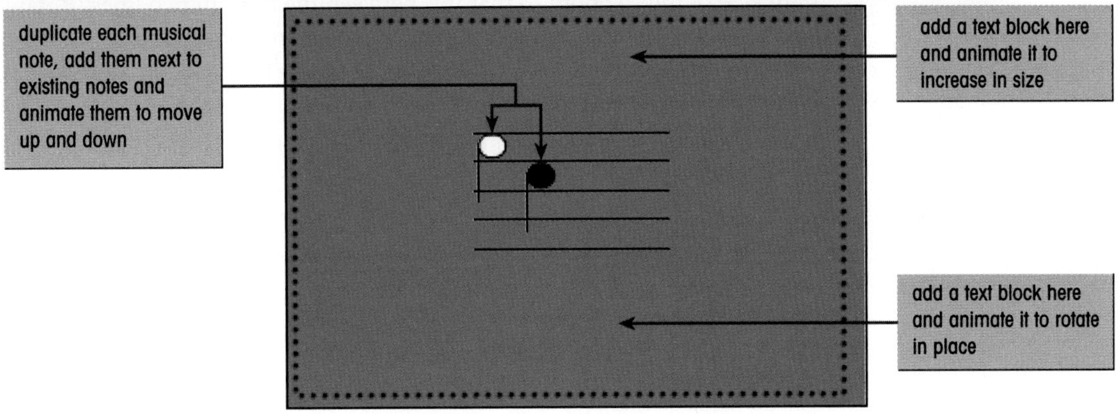

duplicate each musical note, add them next to existing notes and animate them to move up and down

add a text block here and animate it to increase in size

add a text block here and animate it to rotate in place

If necessary, start Macromedia Flash, insert your Data Disk in the appropriate drive, and then do the following:

1. Open the **musicbanner.fla** file from the **Cases** folder under the **Tutorial.03** folder on your Data Disk. The document contains some of the graphic elements that will be used to create the animated banner.

2. Save the banner in the Cases folder of the Tutorial.03 folder on your data disk. Name the banner **musicbanner2.fla**.

3. Select the left musical note on the Stage and convert it to a symbol. Name this symbol **note1**. Select the second musical note and convert it to a symbol also. Name this symbol **note2**.

4. Take note of the positions of the notes within the lines, and then delete them from the Stage. Rename the layer **Background**, and add regular frames so that it extends to Frame 20.

5. Insert a new layer and name it **notes1**. Drag an instance of the note1 symbol to the left side of the lines so that it is in its original position between the top two lines.

6. Create keyframes in each of Frames 5, 10, 15, and 20. In Frames 5 and 15 move the note so that it is between the third and fourth lines from the top. Keep the horizontal position the same. Then create motion tweens between each keyframe. The motion tweens will be in Frames 1, 5, 10, and 15. Test the animation. The note should move up and down.

7. Insert a new layer and name it **notes2**. Drag an instance of the note2 symbol to the left side of the lines so that it is in its original position between the third and fourth lines from the top.

8. Add keyframes in every fifth frame just like you did for the notes1 layer. In frames 5 and 15 move the note so that it is between the first and second lines from the top. Keep the vertical position the same. Now create motion tweens between each keyframe. Test the animation. This note should move up and down.

Explore 9. Insert another layer and name it **notes3**. Drag an instance of the note1 symbol to the right side of the last note so that it is between the second and third lines from the top. You will create motion tweens as before, but before you do, rotate the note 180 degrees so that its stem is pointing up. Then create the keyframes and motion tweens so that it moves up and down like the other notes. When the note moves down it should be between the bottom two lines.

10. Insert another layer and name it **notes4**. Drag an instance of the note2 symbol to the right side of the last note so that it is between the bottom two lines. Rotate the note 180 degrees so that its stem is pointing up. Then create the keyframes and motion tweens so that it moves up and down like the other notes. When the note moves up it should be between the second and third lines from the top.

11. Insert a new layer and name it **title**. In Frame 1 of this layer create a text block with the text *River City Music*. Use a fancy font such as Monotype Corsiva and use a larger text font size such as 36. The text block should be centered on the banner above the notes. Convert the text block to a symbol.

Explore   12. Insert a keyframe in Frame 15 of the title layer and then create a motion tween in Frame 1. Use the Transform panel to reduce the size of the text block in Frame 1 to 25% of its original size. Test the animation. The text block should start out small and grow to its original size.

13. Insert one more layer and name it **sale**. Create a text block in Frame 1 with the text *Piano Sale!* using a smaller font than the title text. Convert this text block to a symbol. Then insert a keyframe in Frame 15 and create a motion tween. Use the Rotate option in the Property inspector to have the text rotate two times in a clockwise direction.

14. Test your animation, save and close the file, and then exit Flash.

Case 3. Creating an Animated Logo for Sonny's Auto Center Sonny Jackson, owner of Sonny's Auto Center, meets with Amanda Lester, who was contracted to update the company's Web site. Amanda shows Sonny the logo she developed and they both agree that the logo could be enhanced by adding some animation.

Amanda decides to revise the logo by adding a shape tween to the company name and a masking effect on the word Autos. She asks you to help her complete the task. The revised logo will use the same graphics as the current logo, but you will animate the Sonny's text and the AUTOS text. Each should be in a separate layer. The banner will look similar to that shown in Figure 3-45.

Figure 3-45   **SONNY'S AUTO CENTER LOGO**

If necessary, start Macromedia Flash, insert your Data Disk in the appropriate drive, and then do the following:

1. Open the logo file you created in Case 3 of Tutorial 2 for Sonny's Auto Center. The file is **saclogo** and should be in the Cases folder under the Tutorial.02 folder on your Data Disk. Save this file as **saclogo2** in the Tutorial.03\Cases folder on your Data Disk. If you did not complete this case problem in Tutorial 2, see your instructor for assistance.

2. Rename Layer 1 to **Background**, and add regular frames so that the layer extends to Frame 30.

3. Insert a layer and name it **Sonny**. Insert another layer and name it **Autos**.

Explore ▶ 4. Select the **Sonny's** text block. Use the Cut command on the Edit menu to cut the text block. Then on Frame 1 of the Sonny layer, use the Paste in Place command on the Edit menu to place the text in the same relative position as it was in the Background layer.

Explore ▶ 5. Select the Sonny's text and use the Break Apart command to break the text apart into individual letters. Use the command a second time to break the letters into filled shapes.

Explore ▶ 6. Insert a keyframe in Frame 20 of the Sonny layer. In the first frame draw a black filled rectangle over the Sonny's text block. The size of the rectangle should be just slightly larger than the text block itself. Insert a shape tween in Frame 1. Test the animation. The rectangle should transform into the text Sonny's.

7. Select the **AUTOS** text block in the center of the Stage. Make sure you do not select any other graphics besides the text. Use the Cut command to cut the text block. Then on Frame 1of the Autos layer, use the Paste in Place command to place the text in the same relative position as it was in the Background layer.

8. Convert the AUTOS text block into a symbol. Name the symbol Autos. Edit the symbol in symbol-editing mode. Rename Layer 1 to **autotext1** and extend it to 20 frames. Insert a new layer and name it **gradient**. Insert another layer and name it **autotext2**.

Explore ▶ 9. In the Gradient layer, create a rectangle with a gray radial gradient fill. The rectangle should be the same height as the text block and about 200 pixels in width. Convert the rectangle into a symbol. Create a motion tween so that the rectangle moves from left to right over the text. Start the tween so that the position of the rectangle only covers the letter **A** and end it so that it only covers the letter **S**.

Explore ▶ 10. Convert the autotext2 layer to a mask layer. The gradient layer should be automatically converted into a masked layer and indented under the autotext2 layer. Exit symbol-editing mode and return to the document. Test the animation.

11. Save the changes you have made to the logo.

Case 4. Creating an Animated Banner for LAL Financial Christopher Perez, head of Marketing at LAL Financial Services, meets with webmaster Elizabeth Danehill to discuss progress in the development of the new banner for the company's Web site. They decide that adding some animation to the banner will enhance its appearance. Elizabeth meets with the graphics designer, Mia Jones, and they decide to ask you to help revise the banner. The banner will look similar to that shown in Figure 3-46, but the square, triangle, and circle shapes will be animated.

Figure 3-46   **LAL FINANCIAL BANNER**

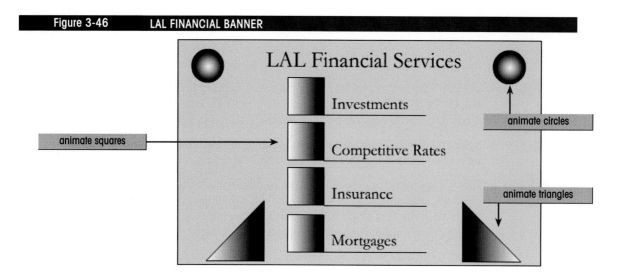

If necessary, start Macromedia Flash, insert your Data Disk in the appropriate drive, and then do the following:

1. Open the banner file you created in Case 4 of Tutorial 2 for LAL Financial Services. The file is **lfsbanner** and should be in the Tutorial.02\Cases folder on your Data Disk. Save this file as **lfsbanner2** in the Tutorial.03\Cases folder on your Data Disk. If you did not complete Case 4 of Tutorial 2, then see your instructor for assistance.

2. Start by selecting one of the circles on the banner. Convert the graphic to a symbol and name it **circle**. Also select one of the triangles and convert it to a symbol. Name the symbol **triangle**. Then select one of the squares and convert it to a symbol. Name it **square**. Then delete all of the circles, triangles, and squares from the banner.

3. Rename the Layer 1 to **background** and extend it so that it has 30 frames.

4. Use the circle symbol to create a motion tween where the circle moves from the lower-left corner of the banner to the upper-left corner. Create another motion tween using the circle symbol to have a circle move from the lower-right corner of the banner to the upper-right corner. Both of these tweens should occur at the same time and cover the first 20 frames.

5. Create four motion tweens using the square symbol. Each instance of the square should move individually from the left side of the banner, starting outside the Stage. Each square should move to the right and end up just to the left of the horizontal line for each text block. The bottom of the square should line up with the horizontal line. The squares should move in a straight horizontal line and should also rotate one time as they move. (*Hint*: For the top square, the motion tween should span frames 1 through 5. For the next square, the motion tween should span frames 1 through 10. The third square should have a motion tween that spans frames 1 through 15. And the motion tween for the bottom square should span frames 1 through 20.)

6. Create two motion tweens for the triangle symbol. Have each instance of the triangle move from the top of the banner to the bottom. One starts to the left of the banner's title and the other starts to the right of the banner's title. The triangle on the right should be flipped horizontally before creating its motion tween. Test the animation.

7. Save and close the file, and then exit Flash.

QUICK | CHECK ANSWERS

Session 3.1

1. The purpose of the Timeline is to coordinate and control the frames that make up an animation. It is also used to organize the layers that contain the different elements of a document.

2. You can tell what the current frame is by looking at the location of the playhead on the Timeline header. You can also see the current frame number displayed at the bottom of the Timeline.

3. The default frame rate is 12 fps.

4. Frames contain content that is displayed for an instant in time. Frames are displayed one after another to create the perception of movement. Layers are made up of one or more frames and are used to organize the graphic elements of a document.

5. You can insert a new layer by using the Layer command on the Insert menu. You can also insert a new layer by clicking the Add Layer button on the Timeline.

6. The Library panel stores and organizes the symbols contained in a document.

7. You delete a symbol by selecting it and then clicking the trash can icon at the bottom of the Library panel.

8. The Wide State button and the Narrow State button change the view of the Library panel.

9. Symbols are reusable elements such as graphics, buttons, and sound files that can be used more than once in your document. An instance is a copy of a symbol.

10. False. Modifying a symbol will also change the instances created from that symbol.

Session 3.2

1. A frame-by-frame animation requires that you create the content for each of the frames. With a tweened animation, Macromedia Flash creates the frames between the beginning and ending keyframes.

2. A layer with a motion tween can only have one object.

3. Create the animation in the symbol's Timeline instead of in the document's Timeline. Each instance of the movie clip symbol then automatically contains the animation.

4. To have an object move from one side of the Stage to the other, you would create a motion tweened animation.

5. False. An object used in a shape tween must not be converted to a symbol.

Session 3.3

1. You can insert a motion guide layer by using the Motion Guide command in the Insert menu or by clicking the Motion Guide icon in the Timeline.

2. To create a path in a motion guide layer you can use the pencil, pen, oval, rectangle, or brush tool.

3. To see the effect that a mask layer has on a masked layer when testing an animation within the program window, lock both layers.

4. False. Text blocks should not be converted to fills with the Break Apart command before applying a motion tween to them. They should be converted to symbols.

5. A text block like any other object must be converted to a symbol before it can be animated using a motion tween.

In this tutorial you will:

- Create buttons and add them to a document

- Learn about actions and how to use the Actions panel to add actions to buttons

- Use the Actions panel to add actions to frames

- Learn about different types of sound effects and how to acquire sounds for your documents

- Add sound effects to buttons

- Add a background sound to a document

ADDING
BUTTONS, ACTIONS, AND SOUNDS

Making the Flounders Pet Shop Banner Interactive

CASE

Actions Web Design

The staff of Actions Web Design holds a meeting every week to discuss the status of projects they are working on for their clients. During a recent meeting, Aly presented the results of the animated banner developed for their client, Flounders Pet Shop. Everyone was impressed with the work done to develop this banner and with the capabilities of the Macromedia Flash program. They were able to see what can be created with the program, and they were excited about how their other client Web sites could be improved with the use of animation. Aly reports that Joe Flounders approved the animated banner, and that Chris has added the banner to the Flounders Pet Shop Web site home page.

Joe was so excited about the banner that he contacted Aly to request a new banner for a fish supplies page being developed for his shop's Web site. He wants the new banner to have a similar design to the animated banner and to include a background sound in addition to animation. Aly suggests that since the banner will be on a page where visitors may have to spend some time reviewing the available fish supplies, it may be a good idea to give the visitor the option to turn off the animation and the background sound. This can keep the visitor from getting distracted while they view the information on the page. She suggests adding several buttons to the banner to control the animation and to mute the sound. She also suggests that the buttons can include their own sound effects to help the visitor know when the button has been clicked. Joe agrees to Aly's suggestions and approves the development of the new banner.

Aly then holds a planning meeting with you to discuss the requested banner for the fish supplies Web page. In discussing the new banner requested by Joe, Aly explains how Flash allows you to add buttons to a movie to allow the user to control it. She states that buttons can be an easy way to make an animation interactive and that they can take many forms, can include sound effects, and can even change in appearance or behavior when the user places the mouse pointer over them. Aly also mentions that she has recently seen some Web sites that use background sounds and thinks the same can be done for the banner. She has developed the initial design of the banner and gives you a printout with instructions on what needs to be done to complete it. See Figure 4-1.

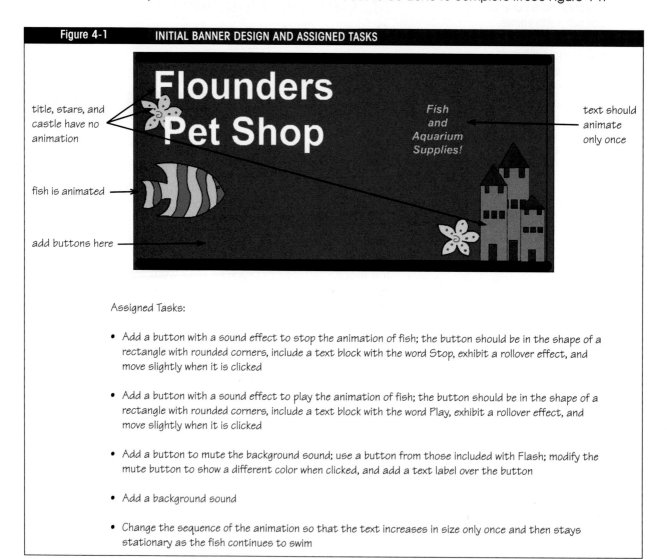

Figure 4-1   INITIAL BANNER DESIGN AND ASSIGNED TASKS

title, stars, and castle have no animation

text should animate only once

fish is animated

add buttons here

Assigned Tasks:

- Add a button with a sound effect to stop the animation of fish; the button should be in the shape of a rectangle with rounded corners, include a text block with the word Stop, exhibit a rollover effect, and move slightly when it is clicked

- Add a button with a sound effect to play the animation of fish; the button should be in the shape of a rectangle with rounded corners, include a text block with the word Play, exhibit a rollover effect, and move slightly when it is clicked

- Add a button to mute the background sound; use a button from those included with Flash; modify the mute button to show a different color when clicked, and add a text label over the button

- Add a background sound

- Change the sequence of the animation so that the text increases in size only once and then stays stationary as the fish continues to swim

In this tutorial you will continue your training in Macromedia Flash by learning how to create buttons, including buttons that change in response to the mouse pointer. You will add buttons to a document and then add actions to the buttons so they can be used to control the animation. You will also learn how to change the way the animation plays by using frame actions, and finally you will add sound effects to the buttons and a background sound to the animation.

In this session you will create buttons that will be used to control the animation of the Flounders Pet Shop fish supplies banner. You will use a button from a library of existing buttons that are included with Flash, and you will also create your own buttons. You will align these buttons using the Align panel, and you will review the visual effects of the buttons.

Buttons

An exciting feature of Macromedia Flash is its ability to make a movie interactive. **Interactive** means that the user has some level of control over the movie, such as being able to stop or play its animation. Adding interaction to a movie draws the viewer in because the viewer is able to do more than passively watch the movie. One of the easiest ways to do this is to add buttons that perform an action. **Buttons** are symbols that contain a Timeline with only four frames. Each frame represents a different state of the button and may contain different content as shown in Figure 4-2.

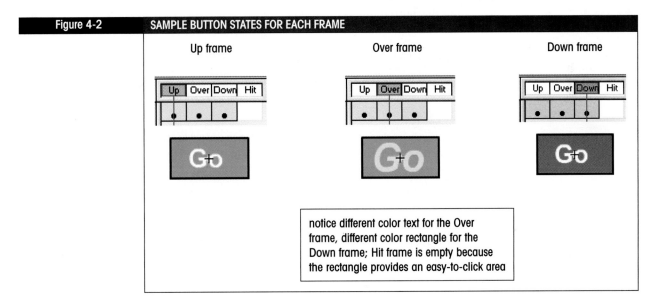

| Figure 4-2 | SAMPLE BUTTON STATES FOR EACH FRAME |

notice different color text for the Over frame, different color rectangle for the Down frame; Hit frame is empty because the rectangle provides an easy-to-click area

The content in each frame is displayed in response to the mouse pointer's action. The **Up** frame contains the button's default state. This is what the button initially looks like to the user, before the user has used the button to take an action. When the pointer is over the button, the content in the **Over** frame is displayed. If you make the contents of the Over frame different from that in the Up frame, you create a **rollover effect**—that is, when the user rolls the pointer over the button, the button changes to show what is in the Over frame. The contents of the **Down** frame show what the button looks like when you click it. Making the contents of the Down frame different from the other frames gives the user a visual clue that the button has been clicked. Finally, the **Hit** frame does not change the appearance of the button. Instead, it represents the clickable or active area of the button. This is the area of the button that responds to a mouse click and displays the hand pointer ᵈʰᵐ when the mouse pointer is over it. This is useful when the button is not a solid shape. For example, if the button consists of text, then the user has to click the letters in the text in order to activate the button. This may be difficult if the text is small. You can make it easier for the user to click the button by drawing a rectangle in the Hit frame. The rectangle represents the area that can be clicked to activate the button.

You will create buttons from scratch later in this session, but first you will use prebuilt buttons found in the Buttons library.

Adding a Button from the Common Libraries Buttons

A quick way to add buttons to your document is by using one of the buttons in the Buttons library. The Buttons library is one of the Flash Common Libraries. The Common Libraries have symbols that install with Flash and can be copied to your documents. These libraries include Buttons, Learning Interactions, and Sounds. Learning Interactions are not covered in this book. You will use the Sounds library later in this tutorial. The Common Libraries can be accessed from the Windows menu. To use the Buttons library you click Buttons from the Common Libraries menu. The library opens and its button symbols can then be copied to your document's library and used within your document. Recall from Tutorial 3 that symbols are stored in the document's library and then copies of the symbol, called instances, are added to the Stage.

Aly has asked you to make the Flounders Pet Shop banner interactive by adding buttons to control the animation. She also wants a button added that allows the user to mute the background sound that will be added later. She indicates this would be a good option to give the user because not everyone will want to listen to background sounds when visiting the Web site. She instructs you to add a button from the Buttons library and to add a text block indicating this button mutes the sound.

To add a button from the Buttons library:

1. Make sure that your computer is turned on, that the Windows desktop is displayed, and that your Data Disk is in the appropriate drive. Now you can start Flash and open the banner.

2. Start Flash and open the **petshop.fla** file located in the Tutorial.04\Tutorial folder on your Data Disk. Next you want to change the view so that the complete contents of the Stage are visible.

3. Change the magnification level of the Stage to **Show All**, position the panels to their default layout, and display the Rulers. The view of the Stage changes to show all of the contents, and the panels are positioned in their default layout. See Figure 4-3. Now save this file with a new name, leaving the original file intact on your Data Disk in case you want to repeat the steps in this session at another time.

Figure 4-3   PETSHOP DOCUMENT

4. Save the petshop.fla document as **petshop2.fla** in the **Tutorial.04\Tutorial** folder on your Data Disk. You will now add a new layer to the Timeline where the buttons will be placed. It is best to keep different elements of a Flash document in separate layers. This helps you keep them organized.

5. Click the **Store** layer in the Timeline, click **Insert** on the menu bar, and then click **Layer** to add a new layer. Change the name of this new layer to **Buttons**. The button you are going to add is part of the Common Libraries. Once you add it to your document, it is copied into your document's library of symbols.

6. Click **Window** on the menu bar, and then click **Library** to open the document's Library panel. The document's library contains five items, including the castle, fish, star, supplies text, and title symbols.

7. Click **Window** on the menu bar, point to **Common Libraries**, and then click **Buttons**. The Buttons library panel opens below the document's Library panel. The library contains 122 items organized into folders which represent categories of buttons such as Key Buttons or Circle Buttons. See Figure 4-4. You double-click a folder to list the buttons inside that folder.

Figure 4-4   BUTTONS LIBRARY

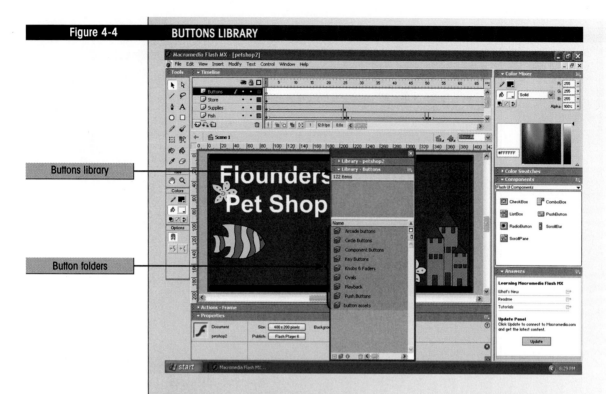

Buttons library

Button folders

8. Locate the Playback folder in the Buttons library panel. Double-click the **Playback** folder icon 📁 to display the list of buttons contained in that folder. Scroll down until you see the playback - stop button. Now you will copy the button to your document.

9. Make sure that the Buttons layer in the Timeline is still selected and then drag the **playback - stop** button from the Buttons library panel to the lower-left corner of the Stage to create an instance of the button. Place the button instance approximately 10 pixels from the left edge of the Stage and approximately 170 pixels from the top. Once you add the button instance to the Stage, the button symbol is also added to your document's library. You do not need the Buttons library any more, so you should close it.

10. Click the **Buttons Library panel options menu** control 📋 and click **Close Panel**. If necessary, click the document's Library panel title bar to expand it and move the Library panel off and to the right of the Stage. Notice that the document's Library panel now contains six items. The playback - stop button has been added as a symbol with a Button behavior type as shown in Figure 4-5.

Figure 4-5   **DOCUMENT'S LIBRARY WITH NEW SYMBOL**

new symbol

Once you have added a button instance to a document, it is a good idea to see how it works. You can do this within the Flash program window by turning on the Enable Simple Buttons command on the Control menu. When you turn this command on, the button exhibits its behavior on the Stage. When you move the mouse pointer over the button it changes to a hand pointer 🖑 and displays any rollover effects that are part of the button. You can use this feature to make sure that the button works properly. Once you have reviewed the button's behavior, you need to turn the Enable Simple Buttons command off if you want to select the button instance. You cannot select it with the hand pointer 🖑.

Use the Enable Simple Buttons command to see how the new button instance works.

To view the playback - stop button's behavior:

1. Click **Control** on the menu bar, and then click **Enable Simple Buttons**.

2. Click a blank area of the Stage away from the button to deselect the button. Now see what happens when the mouse pointer is over the button.

3. Position the pointer over the playback - stop button instance on the Stage. The pointer changes to a hand 🖑 indicating to the user that when the button is clicked, an action will occur.

4. Click the **playback - stop** button. When you click it, the button shifts in such a way that it appears as if the button was depressed and released.

Now you are going to edit the button. Recall Aly's instructions that you are to modify the playback - stop button so that it uses a different color for its Down frame. This is the frame that is displayed when the button is clicked, thus giving the user visual feedback that the button has been clicked. Since the button is a symbol, you need to be in symbol-editing mode to make changes to it.

To edit the playback - stop button to change its color:

1. Double-click the **playback - stop** button's icon 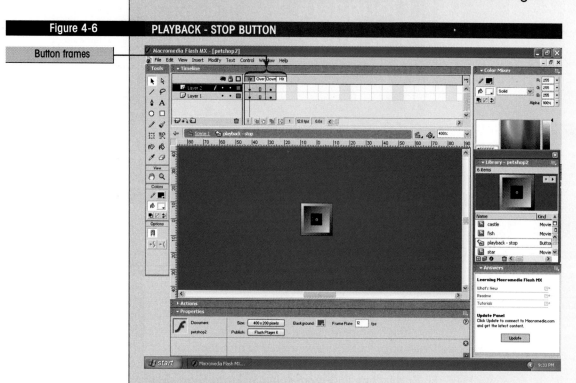 in the Library panel to open the button in symbol-editing mode. The button is displayed on the Stage along with its four-frame Timeline. Change the magnification level and examine the button's frames.

2. Increase the magnification level to **400%** to get a better view of the button as shown in Figure 4-6. Drag the playhead back and forth between the Up frame and the Down frame in the Timeline to see how the button changes.

Figure 4-6	PLAYBACK - STOP BUTTON

Button frames

3. Click the **Down** frame of Layer 2 on the Timeline. The small black square in the center of the button appears selected, which is indicated by the fine dot pattern. Change the color of this square to **green** using the Fill Color pop-up window in the toolbox as shown in Figure 4-7.

Figure 4-7	CHANGING THE BUTTON

Down frame

color will affect
small square in
button's Down frame

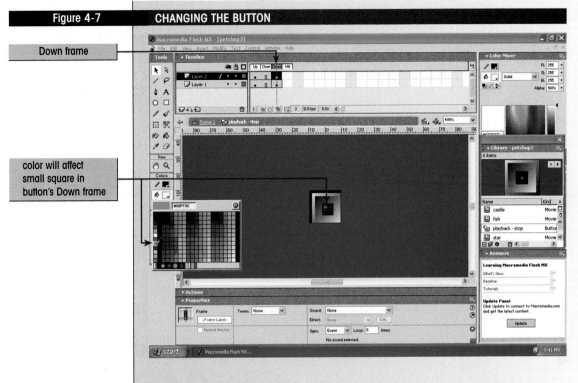

4. Click the **Scene 1** link in the Address bar to exit symbol-editing mode and return to the document

   Now you can see how the button works with the change you made.

5. Click the **button** instance on the Stage. When you click the button instance, the small black square in its center turns green. Now you will turn off the Enable Simple Buttons command.

6. Click **Control** on the menu bar, and then click **Enable Simple Buttons** to deselect this option.

Now that you have modified the button, you should add text above the button instance on the Stage that labels it as the Mute button. This tells the viewer what happens when the button is clicked. Otherwise, the viewer may not know what purpose the button serves. Providing this visual clue is an element of good design.

To add text to identify the button instance:

1. Set the magnification level to **200%**, and then use the **Hand** tool 🖐 to move the view of the Stage so that the button instance is centered in the Stage window. Now you will set the text properties, and add a text block above the button.

2. Using the **Text** tool A, add a text block above the button with the text **Mute**. Use **Arial** for the font, **10** for the font size, **white** for the text color, and **bold** for the text style. See Figure 4-8.

Figure 4-8　　**TEXT ADDED ABOVE BUTTON**

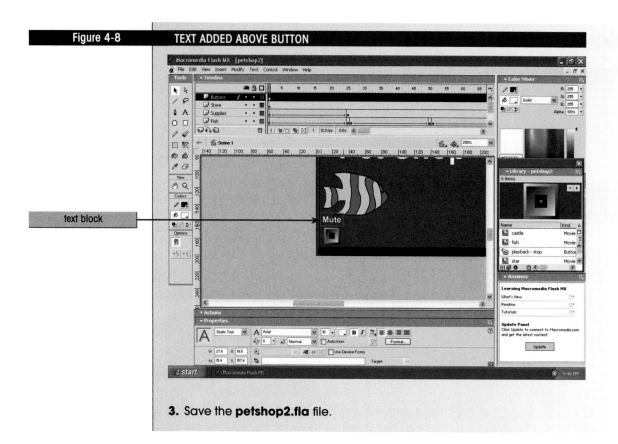

text block

3. Save the **petshop2.fla** file.

You have added a button from the Buttons library. Now you will create a button from scratch.

Creating a Button

The buttons in the Common Buttons Library provide you with many choices to use in your documents. However, you often need to create unique buttons that match your project's design. Macromedia Flash has the tools to create almost any kind of button you need. Buttons can be in the shape of rectangles, ovals, or even in the form of text. You are limited only by your imagination.

To create a button, you can use the Convert to Symbol command or the New Symbol command, both found on the Insert menu. If you first create an object on the Stage, such as a rectangle, you can convert it into a button symbol and then edit it in symbol-editing mode. If you use the New Symbol command to create the button, you do so in symbol-editing mode. In either case, you name the button just like you do any other symbol you create, and you assign Button as its behavior. Recall that symbols can have one of three behavior types, Movie Clip, Button, or Graphic. In symbol-editing mode you create or modify the content for each of the button's four frames. Once you create the button it is stored in the document's library. To use the button in your document, you must create instances of the button. If you convert an object on the Stage to a button symbol, then the object on the Stage becomes an instance once the button symbol is added to the library. If you create a new button symbol in symbol-editing mode, the button is stored in the document's library but no instances are created on the Stage.

REFERENCE WINDOW   **RW**

Creating a Button
- Create the button's shape on the Stage and select the shape.
- Click Insert on the menu bar, and then click Convert to Symbol.
- In the Convert to Symbol dialog box, name the symbol and assign the Button behavior to it.

or
- Click Insert on the menu bar, and then click New Symbol.
- In the New Symbol dialog box, name the symbol and assign the Button behavior to it.
- Create the button's shape on the Stage.

After reviewing the tasks assigned to you by Aly, you see that you now need to create two new buttons and then add these buttons to the banner. These buttons have the same general appearance in that they are both rectangles with rounded corners. However, one button is a Stop button, which the user clicks to stop the animation while it is playing. The second button is a Play button, which the user can click to start the animation playing at any time. Because these two buttons have a similar appearance, you can create the Stop button, and then make a copy of it that you can then modify to create the Play button. You will then add instances of these buttons to the banner.

To create a new button:

1. Click the **Buttons** layer in the Timeline. Before drawing the button on the Stage, select the appropriate settings using the Property inspector.

2. Click the **Rectangle** tool ☐ in the toolbox. In the Property inspector, select **black** for the stroke color and **red** for the fill color. Also, make the stroke height **2** and be sure the stroke style is set to **Solid**. In order to have rounded corners for the rectangle, you need to specify how much rounding to apply.

3. Click the **Rectangle Radius** modifier 🔲 in the options area of the toolbox to open the Rectangle Settings dialog box, and then enter **10** for the Corner Radius. Click the **OK** button to close the dialog box.

4. Create a rectangle in the lower left of the Stage to the right of the Mute button as shown in Figure 4-9. This rectangle represents the default state of the button. Now that you have created the button shape, you need to convert it to a symbol.

Figure 4-9	RECTANGLE

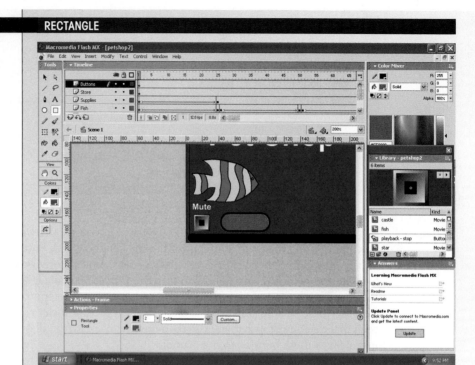

5. Click the **Arrow** tool ▶ in the toolbox. Double-click the **rectangle** to select both its fill and its stroke.

6. Click **Insert** on the menu bar, and then click **Convert to Symbol**. In the Convert to Symbol dialog box enter **Stop** in the Name textbox to name the symbol, and then make sure that **Button** is selected as the behavior type. Click the **OK** button. The new button is added to the document's library.

Now you need to edit this button to add a text label and to create the different states of the button. The button should have a rollover effect. When you roll the pointer over the button, it should change from a red fill to a red radial gradient fill. This provides a visual clue to the user that something will happen if the button is clicked. The button should also move when it is clicked, providing visual feedback that reinforces the user's action. Remember that the button is a symbol, and to edit a symbol, you need to first enter symbol-editing mode.

To add text to the Stop button and create the different states of the button:

1. Double-click the **Stop** button icon 🖼 in the Library panel to open it in symbol-editing mode. Set the magnification level to **200%**. See Figure 4-10.

Figure 4-10   **BUTTON IN SYMBOL-EDITING MODE**

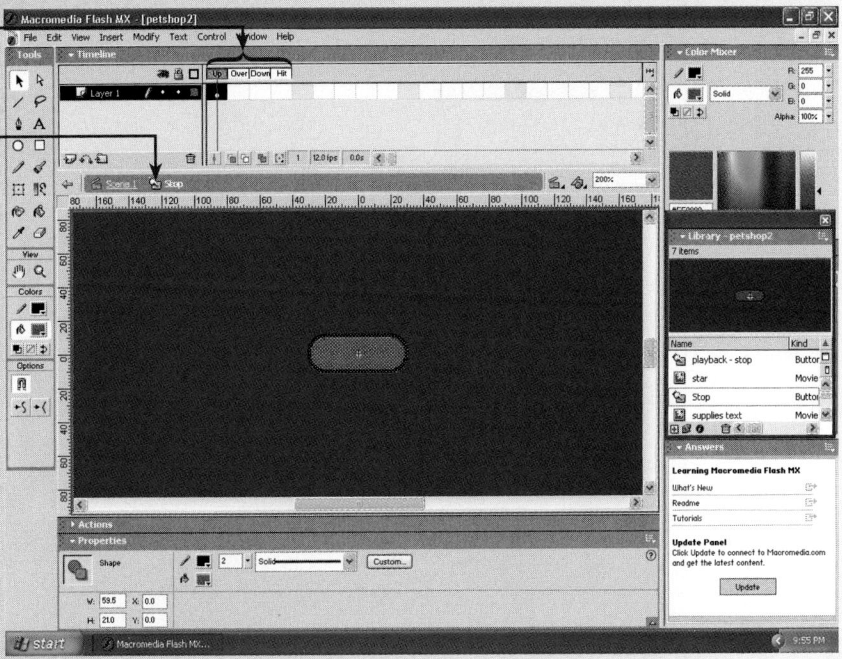

button's four frames

button name

There are four frames in the Timeline for the button. The Up frame has a keyframe and contains the rectangle you created which represents the default state of the button. You will now add text to the button and then add keyframes to the Over and Down frames to create the different states of the button. First set the text properties.

2. Click the **Text** tool A in the toolbox. In the Property inspector, select **Arial** as the font, **10** as the font size, **white** as the text color, and **bold** as the text style.

3. Create a text block inside the rectangle with the word **Stop**. Next you will position the text block such that it is centered inside the rectangle.

4. Click the **Arrow** tool and if necessary, click the **Snap to Objects** modifier on the options area of the toolbox to deselect this option. Use the to move the text block so that it is centered inside the rectangle as shown in Figure 4-11. Now you can create the contents for the Over frame.

Figure 4-11 TEXT ADDED TO RECTANGLE

5. Click the **Over** frame in the Timeline to select it. Insert a **keyframe**. The contents of the Up frame are automatically copied to the Over frame. Recall from Tutorial 3 that each time you add a regular frame or a keyframe in a layer the contents of the previous frame are copied into the new frame.

You want the button's appearance to change from the default state to the Over state, meaning when the user moves the pointer over the Stop button, you want the color of the button to change. So, now you will change the button's fill color in the Over frame.

6. With the rectangle still selected, click the **Fill Color control** list arrow in the tool- box to open the color pop-up window. Click the **red radial gradient** located at the bottom of the pop-up window. It is the third swatch from the left in the bottom row. The red radial gradient replaces the rectangle's red fill as shown in Figure 4-12. Now add content to the Down frame.

| Figure 4-12 | RECTANGLE'S FILL CHANGED IN OVER FRAME |

Over frame

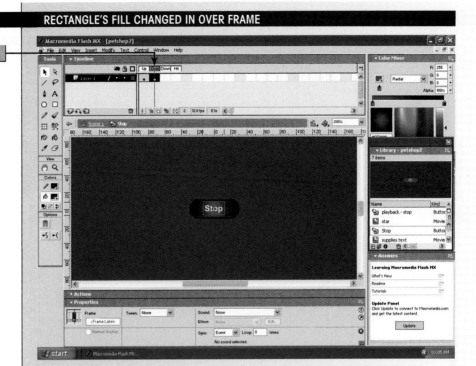

7. Click the **Down** frame in the Timeline. Insert a **keyframe**. The contents of the Over frame are copied to the Down frame. When the user clicks the Stop button, you want the button to appear as if it has been depressed and released. To create this effect, you need to change the button's position in the Down frame.

8. With the rectangle and text block still selected, press the **Down Arrow** key on your keyboard three times, and then press the **Right Arrow** key three times. This changes the position of the rectangle three pixels down and three pixels to the right. Now you will exit symbol-editing mode. There is no need to add anything to the Hit frame because the rectangle shape provides the clickable or active area for the button.

9. Click the **Scene 1** link to exit symbol-editing mode and return to the document.

Now that you have finished creating the button and its different states, preview the button instance's behavior on the Stage to make sure the different effects you have created appear correctly. You use the Enable Simple Buttons command to preview the effects.

To test the button instance's rollover effects:

1. Click **Control** on the menu bar, click the **Enable Simple Buttons** command to select this option, and then click a blank area of the Stage to deselect the button.

2. Move the pointer over the **Stop** button to see the rollover effect as shown in Figure 4-13, and then click the **Stop** button to see how it changes and moves. The rollover effects work well. Now that you are done creating and testing the visual effects of the button, you can turn off the Enable Simple buttons command.

Figure 4-13	BUTTON'S ROLLOVER EFFECT

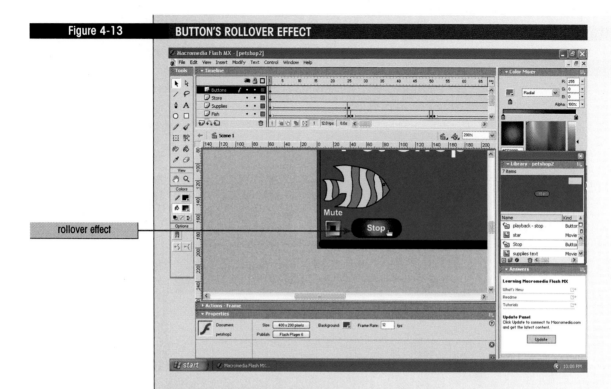

rollover effect

3. Click **Control** on the menu bar, and then click the **Enable Simple Buttons** command to deselect it.

You have created the Stop button and reviewed its rollover effects. Now you need to create one more button—the Play button. Recall from Aly's instructions, the Play button should look very similar to the Stop button. Therefore, instead of creating a new button, you can make a copy of the Stop button you just created, and modify it appropriately to create the Play button.

To create a copy of the Stop button:

1. In the Library panel, click the **Stop** button. Now use the options menu to create a copy of the button.

2. Click the Library panel's **options menu** control ▤ and then click **Duplicate**. The Duplicate Symbol dialog box opens showing the duplicate button's name, Stop copy. You want to change the name of the button.

3. In the Duplicate Symbol dialog box, select the **Stop copy** text in the Name text box, type **Play**, and then click **OK** to close the dialog box. A new symbol is added to the document's library as shown in Figure 4-14.

Figure 4-14	PLAY BUTTON SYMBOL

Now that you have created the Play button by making a copy of the Stop button, you need to modify the Play button so that it is green in its default state and so that it changes to a radiant green color when the user positions the mouse pointer over the button.

To edit the Play button:

1. Double-click the **Play** button icon 🗋 in the Library panel. The button opens in symbol-editing mode.

2. Increase the magnification level to **200%** to make it easier to edit the button.

   To make changes to the button's colors you need to be sure you have selected the appropriate frame. You also want to make sure you do not change the text block. For the Up frame you only want to change the color of the rectangle's fill to green. So make sure the Up frame is selected and the button is deselected.

3. If necessary, select the **Up** frame and deselect the button by clicking a blank area of the Stage. Now select the color to be applied to the button.

4. Using the Fill Color control in the toolbox, change the fill color to a **dark green** (choose the swatch in the fourth column, first row) as shown in Figure 4-15.

| Figure 4-15 | FILL COLOR POP-UP WINDOW |

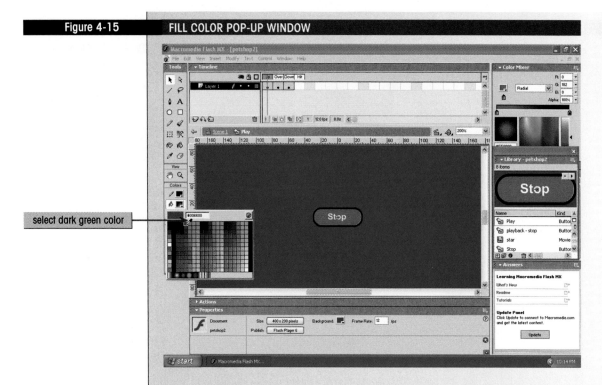

select dark green color

5. Click the **Paint Bucket** tool and then click the **Play** button on the Stage to apply the green color to the button's fill, replacing the button's red color. Now you need to change the text block on the button.

6. Click the **Text** tool A in the toolbox, click the **Stop** text block, and then change the text to **Play**. Make sure the text font is Arial, the text height is 10, the text color is white, and the text style is bold.

   You have only changed the color and text of the Up frame. The Over and Down frames still contain the red fill and the Stop text. Now you need to also change the color and text of the button's Over and Down frames.

7. Drag the playhead to the **Over** frame in the Timeline. Click the **Arrow** tool in the toolbox, and then if necessary, click a blank area of the Stage to deselect the button.

8. Using the Fill Color control in the toolbox, select the **green radial gradient** for the fill color. It is the fourth gradient swatch from the left in the bottom row of the color palette.

9. Click and then click the button on the Stage to apply the gradient to the button's fill. Finally, you need to change the button's text.

10. Change the Stop text to **Play** as you did for the Up frame. See Figure 4-16.

Figure 4-16	OVER FRAME CHANGED

11. Drag the playhead to the **Down** frame in the Timeline. If necessary, deselect the button, and then repeat Steps 9 and 10 to apply the green radial gradient to the button's fill and change the text to Play.

12. Click the **Scene 1** link to exit symbol-editing mode.

You have modified the Play button by changing its color and its text label. Recall that a button symbol resides in the document's library. To use it in the document you need to create an instance of the button symbol. You can easily create an instance by dragging the button from the Library panel to the Stage. Now you can add an instance of the Play button to the document.

To add an instance of the Play button to the Stage:

1. Drag the **Play** button from the Library panel to the Stage. Place the instance to the right of the Stop button instance as shown in Figure 4-17.

Figure 4-17   **PLAY BUTTON INSTANCE ADDED TO DOCUMENT**

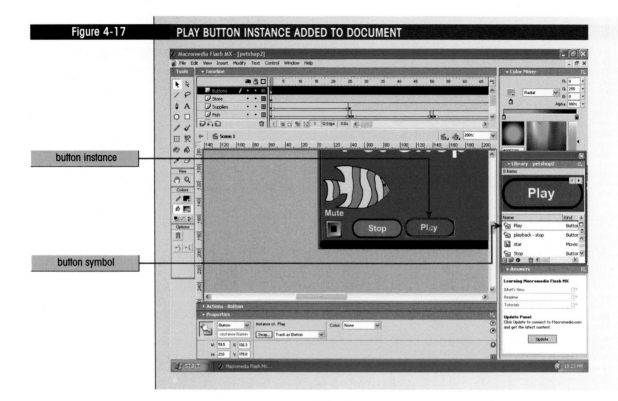

button instance

button symbol

You have changed all of the Play button's frames by making them different from those in the Stop button, and you have added an instance of the Play button to the banner.

Aligning the Buttons

When adding several similar objects to a document you should align the objects. A set of objects like buttons that are close to each other on the Stage should be lined up vertically or horizontally and they should be evenly spaced to give your document a professional appearance. You can accomplish this alignment using the Align panel. The Align panel includes different options used to align a group of selected objects on the Stage. You can align objects by their edges or centers and you can also distribute them so that they are evenly spaced. In order to align objects you need to select them first. You then click one of the buttons in the Align panel. Figure 4-18 describes the different alignment options on this panel.

Figure 4-18   **ALIGN PANEL OPTIONS**

BUTTON	BUTTON NAME	DESCRIPTION
ALIGN		
	Align Left	Align selected objects vertically along their left edges
	Align Horizontal Center	Align selected objects vertically along their horizontal centers
	Align Right	Align selected objects vertically along their right edges
	Align Top	Align selected objects horizontally along their top edges
	Align Vertical Center	Align selected objects horizontally along their vertical centers
	Align Bottom	Align selected objects horizontally along their bottom edges

Figure 4-18		ALIGN PANEL OPTIONS (CONTINUED)
BUTTON	**BUTTON NAME**	**DESCRIPTION**
DISTRIBUTE		
	Distribute Top	Distribute selected objects so that their top edges are evenly spaced
	Distribute Horizontal Center	Distribute selected objects so that their horizontal centers are evenly spaced
	Distribute Bottom	Distribute selected objects so that their bottom edges are evenly spaced
	Distribute Left	Distribute selected objects so that their left edges are evenly spaced
	Distribute Vertical Center	Distribute selected objects so that their vertical centers are evenly spaced
	Distribute Right	Distribute selected objects so that their right edges are evenly spaced
MATCH SIZE		
	Match Width	Resize selected objects so that the widths of all objects match those of the largest selected object
	Match Height	Resize selected objects so that the heights of all objects match those of the largest selected object
	Match Width and Height	Resize selected objects so that the widths and heights of all objects match those of the largest selected object
SPACE		
	Space Horizontally	Evenly spaces the selected objects horizontally
	Space Vertically	Evenly spaces the selected objects vertically
TO STAGE		
	To Stage	Applies alignment relative to the Stage dimensions

Aly reviews the three button instances you have created and instructs you to align them by their bottom edges. She also tells you to make sure that they are positioned with an equal amount of space between them. You will use the Align panel to horizontally align and evenly space the Mute, Stop, and Play buttons.

To align the three buttons using the Align panel:

1. Click **Window** on the menu bar, and then click **Align** to open the Align panel. If necessary, move the panel so that you can see the three buttons on the Stage. Before you can align the three buttons, you must select them.

2. Using the **Arrow** tool , click the **Mute** button instance on the Stage, and then while holding down the **Shift** key on the keyboard, click the **Stop** button instance and click the **Play** button instance to select all three buttons instances at one time, as shown in Figure 4-19.

Figure 4-19	THREE BUTTONS SELECTED

3. Make sure the **To Stage** button on the Align panel is not selected. To Stage aligns the selected objects relative to the Stage and not relative to each other. You want to align the button instances by their bottom edges.

4. With the three button instances selected, click the **Align Bottom Edge** button in the Align panel. This icon is the far-right button in the Align section. Now apply an even amount of space between the button instances.

5. Click the **Space Horizontally** button. This is the far-right button in the Space section. The button instances should now have an equal amount of space between them.

6. Close the **Align** panel, and save the changes you have made to your document. You can either close the file and exit Flash, or leave it and Flash open for the next session.

The buttons you have added to the banner do not control anything yet. When you click them the animation does not change. In order for the buttons to control the animation, they need some programming instructions called Actions. **Actions** are precoded instructions that are used to control how a movie plays and are added using the Actions panel. For example, if you create a button that stops an animation, you need to add a Stop action to the button instance. You will add Actions to the buttons in the next session.

Session 4.1 QUICK CHECK

1. What is a button?

2. Why would you add buttons to a document?

3. How can you add a button from the Buttons library to your document's library?

4. How many frames are in a button's Timeline? List their names.

5. How do you create a rollover effect for a button?

6. How can you test a button in your document while in Macromedia Flash?

7. Which Macromedia Flash tool can help you to easily align several objects on the Stage?

SESSION 4.2

In this session you will use the Actions panel to add actions to the buttons you created in the previous session. You will add a Play action to the Play button and a Stop action to the Stop button. You will also add an action to a frame. Finally, you will test these actions in your browser.

Understanding Actions

The buttons you added to the banner in the previous session look great and have some nice effects such as the rollover effect, but they do not yet allow the user to control the movie's animation. When the button is clicked the movie does not change. The movie still plays sequentially one frame after another until it reaches the end. According to Aly's instructions, the buttons should allow the user to stop and play the movie's animation. In order for the buttons to be fully functional and interactive you need to add instructions called Actions. **Actions** are instructions that are used to control a movie while it is playing. Actions are part of Macromedia Flash's programming language called **ActionScript**. The ActionScript language is very similar to the Web language **JavaScript**, which is used to add interactive elements to Web pages. If you are already familiar with JavaScript, then ActionScript should be familiar to you. However, you do not need any experience with computer programming or Web languages to use ActionScript in your Flash documents. Even though ActionScript is a very powerful language, you can use many of its basic actions without fully understanding all of the language and without manually writing any code. Instead, you can use many of the precoded actions available in the Actions panel. Many of these actions are simple and can be used to create basic navigation controls to control a movie's animation. For example, you can add actions that stop or play a movie. With ActionScript you create scripts that tell the movie what action to take when a certain event occurs. A **script** is a set of one or more actions that perform some function. An **event** is a situation where the user is interacting with a button such as clicking a button with the mouse and then releasing it. These events can be recognized by Flash and can be used to trigger or start the execution of the actions in a script. A sample script is shown in Figure 4-20. Notice that this script contains the Stop action. This script will be added to the instance of the Stop button in the banner.

Figure 4-20   SAMPLE SCRIPT

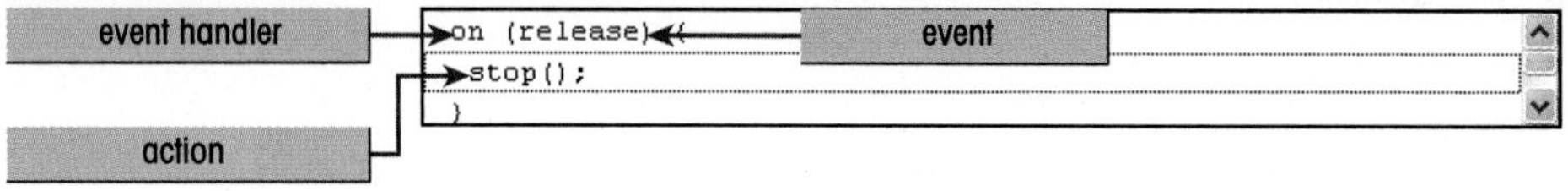

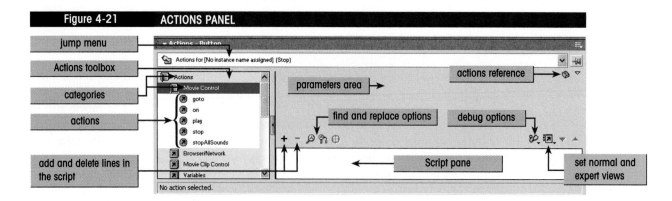

The script consists of three lines of code. The first line has the mouse event handler on followed by the event **release** in parentheses. An **event handler** tells Flash how to handle an event. In the Stop button example, the event handler is triggered when the user clicks and then releases the button causing the stop action to execute. The movie then stops playing. You do not need to create this script yourself. Flash creates it for you when you select actions from the Actions panel.

Adding Actions Using the Actions Panel

As mentioned before, you do not need to fully understand ActionScript to use its basic actions. You also do not need to manually write the scripts yourself. Instead, you access precoded actions in the **Actions** panel shown in Figure 4-21. Flash creates the scripts needed for these actions to work in your document.

Figure 4-21   ACTIONS PANEL

You can use the Actions panel in either normal mode or expert mode. In expert mode, which is not covered in this tutorial, you write the scripts yourself. This requires a deeper understanding of the ActionScript language. You can use other resources to learn more about ActionScript. A good place to start is the Introduction to ActionScript tutorial in the Flash Help system. You can access this tutorial through the Tutorials command on the Help menu. In normal mode, which is the default mode, Flash provides precoded actions you select from the **Actions toolbox**, located on the left side of the Actions panel. The Actions toolbox contains a list that represents different action categories. You click a category to display additional categories or actions. For example, the Actions category contains a list of the different Action categories. One of these categories is Movie Control. When you click Movie Control, a list of the movie control actions is displayed. To select a specific action, you can drag it to the **Script pane**, located on the right side of the Actions panel. The Script pane is where the script is created. You can also double-click the action in the Actions tool-box to add its code to the Script pane. If you make a mistake and you need to delete an action from the script, select it first, and then click the Delete (-) button located above the Script pane. Then you can add the correct action.

When you plan your document, you also plan what interactions will be part of the document and where these interactions will be placed. If you plan to use buttons to give the user control over the animation, then you need to also plan what actions will be needed to make the buttons functional. Once you create the buttons and add instances of them to the document, you can add the appropriate actions to the instances.

Before adding actions to your document, you need to specify where to add the actions. If you want the user to click a button you created and for that button to cause the action to execute, then the action must be attached to the button instance. When adding actions to a button you add them to the button instance on the Stage and not to the button symbol in the library. If you want an action to execute at a certain point in the animation, then attach it to the frame where you want it to start. Adding actions to frames is discussed later in this session.

Aly likes the buttons you have added to the banner. She tells you that the buttons now need actions so they can be used to control the animation as originally planned. She instructs you to add the Stop action to the Stop button and to add the Play action to the Play button.

To add actions to the Stop and Play buttons:

1. If necessary, start Flash and open the **petshop2.fla** banner stored in the Tutorial.04\Tutorial folder on your Data Disk.

2. Set the panels to their default layout and change the magnification level to show all of the Stage.

3. Click the **Stop** button instance on the Stage to select it. Make sure no other buttons or banner elements are selected.

4. Click the **Actions** panel title bar to expand this panel. The Actions panel is located just below the Stage. A list of action categories is displayed in the Actions toolbox located on the left side of the Actions panel. You need to expand the Actions category.

5. Click **Actions** or its **book** icon 🔼 in the Actions toolbox to display its available categories. The Stop action is a movie control, so next display the movie control actions.

6. Click the **Movie Control** icon 🔼 in the Actions toolbox. A list of the available basic movie control actions displays.

7. Double-click the **Stop** action to add the stop action to the Stop button instance. The Stop action and its script are visible in the Script pane as shown in Figure 4-22.

Figure 4-22   STOP SCRIPT

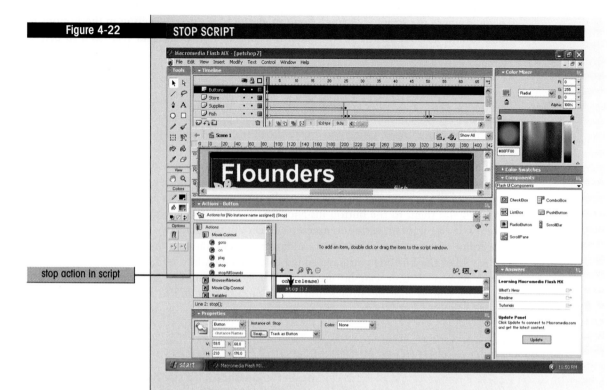

stop action in script

Now you can add the Play action script to the Play button. To do so, you first need to select the button instance.

8. Click the **Actions panel title bar** to collapse it so that you can see the buttons on the Stage.

9. Using the **Arrow** tool , click the **Play** button instance on the Stage to select it. Expand the Actions panel again, and double-click the **Play** action in the Actions toolbox. This action and its script are now added to the Play button instance.

10. Click the **Actions panel title bar** again to collapse it.

Now that you have added the appropriate actions to the Play and Stop buttons, you should test them to make sure they work correctly. You can test them as before by turning on the Enable Simple Buttons command.

To test the button actions:

1. Click **Control** on the menu bar, and then click **Enable Simple Buttons** to turn this command on. First test the Play button.

2. Click the **Play** button to start the animation. While the animation plays, click the **Stop** button to stop the animation. You can click the Play button again to play the animation. The buttons control the movie. Now test the buttons by playing the movie in a Web page.

3. To test the movie in a Web page, click **File** on the menu bar, point to **Publish Preview**, and then click **HTML**. Your computer's default browser opens and the animation plays in a Web page.

4. Test the buttons by clicking them to stop and play the animation.

5. Close the browser window to return to Flash. Save the changes you have made to your document.

Actions that have been added to buttons are executed when certain events occur, such as when the user clicks the button. Another place where you can add actions is in individual frames.

Adding Actions to Frames

Actions in a frame execute when that particular frame is played. Scripts created for frame actions are different from those created for buttons in that no event handler is required. For example, if you add a Stop action to a frame, the script only contains one line with `stop();`. Frame actions do not depend on an event to occur. Instead they execute as soon as the frame they are in is played.

Frame actions can be used to change the sequence in which the frames are played on the Timeline. Ordinarily a movie plays sequentially starting with Frame 1, going through the last frame, and then repeating again at Frame 1. However, you may want to create a different animation effect by playing the frames in a different order. For example, you can create an animation in which a group of frames is played repeatedly by having the playhead go back to an earlier frame. This is called a **loop**. You can do this by placing an action in the last frame of the group that causes the animation to go back to the earlier frame, as shown in Figure 4-23. The frame action is indicated by a small **a** in the frame. Every time the last frame is played the playhead in the Timeline jumps back to Frame 25.

| Figure 4-23 | LOOP CREATED WITH FRAME ACTION |

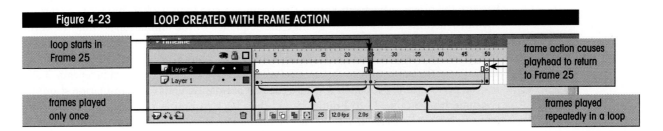

loop starts in Frame 25

frames played only once

frame action causes playhead to return to Frame 25

frames played repeatedly in a loop

In cases like these you need to refer to a specific frame within a script. Although you can refer to frames by their numbers, it is a good idea to assign labels to these frames and to then refer to the labels instead of the numbers. If you use frame numbers in your script and then later add or delete frames from the Timeline, the script may end up referring to the wrong frames. This is because adding or deleting frames causes other frames to be renumbered. You would then have to change each of the scripts that refer to the wrong frame numbers. However, if you use frame labels as shown in Figure 4-24, adding or deleting frames does not affect those frames. They will still have the same labels attached to them. Any scripts that refer to the frames by their labels still work and, therefore, do not have to be changed. Frame labels are added to keyframes using the Frame Label text box in the Property inspector.

Figure 4-24	FRAME LABEL

Frame 25 with a label

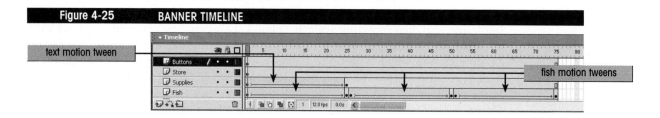

It is also a good idea to create a separate layer in which to add your frame actions. Although this is not required, it makes it easier to keep track of the actions, especially when you have more than one in a document. If you then have to make changes to other parts of the document, the actions are not affected.

Recall from the planning meeting with Aly that the banner contains three motion tweens to make the fish swim back and forth as shown in Figure 4-25. It also contains a motion tween that animates the Supplies text block.

Figure 4-25	BANNER TIMELINE

text motion tween

fish motion tweens

When the banner is published, the text and fish motion tweens repeat continuously because the movie plays from Frame 1 to Frame 75 and then back to Frame 1 to start again. Aly's instructions are for you to change the sequence of the animation so that the text animates only once and then remains stationary as the fish continues to swim. This means that the text motion tween should not be repeated. To accomplish this you need to change the sequence of the animation so that instead of going back to Frame 1 when it repeats, it should instead go to Frame 25, which is where the text animation ends. The animation should then continue from Frame 25 to Frame 75 and then back to Frame 25 to repeat. To do this you add a frame action to the last frame in the document. That frame action causes the playhead to move to Frame 25. The playhead then continues from Frame 25 to Frame 75 again. As a result, the playhead does not replay the text block's animation, but instead continues with the last two fish motion tweens. Since it is possible that frames may be added or deleted from the banner at a later date, the frame action on the last frame should refer to a frame label and not to a frame number. You can add a frame label at Frame 25 that can be referred to by the frame action in Frame 75. To keep things organized in your document, you will place the frame action and the frame label on their own separate layers.

To add actions to a frame:

1. Select the **Buttons** layer in the Timeline. Insert a new layer, and name it **Actions**. Insert another new layer and name it **Labels**. If necessary, make the Labels layer the current layer.

   Before adding a label at Frame 25, you need to make Frame 25 a keyframe. Without a keyframe at Frame 25, the label is added to Frame 1. Anytime there is to be a change in a frame, such as adding a label, a keyframe needs to be inserted at that frame.

2. In the Timeline, click **Frame 25** of the Labels layer, and then insert a keyframe. Now create the label for Frame 25.

3. In the Property inspector, type **Loop Start** in the Frame text box as shown in Figure 4-26, and then press the **Enter** key. The frame label is added to Frame 25 of the Labels layer.

Figure 4-26	ADDING A FRAME LABEL

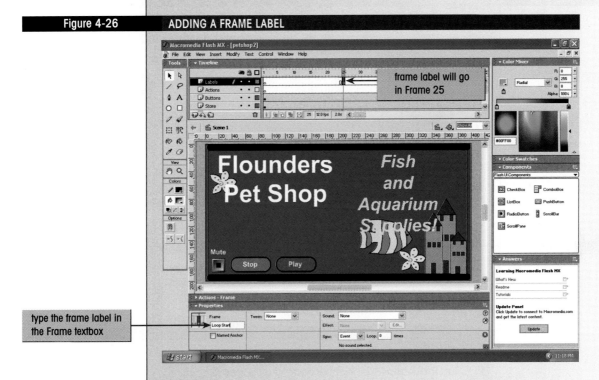

type the frame label in the Frame textbox

Now you will add a frame action to the last frame of the Actions layer. This frame action directs the animation to go back to the Loop Start frame. This last frame also needs to be a keyframe.

4. Click **Frame 75** of the Actions layer, and then insert a keyframe. You may need to use the Timeline's horizontal scroll bar to see Frame 75. Now add the frame action using the Actions panel.

5. Click the **Actions** panel title bar to expand it. If necessary, click the **Actions category** in the Actions toolbox to list the action categories. Also, if necessary, click the **Movie Control** category to list its available actions.

6. Double-click the **goto** action to add it to the Script pane.

Note that the script in the script pane currently reads `gotoAndPlay(1);`. This means that the action causes the animation to go back to Frame 1. You want to change the action so that the animation goes back to Frame 25 instead of Frame 1 because this is where the text block motion tween ends. But rather than referring to a frame number in the script, you want to refer to the frame label you added to Frame 25.

7. In the Actions panel, click the **Type** list arrow to display a list of available types, and then click **Frame Label** from the drop-down list.

8. Click the **Frame** list arrow to display the available labels, and then click **Loop Start** to insert it into the script. The script in the script pane now reads `gotoAndPlay("Loop Start");`. See Figure 4-27. The frame action you just added is indicated by a small **a** in Frame 75 of the Actions layer in the Timeline.

Figure 4-27	FRAME ACTION

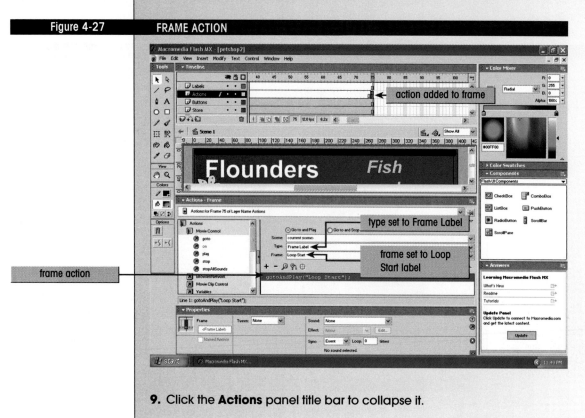

9. Click the **Actions** panel title bar to collapse it.

Now that you have added the frame action, you need to test it to make sure the animation plays properly. You can do this within the Flash program window by turning on the Enable Simple Frame Actions command on the Control menu. With this command on, any frame actions in the document are executed. With the command off, the frame actions are ignored.

To test the frame actions:

1. Click **Control** on the menu bar, and then click **Enable Simple Frame Actions** to select this command. Now play the animation.

2. Click **Control** on the menu bar, and then click **Play**. The animation plays and when the playhead reaches Frame 75, it goes back and starts again at the frame labeled Loop Start, which is Frame 25.

3. Click **Control** on the menu bar, and then click **Stop** to stop the animation.

4. Save the changes you made to the petshop2.fla document. You may either close the file and exit Flash, or leave both the file and the program open for the next session.

In this session you learned how to add actions to button instances and to frames. You learned that actions are part of Macromedia Flash's ActionScript language and that you can add these actions using the Actions panel. You added actions to the banner to control the animation, and you tested the actions. In the next session, you will add sound to the banner.

Session 4.2 QUICK CHECK

1. What is ActionScript?

2. In order to use ActionScript you need to know JavaScript. True or False?

3. What are actions?

4. Which panel is used to add actions?

5. Actions are added to a button symbol and not to an instance of the symbol. True or False?

6. What is an example of an event that triggers an action on a button to execute?

7. Why is it better to refer to a frame label in a script instead of a frame number?

8. What is the difference between a frame action and a button action?

SESSION 4.3

In this session you will learn about the different sound file formats, how to adjust the various sounds you add to your document, and how to compress these sounds before publishing the document. You will add sound effects to the buttons you created in the previous sessions, and you will add a background sound to the Flounders Pet Shop fish supplies banner. You will also add an action to the Mute button to allow the user to stop the background sound.

Sound

Macromedia Flash offers several ways to use sounds. For example, you can add sounds to your document that play continuously and that are independent of the Timeline, such as a background sound. You can add sound effects to instances of buttons to make them more interactive. For example, a sound can be added that plays when a user clicks a button. You can also add sounds that are synchronized with the animation such as a sound simulating a clap of thunder that coincides with an animation of a lightning bolt. Sounds can even be added in the form of a voice narration to supplement the information being displayed on the Web page as text or graphics.

Types of Sounds

There are basically two types of sounds in Flash. These are event and stream sounds. **Event sounds**, which are the default type, will not play until the entire sound has downloaded completely. You add event sounds to keyframes so that the sound plays each time the keyframe is played. Event sounds are not synchronized with the Timeline which means that once an event sound is started it continues to play regardless of the Timeline until all of the sound is played or until the user takes an action to explicitly stop it. If you have a long event sound, it may continue to play even after all of the frames in the Timeline have finished playing.

Stream sounds are synchronized with the Timeline and begin playing as soon as enough data has downloaded. Stream sounds are useful when you need the animation in your movie to coincide with the sound. For example, if you have a voice narration with your animation, and you want the narration to match the text or graphics throughout the document, then you need to make the voice narration a stream sound.

Finding Sounds for Your Documents

Adding sound to an animation can have a very powerful effect, bringing another level of excitement to a well-designed movie. The sound you use can be subtle or loud. You can create sounds with a separate sound-editing program and then import the sounds, or you can acquire prerecorded sounds from other sources. There are many different vendors of prerecorded sound files. Most vendors offer a wide variety of sound effects and music that may be purchased on CD-ROM. Sounds are also available for purchase on the Web. You can even download sounds for free from some Web sites such as Flash Kit's Web site at *www.flashkit.com*. Flash Kit provides a wealth of resources for Macromedia Flash developers. At their site, shown in Figure 4-28, you can find sounds under Sound FX and under Sound Loops.

Figure 4-28   FLASH KIT'S WEB SITE

Sound Loops

Sound effects

You can search for sounds using keywords or browse for sounds by category. Sounds listed at their site can also be previewed before being downloaded. If you download a sound file you may need to decompress the file, using a utility such as WinZip, before using the sounds in your document.

Other Web sites offer sounds for purchase. These Web sites have preproduced sounds from which you can select; they will even create customized sounds for a fee. Two examples of such sites are **Killersound** at *www.killersound.com* and **SoundShopper.com** at *www.soundshopper.com*. These sites also have a few sounds you can download for free to use in your personal projects.

However you acquire sounds, it is important to carefully examine the license agreement that determines how you can use the sounds. Even though a sound file may be downloaded for free there may be restrictions on how you may use it, especially if you plan to distribute the sound with your movie. It is best to look for sounds that are royalty free. **Royalty free** means that there are no additional usage fees when you distribute them with your projects. An alternative to downloading free sounds or purchasing sounds is to record your own. This may not always be possible, but if you record a sound file yourself then you do not have to worry about licensing issues.

Another source of sounds is the Sounds library found in the Common Libraries that install with Flash. Even though the library contains only 36 sounds, it provides a quick way to get a sound to use with your document. Most of these sounds are short and can be used as sound effects for buttons.

Sounds to be used with your documents must first be imported into Flash. The sounds that Flash accepts for import must be in a file format that is compatible with Flash. The file formats that it can import include Windows Waveform (WAV), Audio Interchange File Format (AIFF) used with Macintosh computers, and MP3 which plays on both Windows and Macintosh operating systems. The first two formats are not compressed and tend to be larger in size than MP3 files, which are compressed. Compressed files are smaller because the parts of the sound data that you are not likely to notice have been removed. Compressing a sound file basically means that its size has been reduced without sacrificing too much of the sound quality. The size of sound files is an issue you need to be aware of because adding sounds to your Flash documents can significantly increase the overall size of the published files and will, therefore, affect their download time. You can import a WAV file into your document and then compress it to MP3 format within the program. The MP3 is an ideal format for your Flash movies because it produces very small sound files, retains very good sound quality, and is compatible with both Windows and Macintosh computers.

Adding Sounds to Your Documents

Because you cannot create sounds in Flash, the sound files you use in your documents must first be imported. When you import a sound file it is placed in the document's library along with any symbols and buttons you may already have. You can identify the sound in the library by the sound's icon and also by the waveform that is displayed in the Library panel's preview window as shown in Figure 4-29. A waveform is a graphical representation of a sound.

Figure 4-29	SAMPLE SOUND IN LIBRARY PANEL

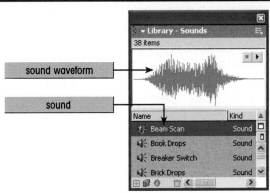

Once you have a sound file in your document's library you can use it as many times as you need in your document. Only one copy of the sound is stored. Before you add a sound to your document it is best to create a separate layer for each sound. This makes it easier to identify the sound in the Timeline. Also, sounds can only be added to keyframes. These can be keyframes in the main Timeline or keyframes in a button's Timeline. To add a sound, first select the keyframe in the Timeline where you want to place the sound, and then drag the sound from the Library panel to the Stage. You can also select the sound from the Sound list box in the Property inspector. The Sound list in the Property inspector lists all the sounds currently in the document's library. Once you add a sound to a keyframe, it will play when the playhead reaches the keyframe.

REFERENCE WINDOW   **RW**

Adding a Sound to a Button:
- Copy the sound from the Sounds Library or import the sound from an external source to the document's library.
- Open the button in symbol-editing mode.
- Create a new layer in the button's Timeline.
- Create a keyframe in the frame where the sound will be placed.
- Select the keyframe.
- Select the sound from the Sound list box in the Property inspector or drag it from the Library panel to the Stage.

Based on the planning discussion for this banner, Aly wants you to add sound effects to the stop and play buttons for the banner. She suggests you use a sound from the Sounds Library.

To add a sound effect to the Stop button:

1. If necessary, start Macromedia Flash and open the **petshop2.fla** document located in the Tutorial.04\Tutorial folder on your Data Disk.

2. Set the panels to their default layout and change the magnification level to show all of the Stage.

3. Click **Window** on the menu bar, and then click **Library** to open the document's Library panel.

4. Click **Window** on the menu bar, point to **Common Libraries**, and then click **Sounds**. The Sounds Library panel opens below the document's Library panel. If necessary, click the document's **Library panel title bar** to expand it.

   You want both the document's library and the Sounds library to be opened at the same time. You can then drag a sound file from the Sounds library to your document's library. Alternately, you can drag a sound from the Sounds library directly to the Stage. Doing so will add the sound to the current keyframe of the current layer and also add it to the document's library.

5. Scroll down the list of sounds in the Sound Library panel to locate the Plastic Button sound. Drag the **Plastic Button** sound from the Sounds library to your document's Library panel. A copy of the Plastic Button sound is now included in your document's library as shown in Figure 4-30. You no longer need to use the Sounds Library panel, so you can close that panel.

Figure 4-30   **PLASTIC BUTTON SOUND IN DOCUMENT'S LIBRARY**

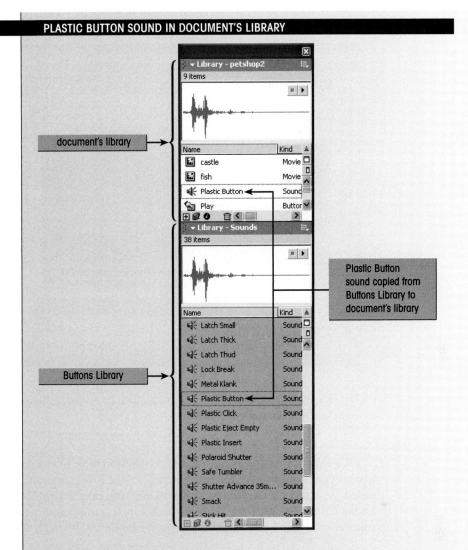

document's library

Buttons Library

Plastic Button
sound copied from
Buttons Library to
document's library

6. Click the **Sound library's options menu** control in the panel's title bar, and then click **Close Panel**. If necessary, move the document's Library panel off and to the right of the Stage. Now open the Stop button in symbol-editing mode.

7. Double-click the **Stop** button's icon in the Library panel to open the button in symbol-editing mode.

8. Insert a new layer in the Stop button's Timeline, and name this layer **Sound**. Now you need to insert a keyframe where the sound will be added.

9. Click the **Down** frame in the Sound layer to select it, and then insert a keyframe.

10. In the Property inspector, click the **Sound** list arrow to display the available sounds, and then click **Plastic Button**. This sound is added to the Down frame as evidenced by the small waveform shown in Figure 4-31.

Figure 4-31	SOUND WAVEFORM IN FRAME

11. Click the **Scene 1** link in the Address bar to return to the document and exit symbol-editing mode.

Now that you have added the sound to the Stop button, you should test it to make sure it works correctly. You can test the sound within the Flash program window the same way you tested the buttons earlier in this tutorial. You turn on the Enable Simple Buttons command on the Control menu and then click the button on the Stage. The button should exhibit its rollover effects and should also play the Plastic Button sound when clicked.

To test the sound effect you added to the Stop button:

1. If necessary, click **Control** on the menu bar, and then click **Enable Simple Buttons** to select this command. Now test the Stop button.

2. Click the **Stop** button on the Stage to hear the Plastic Button sound.

   TROUBLE? If you do not hear a sound when you click the Stop button, make sure your computer's speakers are turned on, and the volume control is turned up.

Now you can add the same sound effect to the Play button. Because you are using the same sound effect, the Plastic Button sound, you do not need to access it from the Common Sounds library. This sound file is already part of your document's library. All you need to do is to add the sound to the Play button the same way you added it to the Stop button. You start by opening the Play button in symbol-editing mode.

To add a sound effect to the Play button and then test it:

1. Double-click the **Play** button's icon 🖼 in the Library panel. First add a new layer for the sound.

2. In the Play button's Timeline insert a new layer and name it **Sound**. Insert a keyframe where the sound will be added.

3. Click the **Down** frame of the Sound layer and insert a keyframe.

4. In the Property inspector, click the **Sound** list arrow, and then click **Plastic Button**. Now, exit symbol-editing mode to return to the document.

5. Click the **Scene1** link in the Address bar to return to the document. You should now test the button.

6. Click the **Play** button on the Stage to hear the sound. Click the **Stop** button to stop the animation.

7. Click **Control** on the menu bar, and click **Enable Simple Buttons** to deselect this command and turn this feature off.

You have added a sound effect to the Stop and Play buttons using a sound from the Sounds Library. In addition to adding sounds to your document you can also apply different settings to the sound files within Flash.

Sound Settings

Once you have added a sound to your document, you can control the way it plays by using the sound settings found in the Property inspector. The settings, shown in Figure 4-32, include **Effects**, **Sync**, and **Loop**.

Figure 4-32   SOUND SETTINGS

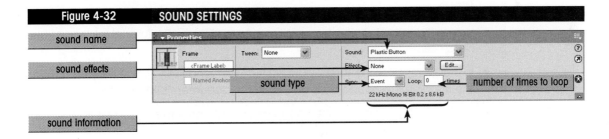

The **Effects** list box offers the settings described in Figure 4-32.

Figure 4-33   SOUND EFFECTS

Left Channel/Right Channel	Specifies that the sound play in only one channel, either the left or the right; if set to left channel, the sound plays in the left speaker; if set to right channel, the sound plays in the right speaker
Fade Left to Right/Fade Right to Left	Specifies that the sound start on one channel (speaker) and then gradually shift to the other channel
Fade In	Specifies that the sound gradually increase in volume over its duration
Fade Out	Specifies that the sound gradually decrease in volume over its duration
Custom	Lets you customize the sound effects by changing the starting point and volume

The **Sync** list box lets you set a sound as an **Event** sound or as a **Stream** sound, the two main types of sounds used in Flash. In addition to this, you can also control event sounds by using the **Start** and **Stop** sync settings. By default, sounds are set to Event. Once an event sound starts it continues to play until it is stopped by the user or until it finishes. As a result, it is possible to have several instances of the same sound playing at the same time. Recall that event sounds play independently of the Timeline. An event sound will start playing when the playhead reaches the sound's keyframe. The sound will play completely until it is finished. If some button or frame action causes the playhead to play the sound's keyframe again before the sound has finished playing, another instance of the sound starts playing at the same time. This means one sound instance will overlap the other. To prevent this, you can change the sync setting of the sound to Start instead of Event. With the Start sync setting, the first instance of the sound will be stopped before a new instance starts, to prevent overlap. Finally, the Stop sync setting stops a sound that is playing. For example, you may have a sound that starts playing in Frame 1 but you want it to stop playing in Frame 10. You can add the same sound to Frame 10 but use a Sync setting of Stop. When the playhead reaches Frame 10, the sound stops playing.

Another sound setting available in the Property inspector is **Loop**. If you want a sound to play continuously for a period of time, then enter a number in the Loop text box that specifies how many times you want the sound to play. For example, if a sound is 10 seconds long and you enter 12 for the number of times to loop, then the sound will play 12 times for a total of 120 seconds or two minutes. It is not a good idea to loop sounds with the Stream sync setting. Recall that a stream sound is synchronized with the Timeline. If you loop the sound and it extends beyond the length of the movie's Timeline, Flash adds frames to the Timeline, thus increasing the size of the movie.

In reviewing the tasks assigned for completing this banner, you see that a sound needs to be added that plays in the background. Aly has acquired a bubbling sound that she wants you to use for this task. This sound file is in the WAV format. You will import it into your document's library and add it as a background sound.

To add a background sound to the banner and then test it:

1. Click **File** on the menu bar, and then click **Import** to open the Import dialog box. In the Import dialog box, navigate to the Tutorial.04\Tutorial folder on your Data Disk.

2. In the file list, click the **Bubbles.wav** sound file, and then click the **Open** button. The Bubbles.wav sound file is added to the document's library.

3. Insert a new layer above the Labels layer, and name this new layer **Sound**. You will add the bubbles sound to the new layer.

4. Click **Frame 1** of the Sound layer. In the Property inspector, click the **Sound** list arrow to view the available sounds, and then click **Bubbles** (or Bubbles.wav). The Bubbles sound is added to the Sound layer as shown in Figure 4-34.

Figure 4-34 | **BUBBLES SOUND WAVEFORM IN LAYER**

waveform

5. In the Property inspector make sure **Event** appears in the Sync text box. Event is the default setting and is used when you do not need the sound synchronized with the Timeline. Enter **10** in the Loop text box to set how many times the sound should repeat.

   As indicated by the information below the Sync list box, the Bubbles sound is 14 seconds long. If you leave the loop setting at 0, the sound ends if the user views the animation for more then 14 seconds. By changing the Loop setting to 10, you are assured that the sound continues playing for a longer period of time. To test the sound you need to play the movie in a Flash Player window or in a Web page. The sound does not play within the Flash program window because it is not synchronized with the Timeline. Test the sound in a Flash Player window.

6. Click **Control** on the menu bar, and then click **Test Movie**. The movie opens in a Flash Player window. If your computer's speakers are on, you will hear the bubbling background sound. Close the Flash Player window to return to your document.

You can modify the way a sound plays by changing the settings in the Effect list box. For example, you can change the sound so that it plays only in the left channel or only on the right channel. The Left Channel setting causes the sound to play only in the left speaker. The Right Channel setting causes the sound to play only in the right speaker. You can also use the Fade Left to Right or Fade Right to Left settings. With Fade Left to Right the sound starts in the left speaker and gradually moves to the right speaker. Fade Right to Left starts the sound in the right speaker and gradually moves to the left speaker. Other effects include Fade In and Fade Out. Fade In will gradually increase the sound while Fade Out gradually decreases the sound. Finally, the Custom setting allows you to create your own sound effects by adjusting the starting point of a sound and by controlling its volume.

Aly suggests you explore the various Effect settings to see how they impact the background sound for the banner.

To explore the Effect settings with the background sound:

1. Click **Frame 1** of the Sound layer to select it. Now change the sound Effect setting.

2. Click the **Effect** list arrow to display the list of effects. Click the **Fade Left to Right** effect. Now test the sound.

3. Click **Control** on the menu bar, and then click **Test Movie** to play the movie and hear the background sound. Close the Flash Player window to return to your document.

4. Select different Effect settings and use the Test Movie command each time to hear how the sound is played.

   Aly listens along with you as the background sound plays with different Effect settings applied. She decides that the Fade In effect fits well with the overall design and purpose of the banner and instructs you to apply that setting.

5. Click the **Effect** list arrow to display the list of effects, and then click **Fade In** to select this effect.

Even though the background sound may be nice to listen to, some viewers may not want to hear it. So you want to give the viewer the option to turn off the sound. You have already added a Mute button, but now you need to add an action to the Mute button instance to turn off the sound. To do this you will select the Mute button and then, using the Actions panel, you will add an Action that will stop all sounds. This Action will not affect the sound effects you added to the Stop and Play buttons.

To add an action to mute the background sound and then test the action:

1. Click **Control** on the menu bar, and make sure that the **Enable Simple Buttons** command is not selected. It must be off for you to be able to select the Mute button with the Arrow tool.

2. Click the **Mute button** on the Stage to select it. Be sure to select the button and not the Mute text block.

3. Click the **Actions** panel's title bar to expand the panel. Now display the basic movie control actions.

4. If necessary, click the **Actions** category in the Actions toolbox, and then click the **Movie Control** category to display the available actions. Select an action to stop the background sound.

5. Double-click the **stopAllSounds** action. The script is added to the button instance and is displayed in the Script pane as shown in Figure 4-35.

Figure 4-35 | **SCRIPT TO STOP ALL SOUNDS**

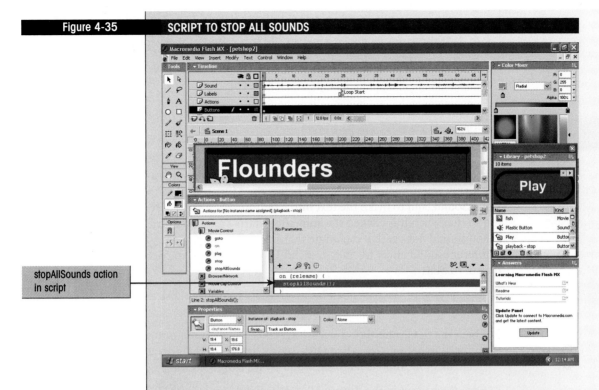

stopAllSounds action in script

6. Click the **Actions** Panel title bar to collapse the panel. Now test the Mute button. Recall that the background sound will not play within the Flash program window. So to test the Mute button, you need to play the movie in a Flash Player window or in a Web page.

7. Click **Control** on the menu bar, and click **Test Movie**. As the animation and the background sound play, click the **Mute** button. The sound stops, but the animation continues to play.

8. Close the Flash Player window to return to the document, save the changes you have made to the banner, and close the file. Exit Macromedia Flash.

In this session you learned how to acquire sounds and how to add them to your documents. You added sounds to buttons and you added a background sound to your document. You used a sound from the Sounds library and you also imported a sound. You learned about the types of sounds that Macromedia Flash uses and about the different sound file formats that can be imported into a document. You also learned how to change the sound settings using the Property inspector and finally, you saw how to add an action to a button to stop all sounds from playing.

Session 4.3 QUICK CHECK

1. List two Web sites from which you can download sounds to use with your documents.

2. What are the two main types of sounds used in a Macromedia Flash document?

3. What are the three sound file formats that may be imported into Flash?

4. When you import a sound into your document, where is it stored?

  5. Sounds can only be added to keyframes. True or False?

  6. List three simple effects you can add to a sound in your document.

  7. What is the purpose of assigning the Start Sync setting to a sound?

REVIEW ASSIGNMENTS

After reviewing the revised interactive banner, Aly asks you to make some changes to it. She wants you to remove the button below the Mute text block, to modify the text to read Mute Sound, and to make the text into a button. She also asks you to change the Play button so that when it is clicked the animation starts again from Frame 1. The background sound should not overlap each time that Frame 1 is played. Finally, she wants you to select a different sound effect for the Stop and Play buttons and to change the text on the Play button to Start.

If necessary, start Macromedia Flash and insert your Data Disk in the appropriate disk drive, and then do the following:

1. Open the **petshop2.fla** banner which you created in the tutorial from the Tutorial.04\ Tutorial folder on your Data Disk, set the panels to their default layout, and set the Stage magnification level to show the entire banner in the Stage window.

2. Save the banner in the Tutorial.04\Review folder on your Data Disk. Name the file **petshop3.fla**.

Explore 3. Select the Mute button instance on the Stage and delete it. Also, delete the playback - stop button from the library. You will not use it in this document.

4. Select the Mute text block and change the text to **Mute Sound,** where the word "Sound" is on a second line. Move the text block down to where the deleted button used to be.

5. Convert the text block to a symbol. Name the symbol **Mute**, and select **Button** as the behavior type.

6. Open the new Mute button in symbol-editing mode. Modify the button so that the text changes to a yellow color when the pointer is over the button.

Explore 7. Add a rectangle to the Hit frame so that it covers the text block. This way the user can click any part of the rectangle to activate the button. The rectangle can be any color because it will not be visible. Exit symbol-editing mode.

8. Use the Actions panel to add a stopAllSounds Action to the Mute Sound button instance.

9. Create a frame label in Frame 1 of the Labels layer. Name this label **Start**.

Explore 10. Select the Play button and open the Actions panel. Delete the play Action in the Script pane and add the goto Action. Select the `gotoAndPlay(1)` script and change its parameters so that instead of referring to a frame number it refers to a frame label. Select Start as the frame label it should refer to. (*Hint*: The Action should read `gotoAndPlay("Start")`.)

11. To prevent the background sound from playing more than once at the same time, change its Sync setting to Start.

12. Open the Sounds library and copy the Breaker Switch sound to the banner's library. Edit the Stop and Play buttons to change the sound in each button from Plastic Switch to Breaker Switch.

13. Edit the Play button to change its text block to read **Start** instead of **Play**. Be sure to change the text in each of its frames.

14. Test the banner to make sure each of the buttons works properly.

15. Save the changes you have made to the petshop3 banner, and close the file.

16. Close the browser window and close Macromedia Flash.

CASE PROBLEMS

Case 1. Making the Banner for Sandy's Party Center Interactive Sandy Rodriquez, owner of Sandy's Party Center is exited about the banner developed for the store's Web site. She asks John Rossini, who developed the banner, to make the banner interactive to generate more interest from visitors to the Web site. Sandy also asks John if sounds can be added to the banner. John agrees to make the banner interactive and to add sounds to it.

John asks you to make the revisions to the animated banner you previously completed. He instructs you to add two buttons from the Buttons library: a Stop button and a Play button. The buttons should be similar in design. You are also to add a short sound effect that plays when the buttons are clicked. Also, add the appropriate actions to the buttons so that they will control the animation. John has provided a sound file that you are to add to the banner as a background sound. Finally, you will add a frame action so that the Grand Opening text block only animates one time.

If necessary, start Macromedia Flash, insert your Data Disk in the appropriate drive, and then do the following:

1. Open the **partybanner2.fla** file that you completed in Case 1 of Tutorial 3. You should have saved it in the Tutorial.03\Cases folder on your Data Disk. If you did not complete Case 1 of Tutorial 3, then see your instructor for assistance. Save the document as **partybanner3.fla** in the Tutorial.04\Cases folder on your Data Disk.

2. Add a new layer and name it **Buttons**.

3. Open the Buttons library, open the Playback folder and scroll down to the gel Stop button. Make sure the Buttons layer is selected and drag the gel Stop button to the lower-left corner of the banner. Also drag the gel Right button so that it is next to the first button.

4. Add a text block below each button instance on the banner. The text for the gel Stop button should read **Stop** and the text for the gel Right button should read **Play**. Use a small font size for the text and make the text black.

5. Edit the gel Stop button. Insert a new layer and name it **Sound**. Insert the Latch Metal Jingle sound from the Sounds library into the Down frame of the Sound layer. Repeat these steps to add the same sound to the Down frame of the gel Right button.

6. Use the Actions panel to add the Stop action to the gel Stop button instance. Add the Play action to the gel Right button.

7. Insert a new layer and name it **Background Sound**. Import the Party sound file from the Tutorial.04\Cases folder on your Data Disk. Add this sound to start at Frame 1 of the Background Sound layer. Make its Sync setting Start, and enter 10 for the number of times to Loop.

8. Insert a new layer and name it **Labels.** Create a label on Frame 10. Enter **Loop** as the label. Frame 10 should be the same frame where the animated text in the Text layer finishes its motion tween.

9. Insert a new layer and name it **Actions.** Add a gotoAndPlay Action on the last frame of the Actions layer. Use the frame label Loop as the destination of the action.

10. Test the changes to the banner. Make sure the buttons work properly and that the sounds play. Also make sure that the balloons and confetti continue to move after the Grand Opening text stops.

11. Save and close the revised banner and exit Flash.

Case 2. Adding Interaction and Sound to the River City Music Banner Janet Meyers, store manager for River City Music, is very pleased with the animated banner developed for their Web site. She meets with Alex Smith who developed the banner and asks if some additional enhancements can be added to the banner. In particular, she thinks musical sounds will make the banner more interesting. Alex agrees to add sound to the banner and suggests adding some interactivity as well.

Alex asks you to help him revise the banner by adding an action that repeats the movement of the musical notes without repeating the text animations. He instructs you to add a button that can be clicked to start the animation from the beginning. The button should resemble a musical note. You also will add a background sound to the banner and a sound effect to the button.

If necessary, start Macromedia Flash, insert your Data Disk in the appropriate drive, and then do the following:

1. Open the **musicbanner2.fla** file that you completed in Case 2 of Tutorial 3. You should have saved it in the Tutorial.03\Cases folder on your Data Disk. If you did not complete Case 2 of Tutorial 3, then see your instructor for assistance. Save the document as **musicbanner3.fla** in the Tutorial.04\Cases folder on your Data Disk.

2. Add a new layer to the Timeline and name it **Labels.** Insert a label in Frame 1 of the Labels layer. Enter **Start** for the label name. Also insert a label in Frame 15. This is where the motion tweens for the text finish. Enter **Loop** for the label name. These labels will be used when you add actions.

3. Insert another layer and name it **Actions.** Add a gotoAndPlay action to the last frame, Frame 20, of the Actions layer. The action should make the playhead go to the Loop frame to repeat the last group of frames that keep the animated musical notes moving.

4. Now add another layer and name it **Music.** Import the Piano loop sound from the Tutorial.04\Cases folder on your Data Disk. Add the Piano loop sound to the first frame of the music layer. Change its Sync setting to Start and have it loop two times.

5. To create a new button, copy the note1 symbol in the library. Name the copy **note button** and make sure its behavior is set to Button. Open the note button in symbol-editing mode.

6. Add a keyframe in the Over frame and change the size of the note graphic so that it is slightly larger. Use the Transform panel and enter a value of 110% for both the height and the width.

7. Add a keyframe in the Down frame and use the arrow keys on the keyboard to move the note graphic three pixels down and three pixels to the right.

8. Add one more keyframe in the Hit frame. Draw a rectangle that covers the note graphic. This will be the clickable area of the button.

9. Insert a new layer into the button's Timeline. Name this layer **Sound**. Import the Piano1 sound from the Cases folder just like you did the Piano loop sound. Add the Piano1 sound to the Down frame of the Sound layer. Exit symbol-editing mode.

10. Add an instance of the note button symbol to the banner. Place the instance in the lower-left corner of the banner. Select the button instance and open the Actions panel. Add the gotoAndPlay Action. Change the Action so that it refers to the Start frame. Now when the button is clicked, the playhead goes to the Start frame and repeats all of the animation.

11. Add a text block over the note button with the text **Start Over**. Use a small font and black text.

12. Test your animation to make sure the background music plays and that the button works.

13. Save and close the revised banner and exit Flash.

Case 3. Enhancing the Logo for Sonny's Auto Center Amanda Lester meets with Sonny Jackson and several of his employees to show them the animated logo for their Web site. The feedback is excellent. Sonny and his employees have several suggestions including adding sound and some interactive components. Amanda takes their suggestions and starts revising the logo.

Amanda asks you to help her complete the revisions by adding a background sound to the logo, adding a stop button and a go button, each with a sound effect. You also will add a frame action to control how the animation plays. The wheels should continue to rotate after the Sonny text shape animation has finished. The stop button will stop the wheel animations, and the go button will start the wheel animations.

If necessary, start Macromedia Flash, insert your Data Disk in the appropriate drive, and then do the following:

1. Open the **sonnylogo.fla** file located in the Tutorial.04\Cases folder on your Data Disk. Save this file as **sonnylogo2.fla** in the same folder.

2. Insert three layers. Name one layer **Actions**, another **StopLabel**, and the third **LoopLabel**.

3. Add a label in Frame 19 of the StopLabel layer. Enter **Stop** for the label. Add a label in Frame 20 of the LoopLabel layer. Enter **Loop** for the label.

4. Add an Action in the last frame of the Actions layer that makes the playhead go to the frame with the Loop label.

5. Import the auto loop sound from the Tutorial.04\Cases folder on your Data Disk. Add this sound to a new layer, and set it to play several times without overlapping itself.

6. Create a new button and name it **Stop**. This button should be in the shape of a circle, about 20 pixels in diameter with a red fill and black stroke. This button represents a red stop light. Add the carhorn sound located in the Tutorial.04\Cases folder on your Data Disk to the button's Down frame.

7. Duplicate the Stop button. Name the duplicate **Go**, and change its fill to green.

8. Insert a new layer and name it **Buttons**.

9. With the Buttons layer selected, add an instance of the Stop button to the logo. Place it to the right of the "S" in AUTOS on the right side of the logo. Also, add an instance of the Go button and place it right below the instance of the Stop button.

10. Add an action to the Stop button instance. The action should cause the playhead to go to the frame with the Stop label and the animation should stop at that point.

11. Add an action to the Go button instance. The action should cause the playhead to go to the frame with the Loop label and continue to play the animation.

12. Test the logo animation making sure the sounds play and that the buttons work properly.

13. Save and close the changes you have made to the logo, then exit Flash.

Explore

Case 4. Adding Sounds and Buttons to the Banner for LAL Financial Christopher Perez is very pleased with the animations added to the banner for LAL Financial Services. He asks webmaster Elizabeth Danehill to add some interaction with appropriate sounds to enhance the impact that the banner can have when viewers visit their Web site.

Elizabeth asks you to modify the banner so that the animation stops when it reaches the last frame. She also instructs you to add a button that will repeat the animation. The button should resemble the circles that are part of the banner's design. She asks you to search the Web to find a background sound for the banner and a sound effect to be added to the button.

If necessary, start Macromedia Flash, insert your Data Disk in the appropriate drive, and then do the following:

1. Open the **lfsbanner2** file that you completed in Case 4 of Tutorial 3. You should have saved it in the Tutorial.03\Cases folder under the folder on your Data Disk. If you did not complete Case 4 of Tutorial 3, then see your instructor for assistance. Save the document as **lfsbanner3** in the Tutorial.04\Cases folder on your Data Disk.

2. Go to the Flash Kit Web site at *www.flashkit.com* or another site of your choice that has sound files you can download. Find two sound files appropriate for your banner. One sound should be short and will be used as a sound effect on a button. The other should be a sound loop that will be used as a background sound. Download the sounds to your Cases folder.

3. Extend the length of the banner by adding regular frames at Frame 45 of each layer in the Timeline.

4. Add a new layer and name it **Sound**. Add another layer and name it **Actions**.

5. Add a Stop action to Frame 45 of the Actions layer. This action should stop the animation and keep it from repeating.

6. Add the sound loop you downloaded to Frame 1 of the Sound layer.

7. Create a new button symbol and name it **Repeat**. Use the circle symbol's shape as the normal state for this button. (*Hint*: Double-click one of the circle symbol instances on the Stage so that you can make a copy of its shape. Then paste the shape into the Up frame of the button.)

8. Change the circle shape in the Over frame so that it has a green gradient fill. Change the shape in the Down frame so that it is offset by a few pixels. Also add the sound effect you downloaded to the Down frame.

9. Add a new layer and name it **Buttons**. Add a Repeat button instance to Frame 45 of this layer. Place the button instance so that it covers the circle symbol in the upper-right corner of the banner. When the animation stops at Frame 45 the button instance should completely cover the circle symbol. It will look the same as the circle symbol until the mouse pointer is moved over it. Then the rollover effect changes the way it looks.

10. Add an action to the button instance. The action should cause the playhead to go to Frame 1 and play the animation again.

11. Test the banner animation making sure the sounds play and that the buttons work properly.

12. Save the changes you have made to the banner and exit Flash.

QUICK | CHECK ANSWERS

Session 4.1

1. A button is a special symbol that contains its own four-frame Timeline.

2. Buttons provide an interactive element to a Macromedia Flash document. They allow the user to control how he or she watches the published movie.

3. Open the Buttons library from the Common Libraries menu in the Windows menu. Then drag a button from the Buttons library to the Stage. The button is automatically added to the document's library. Or drag a button from the Buttons library to the document's library.

4. A button contains four frames in its Timeline. They are the Up, Over, Down, and Hit frames.

5. You can create a rollover effect by making the Over frame's content different from the Up frame's content. When the pointer is over the button, the content in the Over frame is displayed in place of the content in the Up frame.

6. You can turn on the Enable Simple Buttons option found on the Control menu. This allows you to test a button while still in Flash without publishing the movie.

7. You can use the Align panel to easily align several objects on the Stage.

Session 4.2

1. ActionScript is Flash's scripting language and is used to create scripts to control how a movie plays.

2. False, you do not need to know JavaScript or any other scripting language in order to use ActionScript.

3. Actions are precoded instructions that are used to control how a movie plays.

4. Use the Actions panel to add actions.

5. Actions are added to a button instance and not to the symbol.

6. An example of an event that triggers an action on a button to execute is when the user clicks and releases a button.

7. It is better to refer to a frame label in a script instead of a frame number because if you later add or delete frames, the scripts will not have to be changed.

8. You add a frame action to a keyframe, whereas you add a button action to a button's instance.

Session 4.3

1. Many Web sites have sounds you can download. These include *www.flashkit.com*, *www.killersound.com*, and *www.soundshopper.com*.

2. The two main types of sounds used in a Flash document are event and stream.

3. The three sound file formats that may be imported into Flash are WAV, AIFF, and MP3.

4. When you import a sound into your document it is stored in the document's library.

5. True, sounds can only be added to keyframes.

6. Simple effects you can add to a sound in your document can be found under Effect in the Property inspector and include Left Channel, Right Channel, Fade Left to Right, Fade Right to Left, Fade In, and Fade Out.

7. The Start Sync setting can be applied to a sound to prevent several instances of the sound from playing at the same time.

OBJECTIVES

In this tutorial you will:

- Import bitmap graphics into a document

- Change a bitmap graphic's properties

- Convert a bitmap graphic to a vector graphic

- Create a fade effect animation using bitmaps

- Create a new gradient

- Use and transform a gradient

- Convert text to fills

- Apply a gradient fill to text

- Explore and use the Flash Publish settings

- Insert a Flash movie into an existing Web page

USING
BITMAPS, GRADIENTS, AND PUBLISHING

Creating and Publishing a New Banner and Logo for Flounders Pet Shop

CASE

Actions Web Design

Joe Flounders has been very satisfied with the results of the banners created for his fish and aquarium sale and for his Web site's pet supplies page. He and Aly previously discussed the possibility of creating a more permanent banner for his Web site to use after the sale. He also had mentioned developing a new logo that can be used in a variety of areas on the company's Web site. Aly and Joe discuss what he wants in a new banner and logo. Up to now the Flounders Pet Shop banners have only included graphic objects created within Macromedia Flash. Now Joe would like to see photos of some live animals used as part of the banner and logo designs. Aly tells him that it is possible to use photos and even suggests that the photos can be part of an animation.

Aly presents Joe's requests at the regular Actions Web Design staff meeting and suggests that Flash be used to create the banner and logo with photos of pets. Aly also suggests a sample Web page be developed that you can use to place the new banner and logo. Up to now, Chris has taken the banners and added them to the existing Flounder's Web site. As part of your training, Aly would like for you to get some experience incorporating Flash graphics into a Web page. She asks Chris to develop a sample Web page you can use.

Aly holds a planning meeting, with you and invites Chris to attend. As a result of the meeting, some specific needs are outlined. These include the use of pictures or bitmaps that are representative of Flounders Pet Shop. Chris also suggests using a gradient for the background of the banner. He says he has seen some examples of how gradients have been used to create professional-looking designs. Aly agrees to using gradients and states that she will start developing the new Flounders banner. Then, once she completes an initial banner, she will have you complete the banner and create the logo. In particular, you will be working on adding bitmaps, creating gradients, and preparing the final movies for use in the pet shop Web site.

Aly has given you a sketch of the banner and logo requested by Joe Flounders for his Web site, as shown in Figure 5-1.

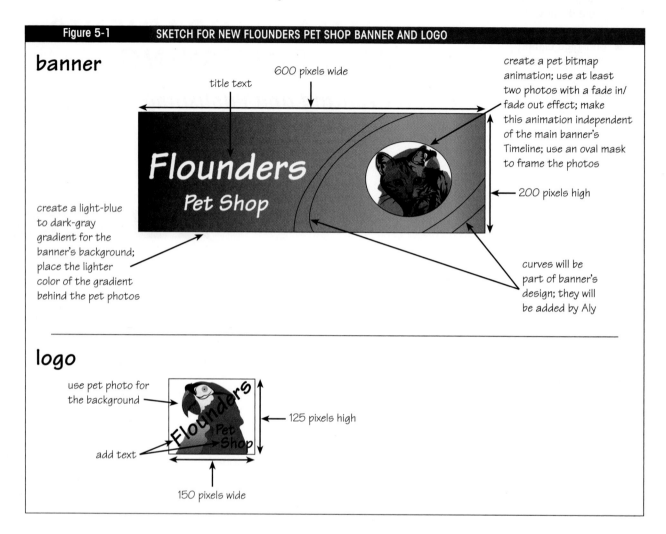

Figure 5-1 — SKETCH FOR NEW FLOUNDERS PET SHOP BANNER AND LOGO

For the banner, she has instructed you to add two photos of pets—one of a cat and one of a parrot. Aly has edited the pictures in a separate image-editing program so that they are both the same size. These pictures will be combined into one animation where each picture is displayed in turn within an oval mask, using a fade in and fade out effect. The pet animation should be independent of any other animation that may be added later to the banner. You are also to create a radial gradient for the banner's background. The gradient will be a blend of a light-blue color that transitions into a dark-gray color. The gradient's light-blue center will be positioned behind the photos of the pets, giving the photos a highlighted effect.

In addition to the banner you are complete, Aly asks you to create the logo Joe has requested. The logo will have the store name over a picture of a pet in the background. You will create a special effect with the picture to make it different from the pictures used on the banner.

In this tutorial you will continue your training in Macromedia Flash by learning how to import bitmap graphics into a Flash document, change the bitmaps' properties, convert a bitmap into a vector graphic, and create animations using bitmaps. You will also learn how to create, modify, and use gradients to add a special effect to the banner. Finally, you will explore the various export and publish options available with Flash, and you will incorporate the banner and logo into an existing Web page.

SESSION 5.1

In this session you will import bitmap graphics into a Flash document. You will change the bitmap properties and then use the bitmaps in an animation. You will also convert a bitmap graphic to a vector graphic and use the resulting graphic to create a logo.

Using Bitmaps

Recall from Tutorial 1 that Flash creates vector graphics that are stored as mathematical instructions. These instructions describe the color, outline, and position of all the shapes in the graphic. Vector graphic files tend to be small and consequently download quickly. They also tend to be mostly geometric in nature, consisting of ovals, rectangles, lines, and curves. In many situations, however, you may want to add more natural looking images such as photographs in your Flash documents. Using a photograph can sometimes greatly enhance the graphics you are creating with Flash. Recall also from Tutorial 1 that a photograph is an example of a bitmap graphic and that a bitmap graphic is stored as a row-by-row list of every pixel in the graphic, along with each pixel's color. Bitmap graphics do not resize well and their file sizes tend to be larger than vector graphics, so using bitmaps in a Flash movie increases the movie's download time. However this should not keep you from using bitmap graphics in your Flash documents; it just means you should make sure that the graphic is really needed in your document's design. You also cannot create or easily edit bitmap graphics within Flash, so you should use another program such as Adobe Photoshop or Macromedia Fireworks to edit and size the bitmaps before bringing them into a Flash document.

Because you cannot create bitmap graphics in Flash, you need to import them into your documents. Once a bitmap has been imported into Flash, you can change its properties, such as its compression settings, use it in animations, and even change it into a vector graphic.

Importing Bitmaps

Importing a bitmap into your Flash document is a fairly straightforward process. You can use the Import command or the Import to Library command, both located on the File menu. Both commands place the bitmap in the document's library. The only difference between these two commands is that the Import command also places an instance of the bitmap on the Stage in addition to placing the bitmap in the document's library. Once the bitmap is in the document's library you can create multiple instances of it on the Stage, yet only one copy of the bitmap is stored with the file. A bitmap in the document's library is not considered a symbol, although the copies you drag onto the Stage are called instances of the bitmap. An instance of a bitmap on the Stage can be converted into a symbol so that it can be used in a motion tween animation. This symbol is then stored in the document's library separately from the original bitmap.

REFERENCE   WINDOW   **RW**

<u>Importing a Bitmap:</u>
- Click File on the menu bar, and then click Import or Import to Library.
- In the Import to Library dialog box, navigate to the location of the bitmap file, and then select the bitmap file in the file list.
- Click the Open button to import the bitmap into the document's library.

Based on the planning sketch shown in Figure 5-1 and Aly's instructions, you are to use two photos of pets in the new Flounders Pet Shop banner. To use these photos you need to import them into the document's library. You will open the partially completed banner that Aly has created and import the parrot and cat photos she has provided.

To import bitmap images into a document:

1. Make sure that your computer is turned on, that the Windows desktop is displayed, and that your Data Disk is in the appropriate drive.

2. Start Flash and open the **floundersnew.fla** file located in the Tutorial.05\Tutorial folder on your Data Disk. Next, save this file with a new name, leaving the original file intact on your Data Disk, in case you want to repeat the steps in this session at another time.

3. Save the **floundersnew.fla** document as **flounders.fla** in the Tutorial.05\Tutorial folder on your Data Disk. Next you want to change the view so that the complete contents of the Stage are visible.

4. If necessary, change the magnification level of the Stage to **100%** and position the panels to their default layout. When you import a bitmap, it is stored in the document's library.

5. Click **Window** on the menu bar, and then click **Library** to open the Library panel.

6. Click **File** on the menu bar, and then click **Import to Library**. In the Import to Library dialog box, click the **Files of type** list arrow, click **All Formats**, and then navigate to the **Tutorial.05\Tutorial** folder on your Data Disk.

7. Click the **cat.jpg** file, press and hold the **CTRL** key on the keyboard, and then click the **parrot.jpg** file. Holding down the CTRL key while you click the filenames allows you to select more than one file at a time.

8. With the two files selected as shown in Figure 5-2, click the **Open** button. The two bitmap files are imported into the document's library and now appear in the Library panel.

Figure 5-2   IMPORT TO LIBRARY DIALOG BOX

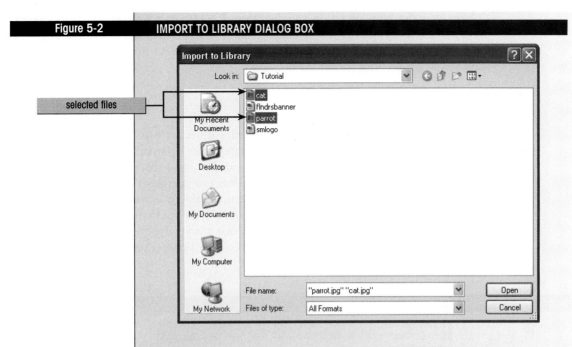

9. Click the **cat** bitmap in the Library panel to display its picture in the preview area. See Figure 5-3.

Figure 5-3   BITMAPS IN THE LIBRARY PANEL

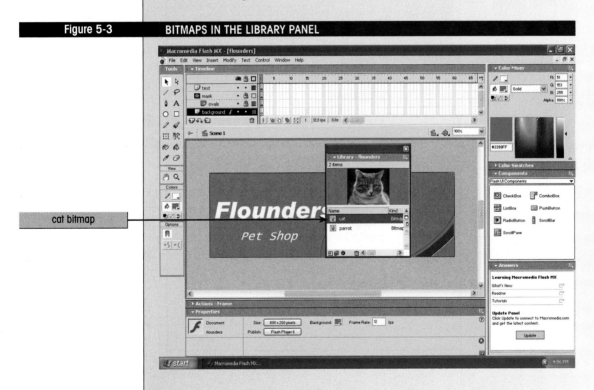

10. Click the **parrot** bitmap in the Library panel to view it in the preview area.

Now that the bitmaps are in the document's library you will change their properties using the Bitmap Properties dialog box. Aly suggests you reduce the JPEG quality to reduce the overall size of the final movie. You can check what effect the new JPEG quality value will have on the pictures within the dialog box.

Setting a Bitmap's Properties

You can modify a bitmap's properties using the Bitmap Properties dialog box. You can change the name of the bitmap, update the bitmap if the original file has been changed, and even change its compression settings. Recall from Tutorial 1 that compression means taking away some of the file's data to reduce its size. You can compress a bitmap while still maintaining its quality. To open the Bitmap Properties dialog box you select the bitmap in the Library panel and then click the Properties icon, or you can double-click the bitmap's icon in the Library panel. The options in the dialog box change depending on the file type of the selected bitmap. Figure 5-4 shows two versions of the Bitmap Properties dialog box, one for a JPEG bitmap and one for a PNG bitmap.

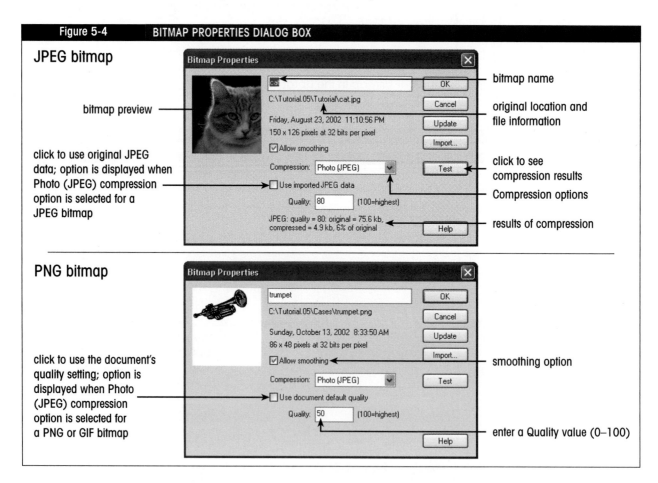

Figure 5-4   BITMAP PROPERTIES DIALOG BOX

The Bitmap Properties dialog box options are described in Figure 5-5.

Figure 5-5	BITMAP PROPERTIES OPTIONS
OPTION	**DESCRIPTION**
Allow Smoothing check box	Smooth the edges of the bitmap so they do not appear jagged
Compression list box	Photo (JPEG): compress the image in JPEG format Lossless (PNG/GIF): compress the image with no data loss
Use imported JPEG data check box	Use the compression quality value specified with the original imported bitmap; check box is displayed for JPEG bitmaps when the Photo (JPEG) compression option is selected
Use document default quality check box	Use the compression quality value specified in the Publish Settings dialog box for the document; check box is displayed for PNG or GIF bitmaps when the Photo (JPEG) compression option is selected
Quality text box	Specify a quality value for compression; higher values (0-100) preserve more of the image and result in larger files; text box is displayed when the Use imported JPEG data check box or the Use document default quality check box is not checked
Location information	Indicates where the original bitmap is stored
Update button	If a bitmap has been modified with an external editor such as Macromedia Fireworks, update the bitmap in Flash without importing it again
Import button	Import a different bitmap to replace the current one; the newly imported bitmap keeps the same name as the one being replaced
Test button	Apply the compression settings; use the preview window to see the resulting image
Compression results	Displays the compressed file size compared to the original file size

In the Bitmap Properties dialog box the name of the bitmap is given, as well as information such as when the file was created or last modified, and its size and current compression rate. You can change the compression settings by choosing either Lossless (PNG/GIF) or Photo (JPEG) from the Compression list box. You can use Lossless (PNG/GIF) compression for bitmaps that are in the PNG or GIF file format or for bitmaps with large blocks of single colors. Use Photo (JPEG) compression for bitmaps with many colors or many color transitions such as photographs.

Imported bitmaps that have a JPEG file format, indicated by a .jpg extension, have the Photo (JPEG) compression option selected in the Bitmap Properties dialog box. The **Use imported JPEG data** check box will also be checked which means the quality JPEG settings of the original bitmap will be used within Flash. When you import bitmaps of other file formats, such as PNG (.png) or GIF (.gif), they will have the Lossless (PNG/GIF) compression option selected in the Bitmap Properties dialog box and the Use imported JPEG data check box will not appear. However, you can change the compression option for a PNG or GIF to Photo (JPEG). Doing so are displaed the **Use document default quality** check box. When this check box is selected, the bitmaps are displayed using the quality value specified for the whole document. This value is set in the Publish Settings dialog box, which is discussed later in this tutorial.

If the Use imported JPEG data check box or the Use document default quality check box is deselected, then the Quality text box is automatically displayed with a default value of 50. You can change this setting using a range of values from 0 to 100, where 0 yields the lowest result and 100 yields the highest. The Quality setting determines how much compression to apply to the bitmap. The more compression that is applied, the more data that is lost. Smaller values apply more compression while larger values apply less compression. You can experiment with this setting by changing the value and then clicking the Test button. When you click the Test button the bitmap's preview changes to reflect the new compression settings. Keep in mind that a bitmap in the JPEG file format has already been compressed and compressing it further degrades the picture. So you need to balance compression with the quality of the picture. You can use the preview of the bitmap in the Bitmap Properties dialog box to see the impact of the selected quality setting on the bitmap. If you move the pointer over the preview area, it turns into a hand pointer ☝ which you can drag to adjust the view of the bitmap. You can also right-click the preview to zoom in to see more detail of the bitmap as you apply compression.

Before placing the bitmaps in the banner, Aly recommends you try to minimize the size of the final movie by changing the compression settings for each bitmap using the Bitmap Properties dialog box. The pictures you are using do not have to be of the highest quality since they are small and will be used as part of a larger graphic, the banner. So you can apply some additional compression to the bitmaps to reduce the overall size of the final movie. You start by selecting a bitmap in the document's Library panel and then clicking the Properties icon to open the Bitmap Properties dialog box.

To change a bitmap's properties:

1. Click the **cat** bitmap in the Library panel, and then click the **Properties** icon ℹ to open the Bitmap Properties dialog box. Now adjust the view of the bitmap in the preview window so you can more readily see the effects of your changes to the picture's properties.

2. Right-click the **bitmap preview** in the upper-left corner and click **Zoom In** on the context menu. Because you want to adjust the compression of the bitmap to suit your needs, you do not want to use the bitmap's imported compression data.

3. Click the **Use imported JPEG data** check box to remove the check and dese-lect this option. The Quality text box shows the default value of 50. Next, see how the bitmap appears with a lower-quality value.

4. Double-click **50** in the Quality text box, type **20**, and then click the **Test** button to apply the new quality value. See Figure 5-6. Notice in the preview window how the quality of the picture is adversely affected. The picture is of poor qual-ity because some of its colors have changed significantly and it has less detail as evidenced by the small blocks that appear throughout the picture. By con-trast, a good quality picture would have most of its original colors and detail.

Figure 5-6   **TESTING A COMPRESSION VALUE**

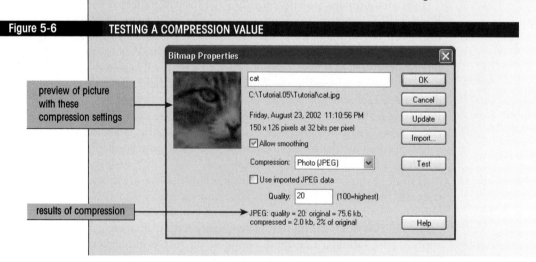

preview of picture with these compression settings

results of compression

Deciding on the best quality value is a subjective effort. There is no specific value that you have to use over another. Instead, you should try several values to compare how the quality of the picture is affected. Select the value that maintains the quality of the picture needed for the particular graphic design while at the same time compressing the bitmap as much as possible. For the cat bitmap, Aly suggests using a quality value of 80.

5. Enter **80** in the Quality text box and then click the **Test** button again. Notice that the compressed size shows the size of the bitmap smaller than the original and that the quality of the picture as seen in the preview window is not adversely affected.

6. Click the **OK** button to accept the compression value. Now you need to adjust the quality for the other bitmap.

7. Click the **parrot** bitmap in the Library panel and open its Bitmap Properties dialog box. Deselect the **Use imported JPEG data** check box and enter a value of **80** in the Quality text box.

8. Click the **Test** button to see how the parrot picture is affected. The parrot picture looks fine with this setting.

9. Click the **OK** button to accept the compression value.

You have changed the compression settings for the two bitmap files. These bitmaps can now be used to create an animation for the new Flounders banner.

Animating Bitmaps

Once you have imported a bitmap into your document you can animate it the same way you animate any other object. For instance, you can create a motion tween that causes the bitmap to move, rotate, change in size (scale), or fade in or out. To animate a bitmap in a motion tween you first need to convert the bitmap instance on the Stage to a symbol. You then create the motion tween the same as you would with any other symbol.

In reviewing Aly's instructions for creating the new banner, you see that you need to use the cat and parrot bitmaps in an animation where one bitmap appears and then fades away while the second bitmap fades in over the first. To accomplish the fade effect you change the alpha amount for each instance. The **alpha amount** controls the transparency of an image. You set the alpha amount by selecting Alpha from the Color list box in the Property inspector and then using the Alpha text box to specify an amount. The alpha amount is a percentage from 0 to 100. An amount of 0% makes the object completely transparent. An amount of 100% makes the object completely opaque, which means it has no transparency. You can create a motion tween that starts the object at an alpha amount of 100% and changes it at the end of the tween to 0%. This makes the object appear to fade out. You reverse the amounts to make the object appear to fade in. Also according to Aly's instructions, this animation of the pet pictures is to be independent of any other animation that may be added to the banner. This means that you should create a movie clip symbol that contains the pet pictures animation within its own Timeline, independent of the main document's Timeline. (Recall that symbols with the Movie Clip behavior have their own independent Timeline.)

To create a new movie clip symbol and convert the cat bitmap into a symbol:

1. Click **Insert** on the menu bar, and then click **New Symbol**. In the Create New Symbol dialog box, enter **pet animation** as the symbol name, and select **Movie Clip** as the behavior type. Click the **OK** button to create the symbol and to enter into the symbol-editing mode. Now you will create an instance of the bitmap on the Stage.

2. If necessary, move the Library panel to the right of the Stage, then drag an instance of the cat bitmap from the Library panel to the center of the Stage. You need to specify an exact location for the bitmap in the Info panel to center the bitmap.

3. Click **Window** on the menu bar, and then click **Info**. In the Info panel enter **0** in both the X and Y text boxes and make sure the center registration point is selected in the Registration icon as shown in Figure 5-7. This centers the bitmap within the editing window.

Figure 5-7	X AND Y COORDINATES SET TO 0

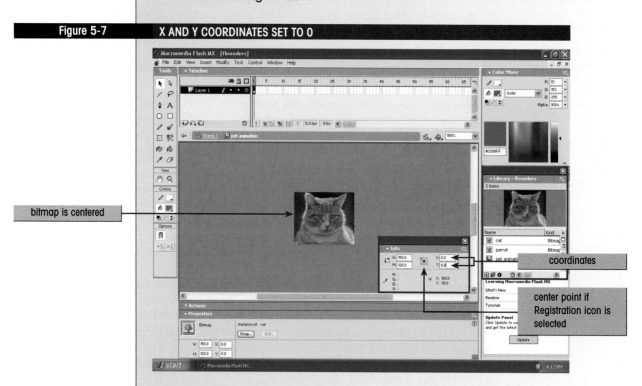

bitmap is centered

coordinates

center point if Registration icon is selected

Now you will convert the cat bitmap instance on the Stage into a symbol so that it may be used in a motion tween animation.

4. If necessary, select the **cat bitmap** instance on the Stage. Click **Insert** on the menu bar, and then click **Convert to Symbol**. In the Convert to Symbol dialog box, enter **cat symbol** for the name, select **Movie Clip** for the behavior, and make sure the center registration point in the Registration icon is selected as shown in Figure 5-8. Click the **OK** button to create the symbol.

Figure 5-8   REGISTRATION POINT SELECTED

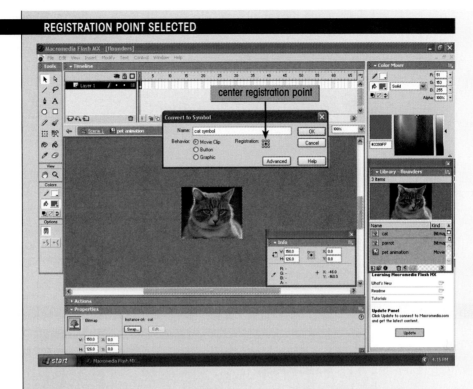

The registration point specifies what part of the symbol is used for alignment. Because the two images, the cat and the parrot, are to be aligned with each other such that they have the same position on the Stage, you want to specify a point in the cat image that can be used for alignment when you position the parrot.

Next you will create an animation in which the cat bitmap fades away after a period of time. Aly has given you a sketch that shows how the animation occurs, as shown in Figure 5-9.

Figure 5-9   FADE ANIMATION

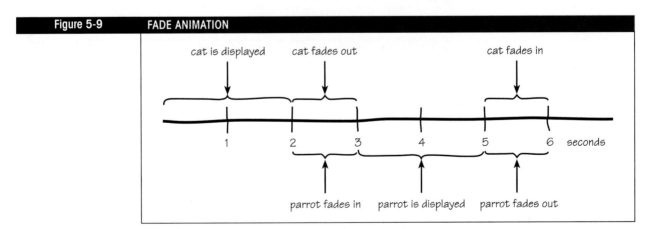

Based on the sketch, the animation of the pictures is to take place over a period of six seconds. During the first two seconds, the cat picture is displayed. Then during the third second, the cat picture fades out, while at the same time the parrot picture fades in. Then during the next two seconds, the parrot picture is displayed. Finally, during the last second, the parrot picture fades out and the cat picture fades back in. Because the frame rate is 12 frames per second, each second requires 12 frames. Converting these time specifications to frame numbers means that you should have keyframes at Frames 1, 24, 36, 60, and 72. These are the frames where a change occurs from the previous frames.

To create the cat animation:

1. Change the name of Layer 1 to **cat layer**. Next you add key frames for the animation.

2. In the cat layer, insert keyframes at **Frame 24** and **Frame 36**. Next, set the alpha values for the cat instance, which control the transparency of the cat, allowing you to create the fade in and fade out effect.

3. Click **Frame 36** in the Timeline and click the **cat instance** to select it. In the Property inspector, select **Alpha** from the Color list box, and enter **0%** for an Alpha amount. The cat instance becomes transparent and thereby no longer appears on the Stage, as shown in Figure 5-10.

| Figure 5-10 | ALPHA AMOUNT SET TO 0% |

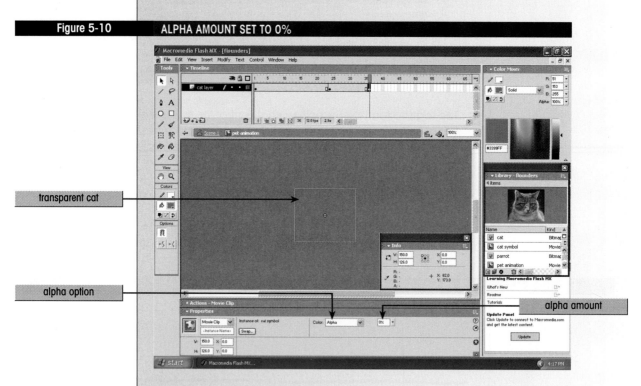

transparent cat

alpha option

alpha amount

4. Click **Frame 24**, click **Insert** on the menu bar, and then click **Create Motion Tween**.

5. Move the playhead to Frame 1, and then press the **Enter** key to preview the motion tween. The cat instance is displayed and then fades out throughout the motion tween. See Figure 5-11. Recall that the cat is supposed to fade out, and then fade back into view at the end of the animation. You will create another motion tween to fade in the cat.

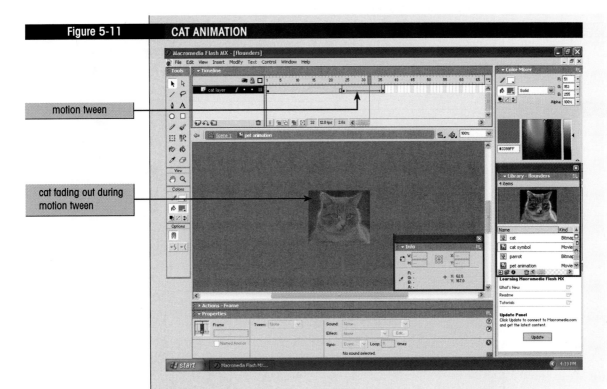

Figure 5-11   **CAT ANIMATION**

motion tween

cat fading out during
motion tween

6. Insert keyframes at **Frame 60** and **Frame 72**. Click **Frame 72** in the Timeline, and then click the cat instance to select it. In the Property inspector, set its Alpha amount to **100%**.

7. Click **Frame 60**, click **Insert** on the menu bar, and then click **Create Motion Tween**. Now preview the two motion tweens.

8. Move the playhead to Frame 1, and then press the **Enter** key. The cat instance is displayed, fades out, and then fades back in at the end of the animation.

You have created an animation where the cat bitmap fades out and then fades in. Now you will repeat similar steps to make the parrot bitmap fade in while the cat bitmap fades out. The parrot bitmap will then fade out while the cat bitmap fades back in. First you need to create a separate layer to hold the parrot animation.

To add the parrot bitmap to the animation:

1. Add a new layer to the Timeline, name it **parrot layer**, and then insert a keyframe at **Frame 24**.

2. Drag a copy of the **parrot bitmap** from the Library panel to the center of the Stage. Next, you use the Info panel to center the parrot bitmap instance and place it in the exact same location as the cat bitmap instance.

3. In the Info panel enter **0** in both the X and Y text boxes and make sure the center registration point is selected in the Registration icon to center the bitmap instance within the editing window as shown in Figure 5-12.

Figure 5-12   PARROT ADDED TO FRAME 24

keyframe in Frame 24

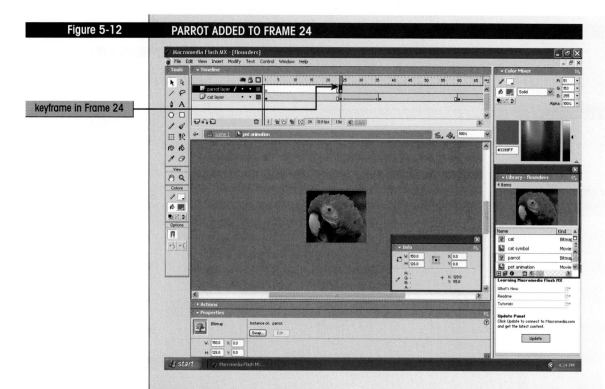

4. Close the Info panel; you will no longer need it. Next you convert the parrot bitmap to a symbol.

5. If necessary, select the parrot bitmap on the Stage. Click **Insert** on the menu bar, and then click **Convert to Symbol**. Enter **parrot symbol** for the name, select **Movie Clip** for the behavior, and make sure the center registration point is selected in the Registration icon. Click the **OK** button. Now add the necessary keyframes.

6. In the parrot layer, insert a keyframe at **Frame 36**. Next, you will set the alpha amount to make the parrot transparent.

7. Click **Frame 24** and, if necessary, select the **parrot instance** on the Stage, and then in the Property inspector select **Alpha** from the Color list box. Enter **0%** for the Alpha amount.

8. Make sure Frame 24 of the parrot layer is selected, click **Insert** on the menu bar, and then click **Create Motion Tween**. Now drag the playhead between Frame 24 and Frame 36 and notice how the parrot is fading in while the cat is fading out. See Figure 5-13. Now create the motion tween for the parrot to fade back in to view.

Figure 5-13	MOTION TWEEN FOR THE PARROT

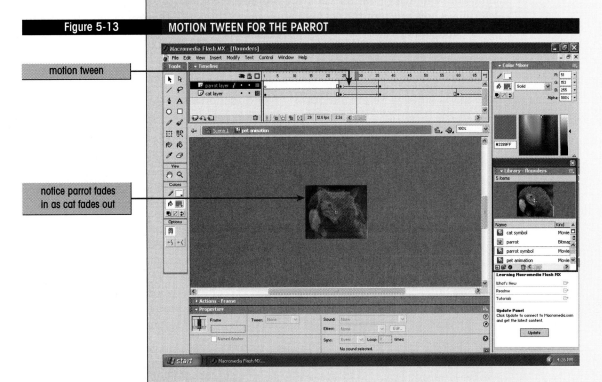

motion tween

notice parrot fades in as cat fades out

9. In the parrot layer, insert keyframes at **Frame 60** and **Frame 72**. Click **Frame 72** and then click the parrot instance to select it. Use the Property inspector to set its Alpha amount to **0%**.

10. Click **Frame 60**, click **Insert** on the menu bar, and then click **Create Motion Tween**.

11. Move the playhead to Frame 1, and then press the **Enter** key. The cat is displayed and then fades out when the parrot fades in. Then the cat fades back in while the parrot fades out.

The pet animation is now complete. Based on Aly's instructions, however, a mask still needs to be added. Recall from previous tutorials that a mask is created on a separate mask layer. The layer below the mask layer becomes the masked layer. The contents of the masked layer that are covered by the shape in the mask layer are displayed when the movie is played. In this case you need to create a mask layer, draw a filled oval that covers the pet animation, and make both the cat layer and the parrot layer masked layers. The filled oval determines how much of the pet animation shows through. This essentially creates a frame for the animation.

To create a mask layer:

1. In the Timeline, select the **parrot layer** and then insert a new layer named **mask**. Now make this new layer a mask layer.

2. Right-click the **mask layer**, and then click **Mask** from the context menu. The mask layer's icon changes to a checkerboard pattern overlaid with an oval shaped frame representing the layer's property. Also, the parrot layer is indented, and its icon changes to a checkerboard pattern indicating it is now a masked layer. Next you need to change the cat layer's properties so that it too is masked.

3. Right-click the **cat layer**, and then click **Properties** on the context menu. In the Layer Properties dialog box, click the **Masked** option button to select this type. Click the **OK** button to close the dialog box. The cat layer is now indented in the Timeline, and its icon also changes to a checkerboard pattern indicating it is now a masked layer. Next, to draw the oval, you need to unlock the mask layer, since it is initially locked to display its effect.

4. Click the **mask layer** in the Timeline, and then click the padlock icon to unlock the layer. Next you draw the shape for the mask. Recall that a mask can be any shape that contains a fill. The area covered by the shape's fill determines what part of the masked layers' content is displayed. The shape's fill can be any color because it is not displayed. You choose a light-blue color.

5. Click the **Oval** tool ⬭ in the toolbox. If necessary, use the Fill Color control in the toolbox to select a light-blue color. You need to draw an oval shape so that the pet animation appears as though it is framed by the oval.

6. Position the crosshair pointer on the upper-left corner of the selection box that appears around the cat, and then drag the pointer to draw an oval to cover the cat as shown in Figure 5-14. Cover as much of the picture as you can but keep the oval inside the picture area.

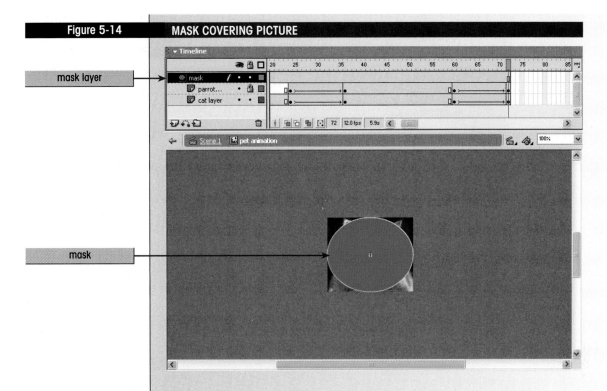

Figure 5-14   MASK COVERING PICTURE

mask layer

mask

7. Lock all of the layers in the Timeline. Locking the layers displays the result of the mask. The cat shows through the mask.

   The mask for the pet animation is now complete. Return to the document and its main Timeline.

8. Click the **Scene 1** link in the Address bar above the Stage to exit symbol-editing mode and return to the document.

9. Save the document.

Now that you have created the pet animation movie clip, you need to add it to the banner. Recall from the specifications for this banner that the pet animation is to be placed on the right side of the banner inside the large curves.

To add the pet animation to the banner and preview it:

1. Click the **background layer** in the Timeline and drag the pet animation symbol from the Library panel to the right side of the Stage and placing it inside the ovals as shown in Figure 5-15.

Figure 5-15   PET ANIMATION IN BANNER

pet animation instance

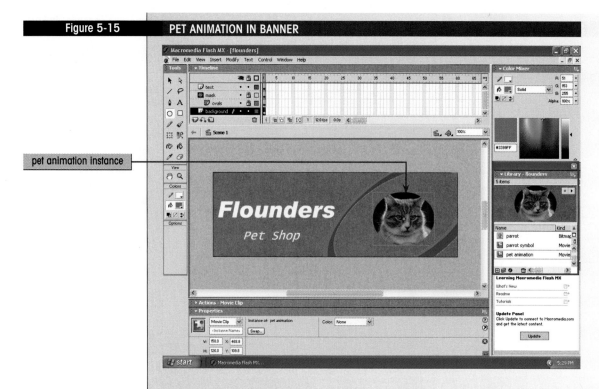

Since the animation was created inside the movie clip's Timeline, you cannot preview it within the main document's Timeline. To preview the pet animation with the banner, you need to create a SWF file and play it in a separate window or in a Web page. Use the Test Movie command to preview the banner.

2. Click **Control** on the menu bar, and then click **Test Movie**. A separate window opens with the banner and the pet animation.

3. After viewing the banner, close the window to return to Flash.

4. Save the banner.

Another option when working with bitmaps is to convert them to vector graphics. The Flash vector drawing and painting tools can then be used to modify the graphics.

Converting a Bitmap to a Vector Graphic

A bitmap instance on the Stage can also be converted to a vector graphic. Once converted, the graphic can be modified just like any other vector graphics created in Flash. Converting a bitmap to a vector graphic may be useful if the imported bitmap is geometric in nature and you can use the Flash editing tools to edit the graphic. It may also be useful if you want to create a different visual effect with the image. Once you convert a bitmap instance on the Stage to a vector graphic, it is no longer linked to the imported bitmap in the document's library. The original bitmap in the library is not affected and can still be used to create instances of the bitmap on the Stage. Converting a bitmap instance to a vector graphic may also help reduce the file size of the final movie.

You convert a bitmap instance on the Stage into a vector graphic using the Trace Bitmap command. When you select the Trace Bitmap command from the Modify menu, the Trace Bitmap dialog box opens, as shown in Figure 5-16. You then specify values and select options to indicate how the bitmap is to be converted. The Trace Bitmap command then compares each pixel in the graphic to assign it a color.

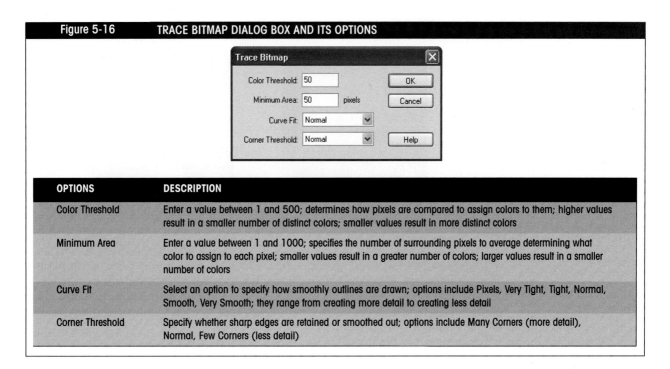

Figure 5-16   TRACE BITMAP DIALOG BOX AND ITS OPTIONS

OPTIONS	DESCRIPTION
Color Threshold	Enter a value between 1 and 500; determines how pixels are compared to assign colors to them; higher values result in a smaller number of distinct colors; smaller values result in more distinct colors
Minimum Area	Enter a value between 1 and 1000; specifies the number of surrounding pixels to average determining what color to assign to each pixel; smaller values result in a greater number of colors; larger values result in a smaller number of colors
Curve Fit	Select an option to specify how smoothly outlines are drawn; options include Pixels, Very Tight, Tight, Normal, Smooth, Very Smooth; they range from creating more detail to creating less detail
Corner Threshold	Specify whether sharp edges are retained or smoothed out; options include Many Corners (more detail), Normal, Few Corners (less detail)

When you convert a bitmap to a vector, pixels with similar colors are converted into areas of one color, essentially reducing the number of colors in the picture. Also, areas of contrasting color are converted to lines and curves. You specify how you want Flash to do this conversion through the settings in the Trace Bitmap dialog box. The **Color Threshold** value determines how pixels are compared to assign colors to them. A higher value means that the colors of adjacent pixels have to vary more before they are considered to be a different color. Higher Color Threshold values result in a smaller number of distinct colors. Smaller values result in more distinct colors. The **Minimum Area** value specifies the number of surrounding pixels to average determining what color to assign to each pixel. Using a smaller value for the Minimum Area means less surrounding pixels are compared and results in a greater number of colors. A larger value means a greater number of surrounding pixels are compared and results in a smaller number of colors. The **Curve Fit** list box provides options for specifying how curves are drawn. The options range from Pixels, which results in more detail, to Very Smooth, which results in less detail. Finally, the **Corner Threshold** list box provides options for specifying how many corners or sharp edges are retained in the converted image. The Many Corners option results in more detail and the Few Corners option results in less detail. Applying different values creates different effects on the end result. For example, applying the Trace Bitmap command on the cat bitmap using a Color Threshold of 50, a Minimum Area of 50, Curve Fit at Normal, and Corner Threshold at Normal creates a special effect as shown in Figure 5-17.

Figure 5-17	THE CAT BITMAP CONVERTED TO A VECTOR

original bitmap   vector graphic

In Aly's discussions with Joe Flounders, Joe indicated that he would like to have a photo of a bird used with the new company logo. Aly instructs you to use the parrot photo as a background for the new logo and to convert the bitmap to a vector graphic to create a special effect. First you will create a new document and set its dimensions as specified in the planning sketch that Aly provided. You will then apply the Trace Bitmap command with values and options suggested by Aly.

To convert the parrot bitmap to a vector:

1. Click **File** on the menu bar, and then click **New**. Now change the new document's dimensions to match those given by Aly in her sketch shown in Figure 5-1.

2. Click **Modify** on the menu bar, and then click **Document**. In the Document's Properties dialog box enter **150** in the width text box and **125** in the height text box. Click the **OK** button to close the dialog box.

3. Save the file as **petlogo.fla** in the Tutorial.05\Tutorial folder on your Data Disk.

4. Change the magnification level of the Stage to **200%**, and then scroll the Stage window so that all of the Stage is visible. If necessary, expand the flounders document's Library panel. The logo will use the parrot bitmap stored in the flounders document's library.

5. Drag a copy of the **parrot bitmap** from the flounders Library panel to the Stage. It should fill all of the Stage. The bitmap is also added to the petlogo document's library. Now you will convert the parrot bitmap to a vector graphic.

   TROUBLE? If the parrot instance on the Stage has a thin blue outline instead of a gray dotted outline, you dragged the parrot symbol instead of the parrot bitmap. Delete the parrot symbol instance from the Stage and repeat Step 5.

6. With the parrot instance selected on the Stage, click **Modify** on the menu bar, and then click **Trace Bitmap**. The Trace Bitmap dialog box opens.

7. Enter a value of **50** in the Color Threshold text box, and then enter a value of **50** in the Minimum Area text box.

8. Click the **Curve Fit** list arrow, click **Very Tight**, click the **Corner Threshold** list arrow, and then click **Many corners**.

9. Click the **OK** button to convert the bitmap to a vector. Deselect the graphic by clicking the Work Area. The parrot picture is now a vector graphic as shown in Figure 5-18.

Figure 5-18	PARROT AS A VECTOR GRAPHIC

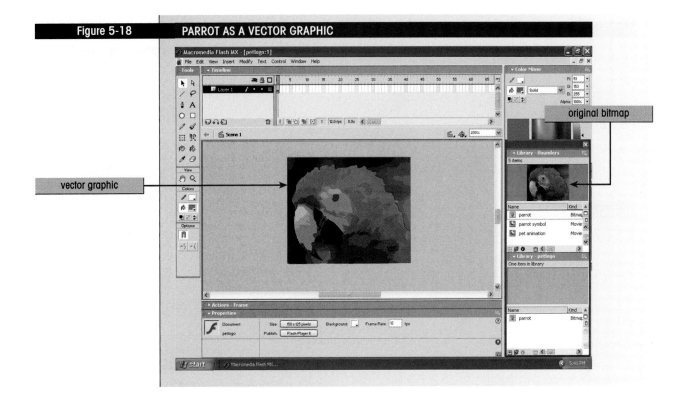

Now that you have converted the parrot bitmap on the Stage to a vector graphic you can complete the logo by adding text on top of the graphic as shown in Aly's planning sketch. The graphic is the background for the logo. You will add the text on separate layers.

To complete the logo by adding text:

1. Insert a new layer and name it **flounders**.

2. Click the **Text** tool A in the toolbox. Before creating the text, set the text properties.

3. In the Property inspector, change the font to **Arial Black**, the font size to **26**, and then use the color pop-up window to change the text color to a shade of **yellow** (last column on the right, third row from the bottom). Click the **Left alignment** button, and make sure the Bold and Italic buttons are not selected.

4. Click the left-center area of the parrot and type **Flounders**. Next you make the first letter in the text block larger.

5. Select the letter **F** and then change the font size in the Property inspector to **42**.

6. Click the **Free Transform** tool in the toolbox, and then click the **Rotate and Skew** modifier in the options area of the toolbox. Drag one of the corner handles on the bounding box around the text to rotate the text box. If necessary, reposition the text block so that it is on the center of the picture. See Figure 5-19.

| Figure 5-19 | ROTATED AND CENTERED TEXT BOX |

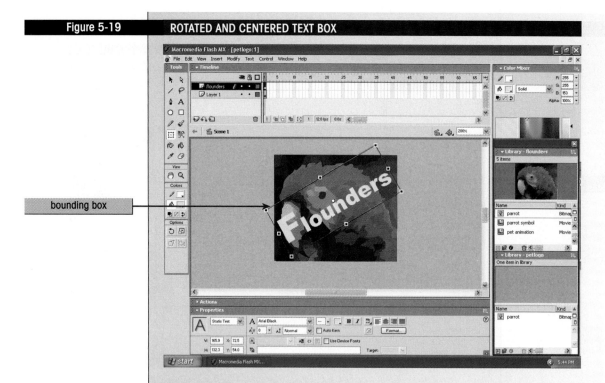

bounding box

Now you need to create two more text blocks, one for the word "Pet" and one for the word "Shop." Each will have a slightly different color.

7. Deselect the Flounders text block. Click A in the toolbox in the Property inspector, change the font size to **16**, the text color to a **gray** (fourth row, first column, in the color pop-up window), and then create a text box at the bottom center of the Stage. Type **Pet** for the text.

8. Use the color pop-up window in the Property inspector to change the text color to a **lighter gray** (fifth row, first column, in the color pop-up window), and then create another text block below the Pet text. Type **Shop** in this text block, and then reposition the two text blocks as shown in Figure 5-20.

Figure 5-20   **LOGO WITH TEXT**

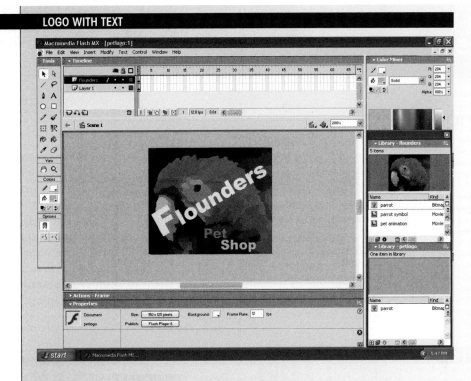

9. Save and close the logo file. You will export this logo and add it to a Web page later in this tutorial. You can either close the flounders.fla file and exit Flash, or leave this file and the program open for the next session.

In this session you learned that in order to use bitmaps in a Flash document, they have to be imported. Once imported, the bitmaps are stored in the document's library and instances can then be created on the Stage. You also learned how to change a bitmap's properties, how to convert a bitmap to a vector graphic, and how to create an animation using bitmaps. Finally, you learned how to use the alpha amount to create a fade effect animation with the bitmaps.

Session 5.1 QUICK CHECK

1. What is a bitmap?
2. What is the difference between the Import and the Import to Library commands?
3. How do you access a bitmap's properties within Flash?
4. For what type of bitmaps should you use the Photo (JPEG) compression setting?
5. What alpha amount makes an object transparent?
6. What command do you use to convert a bitmap to a vector graphic?
7. When converting a bitmap to a vector graphic how does the Color Threshold value affect the resulting graphic?

SESSION 5.2

In this session you will learn how to create and use gradients. You will create a custom gradient using the Color Mixer panel, save the gradient, and then apply the gradient to an object on the Stage. You will also learn how to modify a gradient once it has been applied to an object.

Using Gradients

A **gradient** is a gradual blend or transition from one color to another. Using gradients can help you create special effects and add a professional touch to your documents. For example, you can use a gradient for a banner's background, create a gradient to simulate a sunset or a rainbow, or use a gradient as part of an animation. Gradients can be added as fills to any object the same way you add solid color fills. You can select the gradient first for the fill color and then draw an object such as a rectangle that contains the gradient as a fill. You can also use the Paint Bucket tool to apply a gradient to an existing object.

There are two types of gradients you can create in Flash, linear and radial. A **linear** gradient blends the colors from one point to another in a straight line. A **radial** gradient blends the colors from one point outwards in a circular pattern. Figure 5-21 shows examples of linear and radial gradients.

Figure 5-21	GRADIENT EXAMPLES

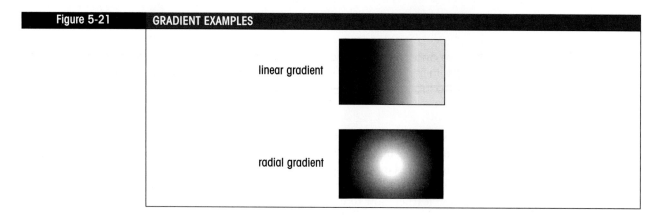

linear gradient

radial gradient

Flash includes several preset gradients located below the color swatches in the color pop-up window. You can use these gradients as fills for any closed shape. You can also create your own custom gradients using the Color Mixer panel.

Creating and Editing Gradients

The Color Mixer panel can be used to create new gradients. With the Color Mixer you specify linear or radial gradient as the fill style and then select the colors for the gradient. Once you select a gradient as the fill style, the gradient definition bar is displayed in the middle of the panel. Gradient pointers are displayed below the gradient definition bar and specify which colors are used in the gradient. If you need to create a gradient with more than two colors, you just add more gradient pointers. You add gradient pointers by clicking the area below the gradient definition bar as shown in Figure 5-22.

Figure 5-22	GRADIENT POINTERS IN COLOR MIXER

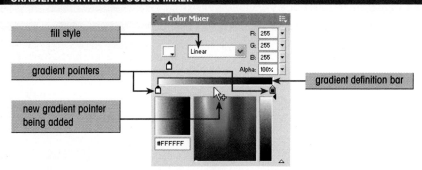

To remove a gradient pointer you drag it down, away from the gradient definition bar. Also, you can reposition a gradient pointer by dragging it to the left or the right. Doing so changes the gradient's **fall off point**, which is the point where the gradient shifts from one color to another.

There are several ways in which you can specify the colors for the gradient. Before specifying a color, however, you should first click the gradient pointer for the color you want to change. You then select a color using the color pop-up window, by entering the color's Red, Green, Blue (RGB) values, or by clicking the Color Space in the Color Mixer. You can also adjust the brightness of a color using the brightness control in the lower-right corner of the Color Mixer.

Once you have created a gradient you can save it with the Add Swatch command located on the Color Mixer's options menu. This command adds the new gradient to the document's color swatches that appear in the color pop-up window. The gradient is only stored with the current document.

Aly's instructions for creating the new banner for the Flounders Pet Shop state that the background should be a radial gradient using a blend of a light-blue color that transitions into a dark-gray color. You need to create the radial gradient and then create a rectangle with the gradient as its fill for the banner's background. You will create the rectangle on a separate layer.

To create a gradient for the banner:

1. If necessary, start Flash, and open the **flounders.fla** document. Change the magnification level of the Stage to **100%** and position the panels to their default layout.

2. Click the **Fill style** list arrow in the Color Mixer panel, and then click **Radial**. Now you can use the Color Swatches panel to view the preset gradients.

3. If necessary, click the **Color Swatches** panel title bar to expand it. You will select a preset gradient as a starting point.

4. Click the **gray radial** gradient in the Color Swatches panel with the eyedropper pointer. This gradient appears as the second gradient from the left below the color swatches. See Figure 5-23.

Figure 5-23   SELECTING A PRESET GRADIENT

The Color Mixer changes to display the preset gray radial gradient and its gradient pointers. Next you change these gradient pointers to create a new gradient based on the colors specified in the planning sketch.

5. Click the **left gradient pointer** below the gradient definition bar to select it. When a gradient is selected, its small triangle appears black.

6. Click the panel's **color control** list arrow to open the color pop-up window.

7. Click the color swatch in the bottom row, seventh column from the left, as shown in Figure 5-24.

Figure 5-24	CHOOSE THE LEFT GRADIENT COLOR

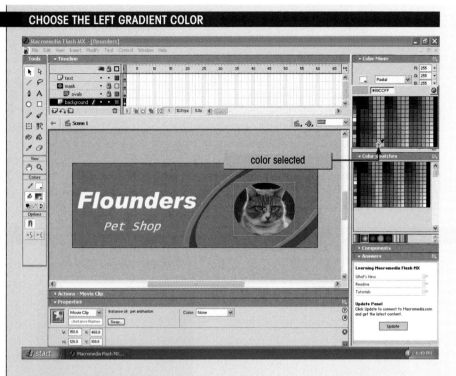

8. Click the **right gradient** pointer under the gradient definition bar, open the color pop-up window, and then click the color swatch in the second row, first column from the left.

   The Color Space in the Color Mixer shows the new gradient based on the colors you selected. You should save this gradient with the document.

9. Click the Color Mixer panel's **options menu control** ▦, and then click **Add Swatch** from the menu. The gradient is now added to the gradients in the Color Swatches panel, as shown in Figure 5-25.

Figure 5-25	NEW GRADIENT IN COLOR SWATCHES PANEL

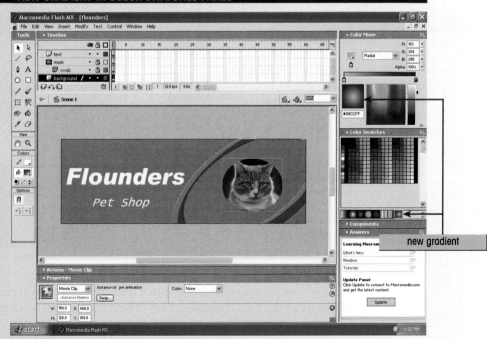

You have created a gradient and added it to the document's color swatches. Now you are ready to use this gradient to create a background rectangle for the banner.

Applying a Gradient Fill

To apply a gradient fill to an object you follow the same process as when applying a solid fill. You can select the gradient for the fill color and then when you draw a shape such as a rectangle, the rectangle has the gradient as its fill. If the shape already exists on the Stage, you can use the Paint Bucket tool to apply the gradient. When using the Paint Bucket tool to apply a radial gradient, you can specify where the gradient's center point should go. The center point of a radial gradient is where the first color begins. The point where you click determines the gradient's center point, as shown in Figure 5-26.

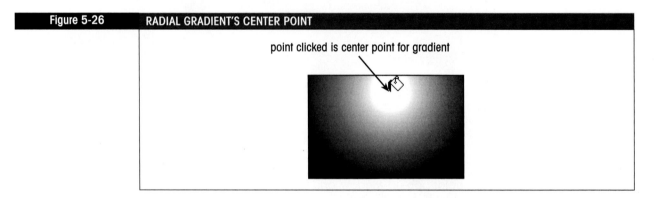

Figure 5-26   **RADIAL GRADIENT'S CENTER POINT**

point clicked is center point for gradient

You can also apply a linear gradient by drawing a straight line with the Paint Bucket pointer. The line you draw determines the direction of the gradient.

Another option you can use when applying gradients is the Lock Fill modifier which is displayed in the options area of the toolbox when the Paint Bucket tool is selected. Using the Lock Fill modifier paints one gradient across several objects on the Stage rather than one gradient for each object. See Figure 5-27.

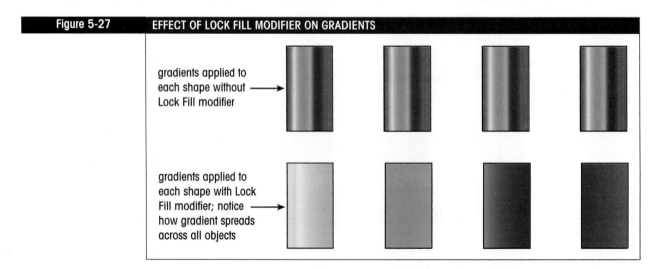

Figure 5-27   **EFFECT OF LOCK FILL MODIFIER ON GRADIENTS**

gradients applied to each shape without Lock Fill modifier

gradients applied to each shape with Lock Fill modifier; notice how gradient spreads across all objects

Now you will create a rectangle that uses the gradient you created earlier. The rectangle will serve as the banner's background. The rectangle will be added to the background layer.

To add a rectangle with the custom gradient:

1. If necessary, select the **background** layer, and then click the **Rectangle** tool in the toolbox.

2. If necessary, select the new gradient you created for the fill. The gradient is located in the bottom row, eighth column, of the color pop-up window in the toolbox. Set the stroke to **no color**.

3. Draw a large rectangle that is the same size as the Stage. The rectangle should cover the entire Stage. See Figure 5-28

| Figure 5-28 | GRADIENT AS BACKGROUND |

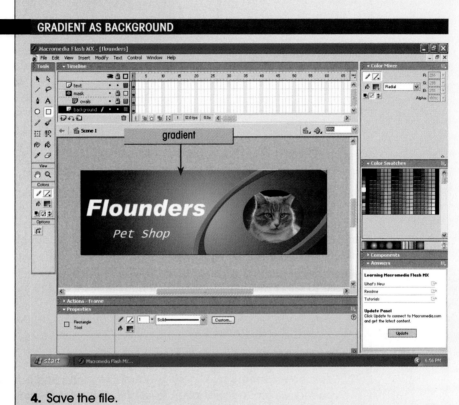

4. Save the file.

You now have a rectangle with the new gradient that serves as a background for the banner. This gradient can be modified to create a different effect using the Fill Transform tool.

Transforming Gradient Fills

A gradient fill in an object can be modified by using the Fill Transform tool in the toolbox. You can move a gradient's center, change its size, or change its direction. When you select a linear gradient with the Fill Transform tool, a bounding box is displayed around it. For a radial gradient a bounding circle is displayed around it. The gradient's center point is also displayed along with editing handles, as shown in Figure 5-29. You drag these handles to transform the gradient.

Figure 5-29	EDITING HANDLES

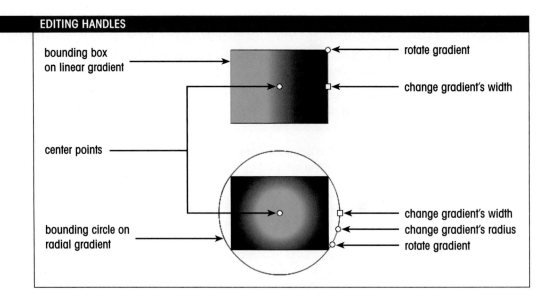

You drag a gradient's center point to reposition it. The linear gradient has a circular handle used to rotate the gradient. It also has a square handle used to change the gradient's width. The radial gradient has a square handle and two circular handles. The square handle is used to change the width of the radius. The middle circular handle is used to change the radius of the gradient and the bottom circular handle is used to rotate the gradient.

In reviewing the gradient you created for the banner, Aly instructs you to modify the gradient so that the lighter color of the gradient is behind the cat. First you will move the gradient's center point to the right side of the banner over the pet animation. You will then increase its radius slightly to spread more of the lighter color to the rest of the banner. You will need to select the gradient with the Fill Transform tool to modify it.

To modify the gradient:

1. Click the **Fill Transform** tool in the toolbox.

2. Click the **rectangle** to display its bounding circle and editing handles. Next you reduce the magnification level of the Stage to make it easier to work.

3. Click the **Zoom control** list arrow to change the Stage magnification level to **50%**. This makes the entire bounding circle visible as shown in Figure 5-30.

Figure 5-30   **GRADIENT BOUNDING CIRCLE**

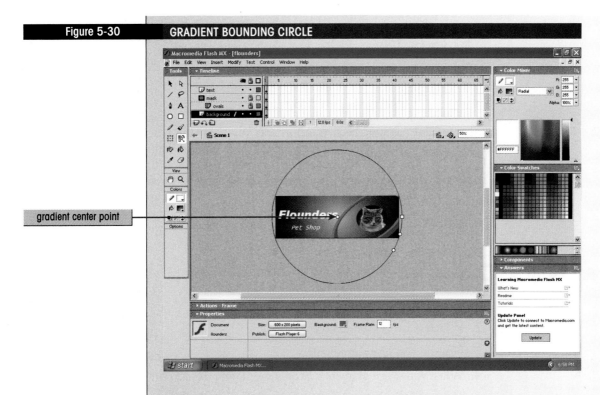

gradient center point

Next you reposition the center point of the gradient to be over the middle of the pet animation.

4. Drag the center point of the gradient to the right and position it over the cat.

5. Drag the middle circular handle to increase the gradient's radius so that the bounding circle's left side is just to the left of the "F" in the "Flounders" text, as shown in Figure 5-31.

Figure 5-31   **INCREASING THE GRADIENT'S RADIUS**

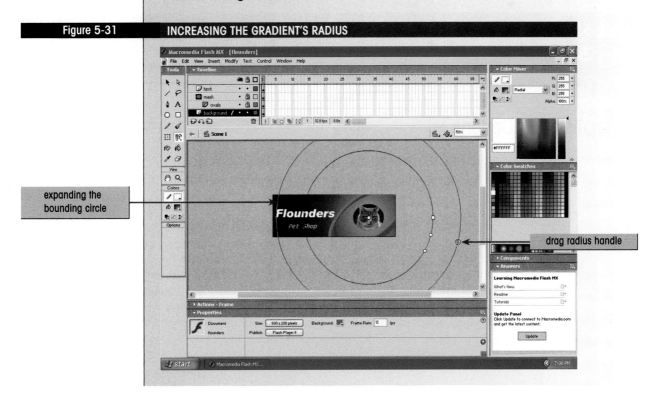

expanding the bounding circle

drag radius handle

6. Click the Work Area to hide the bounding circle, and then return the magnification level to **100%**.

7. Save the flounders.fla banner. You can either close the file and exit Flash, or leave the program and file open for the next session.

The gradient has now been transformed. You show the banner to Aly and she is very pleased with your work and thinks it will look great on the Flounders Pet Shop Web site.

In this session you learned about gradients. You learned how to create a gradient and how to use a gradient by drawing an object or by applying it to an existing object. You also learned how to modify a gradient's position, size, and width using the Fill Transform tool. In the next session, you will publish the banner.

Session 5.2 QUICK CHECK

1. What is a gradient?

2. Which panel is used to create a gradient?

3. How do you save a gradient?

4. When you save a gradient it is only saved with the current document. True or False?

5. If you have a gradient with two colors, how do you add another color?

6. Which tool is used to apply a gradient to an existing object?

7. Which tool is used to modify a gradient fill?

8. Which handle do you change on a linear gradient to rotate the gradient?

SESSION 5.3

In this session you will learn about the publishing options in Macromedia Flash. You will explore the various settings available and then you will publish the new Flounders banner as a SWF file and export the new logo as a JPEG file. You will also learn how to incorporate the banner and logo into an existing Web page.

Publishing Options

As you have learned, the native file format for your Macromedia Flash documents is the FLA format. When you are done creating a FLA document you want to make it available for use on the Web. To do so, the document has to be published or exported into a format readable by a Web browser. You have already done this when you published your FLA documents as SWF movie files in previous tutorials. You have done this using the Test Movie command on the Control menu and also when you used the Default (HTML) command on the Publish Preview menu. Recall the Test Movie command creates a SWF file and plays it in a separate window. The Default-(HTML) command creates both a SWF file and an HTML file to play the movie. The browser uses the Flash Player plug-in to play the movie. In most cases, if you are creating movies for the Web, you want to publish a SWF file. However, there are times when you need to publish or export your document in a different file format. Flash has other publishing and exporting options that allow you to publish your Flash documents in such file formats as JPEG, GIF, and PNG. A Flash file can even be published as a projector file, which is a stand-alone file with an .exe extension. A projector file has the Flash Player incorporated into it and plays the movie in its own window, not in a Web browser.

You specify how you want your FLA documents published using the Publish Settings dialog box.

Publish Settings

The Publish Settings dialog box shown in Figure 5-32 lists the many file formats you can use to publish a Flash document.

Figure 5-32	PUBLISH SETTINGS DIALOG BOX

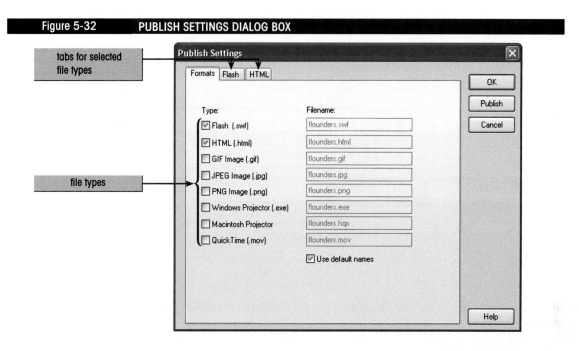

By default, only the first two Type options are selected. These are Flash (.swf) and HTML (.html). Most of the time, the documents you create are meant to be played on a Web page so these two options are the only two you will select. However, if you need to publish a document in a different format, you should select the check box for that format. For example, if you need to publish the document as a JPEG file, then you select the JPEG Image (.jpg) check box. Upon selecting a new Type option, its corresponding tab is displayed at the top of the dialog box. Each of the tabs has additional options for the associated file type. For example, when you click the Flash tab, its options are displayed. The Flash options and the default settings are shown in Figure 5-33.

Figure 5-33   FLASH FORMAT OPTIONS

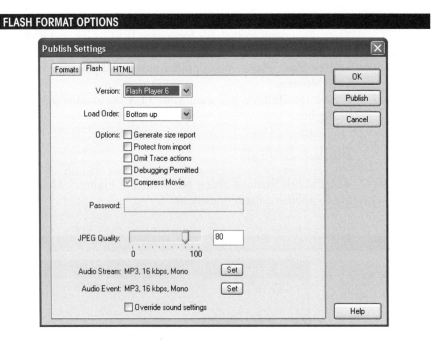

The Flash options are described in Figure 5-34.

Figure 5-34   FLASH FILE OPTIONS

OPTION	DESCRIPTION
Version list box	Select the Flash Player version to publish to
Load Order list box	Select either Bottom up or Top down; determines the order the movie's layers are displayed
Options:	
Generate size report check box	Create text file with information about the size of the published file and its components
Protect from import check box	Prevent the SWF file from being imported and converted back to a FLA file
Omit Trace actions check box	Advanced option used when troubleshooting a movie
Debugging Permitted check box	Advanced option used to troubleshoot a movie
Compress Movie check box	Compress a Flash movie; the resulting movie only plays in Flash Player 6
Password text box	Add password for protection; use when Debugging Permitted is selected
JPEG Quality	Specify the JPEG quality value for all JPEG images in the document; settings applied to individual images with the Bitmap Properties dialog box override this setting
Audio Stream	Specify the compression settings for stream sounds
Audio Event	Specify the compression settings for event sounds
Override sound settings check box	Override the sound settings set for individual sounds with the Sound Properties dialog box

The new banner you created will be added to the home page of the Flounders Pet Shop Web site so it needs to be published as a SWF file. Since the Web page already exists, you are to publish a SWF file only. Aly also instructs you to use the Publish Settings dialog box to specify what to publish and how to publish the movie. She wants you to make the SWF file compatible with all Flash Player plug-ins starting with version 5. You are to accept the

Load Order default setting of Bottom up. This movie contains a small number of layers so the order they are loaded is insignificant. Also, the JPEG quality and sound settings do not have to be changed. Recall the bitmap properties were individually set and they override the JPEG settings in this dialog box. Also, there are no sounds in this movie so the Audio settings are not used. The only option that Aly instructs you to set is the Generate size report option. She wants you to see an example of this report that shows the size of the different parts of the movie. The report is created as a text file and is saved with the FLA file's name plus the word Report and an extension of .txt.

To publish a SWF file:

1. If necessary, start Flash and open the **flounders.fla** file. Change the magnification level of the Stage to **100%** and position the panels to their default layout. Click **File** on the menu bar, and then click **Publish Settings**. The Publish Settings dialog box opens.

2. On the **Formats** tab, click the **HTML (.html)** check box to deselect this option, and then make sure that the **Flash (.swf)** check box is checked. Now you will specify the name for the SWF file.

3. Click the **Use default names** check box to deselect this option, and then enter **banner.swf** in the Filename text box to the right of Flash (.swf), as shown in Figure 5-35. Next you set the publishing options Aly has requested.

Figure 5-35   **ENTERING A NEW NAME FOR THE SWF FILE**

new name

do not select this option

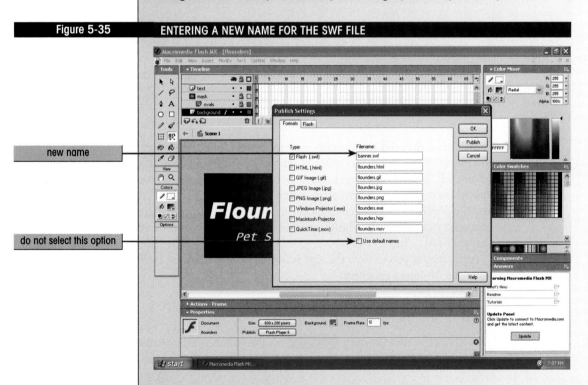

4. Click the **Flash** tab to display the settings for this format. Click the **Version** list arrow, select **Flash Player 5**, and then click the **Generate size report** check box to select it. See Figure 5-36.

Figure 5-36   FLASH PUBLISH SETTINGS

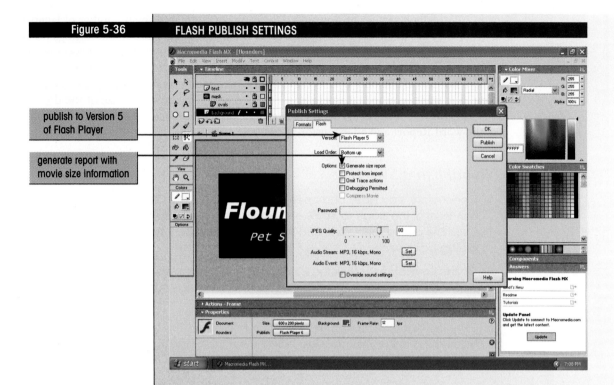

publish to Version 5
of Flash Player

generate report with
movie size information

5. Click the **Publish** button to create the SWF file and the size report. The files are created in the same folder as the FLA file.

6. Click the **OK** button to close the Publish Settings dialog box.

7. Save and close the flounders.fla file.

You have changed the publish settings for this file. The next time you need to publish, you can click the Publish command on the File menu instead of using the Publish Settings command. The Publish command publishes the files according to the settings in the Publish Settings dialog box. Also, since you deselected HTML (.html) from the Formats list, the Publish Preview command on the File menu no longer reads Default (HTML). Instead it reads Default (Flash) indicating that the default now creates a SWF file only and not an HTML file.

Aly instructs you to view the size report text file generated by Flash. You can open the file using the Notepad program.

To open the size report file:

1. Click the **Start** button ![start] on the taskbar, point to **All Programs**, and then point to **Accessories**. Click **Notepad** to start the program.

2. Click **File** on the menu bar, and then click **Open**. In the Open dialog box, navigate to the drive containing your Data Disk, open the Tutorial.05\Tutorial folder, click the **banner Report.txt** file, and then click the **Open** button. The report is displayed in the Notepad window, as shown in Figure 5-37.

Figure 5-37   **MOVIE SIZE REPORT**

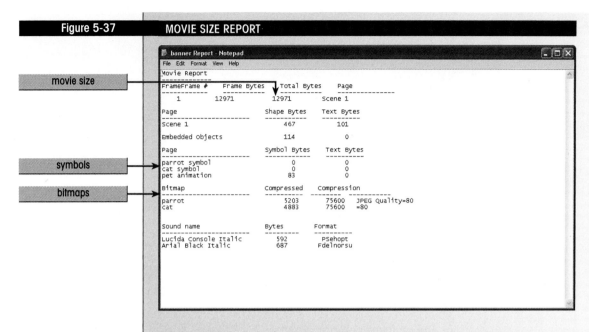

movie size

symbols

bitmaps

The report file shows information about the movie including its number of frames. Recall the main Timeline for the banner only has one frame. It also shows the total size of the movie in number of bytes, a list of the symbols in the movie, and a list of the bitmaps. This information can be useful when optimizing a larger, more complex movie to find ways of reducing its size.

3. Click **File** on the menu bar, and then click **Exit** to close the text file and exit Notepad.

Now that you have published the banner and viewed its size report, you turn your attention to the logo you created earlier in this tutorial. The logo can be published as a SWF file, but because it does not have any animation Aly wants you to export it as a JPEG file.

Exporting an Image

The JPEG and GIF file formats are the most common file formats used for images on Web pages. JPEG format is best for images that include many colors such as the photograph of the parrot. GIF format is best for images with fewer colors. You can use the Publish Settings dialog box to select JPEG or GIF as the format to publish. You can also use the Export Image command on the File menu. The Export Image command allows you to specify the type of format you want to export to and then displays settings you can change based on the file format you select. Some of the formats you can export to are listed in Figure 5-38.

Figure 5-38   **EXPORT FORMATS**

FILE TYPE	EXTENSION
Flash movie	.swf
Enhanced metafile	.emf
Windows metafile	.wmf
Adobe Illustrator	.ai

Figure 5-38	EXPORT FORMATS (CONTINUED)

FILE TYPE	EXTENSION
Bitmap (BMP)	.bmp
JPEG image	.jpg
GIF image	.gif
PNG image	.png

Because the logo you created earlier is static and includes only a picture and some text, you can export it as a JPEG image using the Export Image command. You do this next.

To export the logo as a JPEG image:

1. If necessary, display the Flash program window. Open the **petlogo.fla** document stored in the Tutorial.05\Tutorial folder on your Data Disk. The Export Image command is located on the File menu.

2. Click **File** on the menu bar, and then click **Export Image**. The Export Image dialog box opens.

3. If necessary, navigate to the Tutorial.05\Tutorial folder on your Data Disk. Enter **petlogo** in the File name text box, click the **Save as type** list arrow, and then click **JPEG Image (*.jpg)**.

4. Click the **Save** button. The Export JPEG dialog box opens. See Figure 5-39.

Figure 5-39	EXPORT SETTINGS

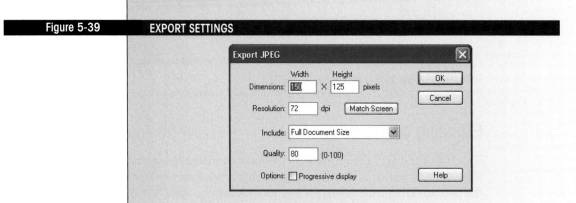

Notice the Include list box has options of **Minimum Image Area** or **Full Document Size**. If the document has empty space, the Minimum Image Area setting will not export the empty space. The Quality value specifies how much compression is applied to the whole image.

5. If necessary, click the **Match Screen** button to change the dimensions to **150** by **125** pixels and the resolution to **72**. Also, if necessary, set the Include option to **Full Document Size** and enter **80** for the Quality value. See Figure 5-39.

6. Click the **OK** button to save the image and close the dialog box.

7. Close the petlogo.fla file and exit Flash.

The published banner and exported logo are now ready to be placed in a Web page.

Adding Flash Graphics to a Web Page

The final outcome of creating movies with Macromedia Flash is a Web page that displays the movies along with text, hyperlinks, and other graphics. Once you complete a Flash graphic such as a banner or a logo you need to incorporate its file information into the Web page's HTML. When you publish a movie with the HTML format option, Flash automatically creates a simple Web page to display the movie. However, to add the SWF file to an existing Web page you need to edit the actual Web page. You can do this with a Web page editing program such as Macromedia Dreamweaver or Microsoft FrontPage. You also can edit the HTML itself in a text editor such as Notepad.

Chris has created a sample Web page for you to use to add the banner and the logo you have created. The Web page has a simple banner and logo that you will replace. You will edit the Web page using Notepad.

To add the banner and logo to a sample Web page:

1. Start the Notepad program.

2. Click **File** on the Notepad menu bar, and then click **Open**. The Open File dialog box opens.

3. Click the **Files of type** list arrow, click **All Files**, navigate to the Tutorial.05\Tutorial folder on your Data Disk, click **sample.htm** in the file list, and then click the **Open** button. The HTML for the sample Web page is displayed in the Notepad window.

4. Click the **Maximize button** 🔲 to maximize the program window. See Figure 5-40.

Figure 5-40 | SAMPLE WEB PAGE HTML

replace image tag

change logo name and dimensions

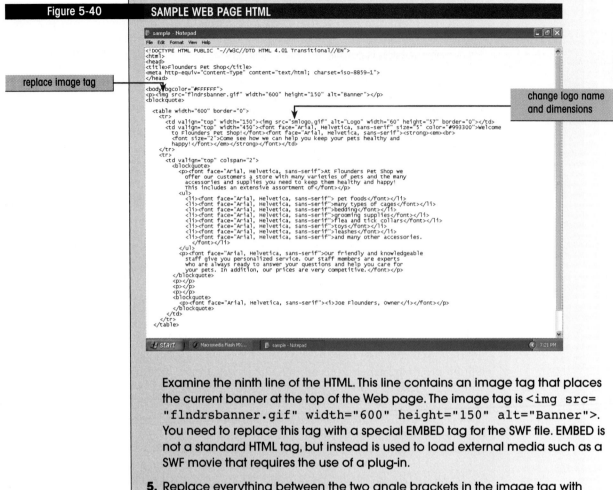

Examine the ninth line of the HTML. This line contains an image tag that places the current banner at the top of the Web page. The image tag is `<img src= "flndrsbanner.gif" width="600" height="150" alt="Banner">`. You need to replace this tag with a special EMBED tag for the SWF file. EMBED is not a standard HTML tag, but instead is used to load external media such as a SWF movie that requires the use of a plug-in.

5. Replace everything between the two angle brackets in the image tag with

```
<embed src="banner.swf" width="600" height="200">
```

Next you need to replace the reference for the current logo with a reference for the new logo file, petlogo.jpg.

6. On the 14ᵗʰ line, replace `smlogo.gif` with `petlogo.jpg`. Next you change the width and height values.

7. On the same line, replace `width="60" height="57"` with `width="150" height="125"`.

8. Save the changes, close the file, and exit Notepad.

Now that you have made the changes to the HTML of the sample Web page, you can test it by opening the page in your browser.

To preview the sample.htm Web page:

1. Start your browser.

2. Click **File** on the menu bar, and then click **Open**.

3. In the Open dialog box, click the **Browse** button, and then navigate to the Tutorial.05\Tutorial folder on your Data Disk.

4. Click **sample.htm** in the file list, and then click the **Open** button. The page is displayed in the browser window, as shown in Figure 5-41.

Figure 5-41 **SAMPLE WEB PAGE WITH FLASH GRAPHICS**

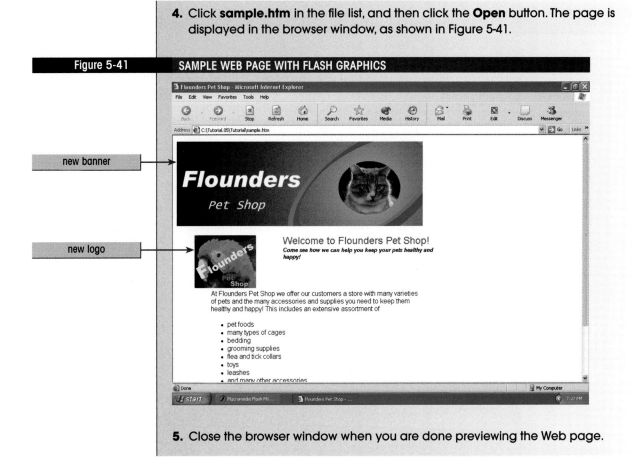

new banner

new logo

5. Close the browser window when you are done previewing the Web page.

In this session you learned about the different options available in Flash to publish and export movies and graphics. You changed the publish settings for the banner and then you published the banner movie. You also changed the export settings to export the logo as a JPEG file. Finally, you edited the HMTL for a sample Web page to incorporate references for the new Flounders Pet Shop banner and logo.

Session 5.3 QUICK CHECK

1. What is the native file format for Flash documents?

2. What is the file format for published Flash movies?

3. How do you get the GIF tab to be displayed in the Publish Settings dialog box?

4. What information is contained in the size report generated when the Generate size report option is selected in the Flash publish settings?

5. What types of files are published by the Publish command?

6. List five file formats you can export with the Export Image command.

7. To add a SWF file to an existing Web page you must use Notepad. True or False?

REVIEW ASSIGNMENTS

Aly is very pleased with the new Flounders banner and asks you to make some changes before she shows it to Joe Flounders. She instructs you to replace the parrot bitmap with a dog bitmap in the pet animation. The dog bitmap will have the same properties as the other bitmaps and will have the same fade effect in the animation. She also asks you to change the Flounder text block so that it has a gradient instead of a solid color for the fill of the letters.

If necessary, start Macromedia Flash and insert your Data Disk in the appropriate disk drive, and then do the following:

1. Open the **flounders.fla** banner file which you created in the tutorial. It is located in the Tutorial.05\Tutorial folder on your Data Disk.

2. Save the banner in the Tutorial.05\Review folder of your Data Disk. Name the file **flounders2.fla**.

3. Import the dog bitmap into the document's library. The bitmap is in the Tutorial.05\ Review folder on your Data Disk. Modify the dog bitmap's properties using a Quality value of 80.

4. Open the pet animation movie clip in symbol-editing mode. Delete the parrot layer and add a new layer above the cat layer. Name this layer dog layer and make sure it is indented under the mask layer just like the cat layer. Temporarily hide the contents of the mask layer while you work with the other layers.

5. Add a keyframe at Frame 24 of the dog layer. At Frame 24 drag a copy of the dog bitmap to the Stage. Use the Info panel to make sure that the position of the dog bitmap is the same as that of the cat bitmap. Convert the dog bitmap into a symbol and name it dog symbol.

6. Add another keyframe at Frame 36 of the dog layer. Change the alpha amount of the dog symbol at Frame 24 to 0%. If necessary, change the alpha amount of the dog symbol at Frame 36 to 100%. Create a motion tween at Frame 24.

7. Add two more keyframes to the dog layer, one at Frame 60 and another at Frame 72. At Frame 72 change the alpha amount of the dog symbol to 0%. Create another motion tween at Frame 60. Exit symbol-editing mode and return to the main document.

8. To add a gradient fill to the Flounders text, you need to convert the text to fills. Select the Flounders text block and apply the Break Apart command twice to convert the text to fills.

9. With the text still selected, create a gradient using the Color Mixer panel. Select linear gradient for the fill style. If necessary, click the gray linear gradient in the Swatches panel. Then in the Color Mixer panel change the color of the right gradient pointer to blue (ninth row, first column).

10. Save the changes you have made to the banner. Set the Flash publish settings to select Flash Player 6 and do not generate a size report. Publish the banner as a SWF file with the name **newbanner.swf**. Do not create an HTML file.

11. Open the **sample2.htm** Web page in Notepad. The file is in the Tutorial.05\Review folder on your Data Disk. Replace the image tag that has the flndrsbanner.gif reference to an EMBED tag with the newbanner.swf reference so that the Web page will display the new banner. Save the sample2.htm file and close Notepad.

12. Preview sample2.htm in Internet Explorer.

13. Close the browser window and close Macromedia Flash.

CASE PROBLEMS

Case 1. Creating a Logo for Sandy's Party Center Sandy Rodriquez, owner of Sandy's Party Center, asks John Rossini to develop a new logo for her store's Web site. She would like a logo with festive colors using some of the elements previously created for the banner such as the balloons and confetti. John suggests also incorporating the use of a picture for the letters on the logo and adding a gradient to the background. Sandy likes John's suggestions and tells John to develop the logo as soon as possible.

John develops an initial draft of the logo and instructs you to complete the logo by adding a bitmap that can be used as a fill for the letters. You also will create a gradient and use it as the background for the logo.

If necessary, start Macromedia Flash, insert your Data Disk in the appropriate drive, and then do the following:

1. Open the **partylogo** file from the Tutorial.05\Cases folder on your Data Disk.

2. Save the document as **partylogo2** in the Tutorial.05\Cases folder.

3. Import the jellybeans.jpg bitmap from the Tutorial.05\Cases folder directly into the document's library. Do not place a copy of the bitmap on the Stage.

4. Modify the bitmap's properties by changing its compression Quality value to 80%.

5. Select and change the text to fills by applying the Break Apart command twice to the text. Keep the text selected.

Explore   6. Use the Color Mixer panel to select bitmap as the fill style, and then if necessary, click the bitmap thumbnail in the Color Mixer panel. The text now has the jellybeans bitmap as its fill. Deselect the text.

7. Insert a new layer and label it background. In the Color Mixer panel create a new linear gradient. Use white as the color for the left gradient pointer and use yellow as the color for the right gradient pointer.

8. Draw a rectangle starting from the upper-left corner of the Stage to the lower-right corner to cover the entire Stage. The rectangle should have no stroke color and have the gradient as its fill.

9. Rotate the gradient using the Fill Transform tool so that the lighter or white area of the gradient is towards the bottom of the Stage.

10. Save the revised banner.

11. Publish the logo as both a SWF file and a JPEG file. Also, let Flash create a temporary HTML file.

12. Preview the logo in your browser using the HTML file created by Flash.

13. Close any open files and exit Flash and your browser.

Case 2. Revising the River City Music Banner with Bitmaps and a Gradient Janet Meyers, store manager for River City Music, is very happy with the interactive banner developed for the store's Web site. She meets with Alex Smith who developed the banner and asks him to add pictures of musical instruments and to change the Piano Sale text to read Instruments. Alex suggests that the pictures of the instruments can also be animated and further suggests that a gradient can be added to the background to enhance the look of the banner.

Alex asks you to help him revise the banner that was previously developed. He instructs you to import two bitmaps of musical instruments, to add one to the left side of the banner and the other to the right side. Each bitmap will be animated to fade in and then to rock back and forth as the musical notes move up and down. He also instructs you to add a rectangle with a radial gradient to cover the banner within the current rectangle in the background. The gradient should start with white and end with the blue color used for the background.

If necessary, start Macromedia Flash, insert your Data Disk in the appropriate drive, and then do the following:

1. Open the **musicbanner3** file that you completed in Case 2 of Tutorial 4. You should have saved it in the Tutorial.04\Cases folder on your Data Disk. If you did not complete Case 2 of Tutorial 4, then see your instructor for assistance.

2. Save the document as **musicbanner4** in the Tutorial.05\Cases folder on your Data Disk.

3. Import the trumpet.png and violin.png bitmaps from the Tutorial.05\Cases folder on your Data Disk to the documents library.

4. Select the background layer and insert a new layer above it. Name the new layer trumpet.

5. Drag a copy of the trumpet bitmap from the Library panel to the left side of the animated musical notes. Convert the trumpet to a symbol and name it trumpet symbol. Add a keyframe at Frame 15 and at Frame 20 of the trumpet layer.

6. Select Frame 1 of the trumpet layer and change the alpha amount of the trumpet symbol instance to 0%. Create a motion tween at Frame 1. The trumpet will fade in throughout the motion tween.

7. Select Frame 20 of the trumpet layer and rotate the trumpet symbol instance slightly to the right. Create a motion tween at Frame 15.

8. Insert a new layer and name it violin.

9. Repeat Steps 5 through 7 using the violin bitmap on the violin layer. The violin should be placed on the right side of the animated musical notes. At Frame 20, the violin should be rotated slightly to the left. This way the trumpet and the violin will rock back and forth in opposite directions.

10. Insert a new layer and name it gradient. Move this layer below the background layer.

11. Create a new radial gradient. The gradient should start with the color white. The second color should be the same as the blue color currently used for the background.

12. Draw a rectangle in the gradient layer. The rectangle should have no stroke and it should use the gradient as its fill. Draw it so that it is the same size as the current rectangle that has a dotted stroke and is framing the banner.

13. Save the revised banner.

14. Publish the banner as a SWF file. Also, let Flash create a temporary HTML file.

15. Preview the banner in your browser using the HTML file created by Flash. Make sure the trumpet and violin fade in and then rock back and forth as the musical notes move up and down.

16. Close any open files and exit Flash and your browser.

Case 3. Revising the Sonny's Auto Center Logo with Bitmaps and a Gradient Sonny Jackson and his staff are excited about the interactive logo developed for their Web site. He talks to Amanda Lester and asks her about the possibility of using pictures of cars as part of the animation. Amanda suggests adding some sample pictures of cars so that he can see how the logo will look. Amanda also suggests changing the title of the logo to make it more dynamic. Sonny agrees to Amanda's suggestions. Amanda asks you to help her complete the revisions by creating an animation with the car bitmaps and adding a new, more dynamic title.

If necessary, start Macromedia Flash, insert your Data Disk in the appropriate drive, and then do the following:

1. Open the **sonnylogo2** file that you completed in Case 3 of Tutorial 4. You should have saved it in the Tutorial.04\Cases folder on your Data Disk. Save this file as **sonnylogo3** in the Tutorial.05\Cases folder. If you did not complete Case 3 of Tutorial 4, see your instructor for assistance.

2. Delete the Sonny, Autos, Tire1, and Tire2 layers. Also, in Layer 1, delete the Auto and Center text blocks, as well as the blue gradient rectangle. Leave the larger rectangle, but delete the small vertical line that is inside it.

3. Edit the masked Autos symbol. Change the text in the text block of the autotext1 layer and the autotext2 layer. The text should read Sonny's Autos. Use the same font, keep it italic, and make sure the Center Justify button is selected in the Property inspector before you type the new text. Both text blocks should be exactly the same and in the same position.

Explore ⟩ 4. Change the gradient as follows. Make it linear and select the gray linear gradient from the Swatches panel as a starting point. Add two more gradient pointers in the center of the gradient definition bar. Make these two new gradient colors white. Make the far left gradient color black. You should have a narrow white band in the middle of the gradient. Apply this new gradient to the rectangle on the Stage.

5. In the main document, in Layer 1, Frame 1, add an instance of the masked Autos symbol to the Stage so that it is inside the top rectangle. This is the title for the logo.

Explore ⟩ 6. Import the view1.png, view2.png, and view3.png files which are stored on the C: drive in the \Program Files\Macromedia\Flash MX\Tutorials\FlashIntro\assets folder. If Flash was installed on a different drive, then look for the files on that drive. These bitmaps are part of the Flash MX tutorial installed with the program. Import to the library only and not to the Stage.

Explore ⟩ 7. Create a new symbol, name it car animation, and use Movie Clip as its behavior. In the car animation edit window drag a copy of the view1 bitmap onto the Stage, center it, and then reduce its size to 30%. (*Hint*: Use the Property inspector and the Transform panel.)

Explore ⟩ 8. At Frame 15 delete the view1 instance and add a view2 instance. At Frame 30 delete the view2 instance and add a view3 instance. The view3 instance should exist through Frame 45. Make sure each instance is centered and reduced to 30%. The resulting animation has each view of the car appear for 15 frames and then be replaced by a different view.

9. In the document's main Timeline, insert a new layer and name it car. Drag an instance of the car animation symbol to Frame 1 of the car layer. Center the car animation instance on the Stage.

10. Save the revised logo.

11. Publish the logo as a SWF file. Also, let Flash create a temporary HTML file.

12. Preview the logo in your browser using the HTML file created by Flash. Make sure the views of the car change and the Sonny's Auto text has the gradient moving through its letters.

13. Close any open files and exit Flash and your browser.

Case 4. Modifying the LAL Financial Banner with Gradients Christopher is very pleased with the interactive banner created for LAL Financial Services. He asks webmaster Elizabeth to modify the banner so that it has more of a green color instead of the gray color. He also asks Elizabeth if she can find a way to highlight the company name more than it is in the current banner. Elizabeth tells him that a motion tween with a gradient can be used to provide a highlight effect and agrees to modify the banner.

Elizabeth asks you to help her modify the various gradients on the different banner elements and to create a motion tween with a gradient that will highlight the company name.

If necessary, start Macromedia Flash, insert your Data Disk in the appropriate drive, and then do the following:

1. Open the **lfsbanner3** file that you completed in Case 4 of Tutorial 4. You should have saved it in the Tutorial.04\Cases folder on your Data Disk. If you did not complete Case 4 of Tutorial 4, then see your instructor for assistance.

2. Save the document as **lfsbanner4** in the Tutorial.05\Cases folder on your Data Disk.

3. Rename the background layer as text. Insert a new layer and name it background. Move the background layer below the text layer.

4. In the background layer create a rectangle that covers all of the Stage. Use no color for the stroke and a dark green for the fill (use the swatch on the sixth column, first row, or hexadecimal #009900).

5. Insert a new layer above the background layer. Name this layer highlight. Draw a rectangle in the highlight layer. Draw it below the Stage in the Work Area, with no stroke and the same fill color as before. This fill color will be replaced. The rectangle should be at least as wide as the Stage and should be about 100 pixels high.

6. Create a new linear gradient. Use the gray linear gradient from the Swatches panel as a starting point. Add one more gradient pointer to the middle of the gradient definition bar. Use the dark-green color (#009900) for the left gradient pointer. Use the same color for the right gradient pointer. Use white as the color for the middle gradient pointer. Add this gradient to the Swatches panel.

7. Apply the new gradient to the rectangle you created in Step 5. You want the top and bottom areas of the rectangle to have the dark-green color and the middle to have the white color. The result should be a narrow horizontal white band across the width of the rectangle. (*Hint*: Draw a vertical line with the Paint Bucket tool.)

8. Convert the rectangle with the gradient to a symbol. Name the symbol highlight and use Movie Clip as its behavior type.

9. Create a motion tween in the highlight layer that moves the highlight symbol from below the Stage to the top of the Stage. It should stop right over the LAL Financial Services text block. The motion tween should span Frames 1 to 45.

10. Change the text color to white in each of the text blocks in the text layer. Then in the last frame of the text layer, change the LAL Financial Services text color to black. (*Hint*: Add a keyframe where you make the change.)

11. Edit the circle symbol. Replace its gradient fill with the green radial gradient found in the fill color pop-up window. It is the fourth gradient from the left. Then move the gradient's center point to the upper-left part of the circle.

12. Edit the repeat button. Replace the circle in the Up Frame with the circle symbol from the library. Center the circle symbol instance.

13. Edit the square symbol. Replace its gray gradient fill with a new linear gradient. Use green (eighth row, first column, or #00FF00) for the left gradient pointer and use black for the right gradient pointer. Rotate the gradient fill on the square so that the green area is in the lower-right corner of the square.

14. Edit the triangle symbol. Change the linear gradient you used for the square so that its left gradient pointer is moved to the middle of the gradient definition bar effectively increasing the green area of the gradient. Replace the triangle's gray gradient fill with the new gradient.

15. Save the revised banner.

16. Publish the logo as a SWF file. Also, let Flash create a temporary HTML file.

17. Preview the logo in your browser using the HTML file created by Flash. Make sure the highlight gradient moves throughout from the bottom to the top and stops on the title text.

18. Close any open files and exit Flash and your browser.

QUICK | CHECK ANSWERS

Session 5.1

1. A bitmap is a graphic that is stored as a row-by-row list of pixels, along with each pixel's color information.
2. Both commands place the imported bitmap into the library. The Import command also places an instance of the bitmap on the Stage.
3. Select the bitmap in the library and then double-click the bitmap icon in the Library panel, or single-click the properties icon.
4. Use Photo (JPEG) compression for bitmaps with many colors or many color transitions such as photographs.
5. The alpha amount that will make an object transparent is 0%.
6. Use the Trace Bitmap command to convert a bitmap to a vector graphic.
7. The Color Threshold value determines how many colors are used. A smaller value results in more colors.

Session 5.2

1. A gradient is a gradual blend or transition from one color to another.
2. Use the Color Mixer panel to create a gradient.
3. Click Add Swatch from the options menu in the Color Mixer panel.
4. True. A gradient is only saved with the current document.
5. To add another color you add another gradient pointer by clicking below the gradient definition bar.
6. Use the Paint Bucket tool to apply a gradient to an existing object.
7. Use the Fill Transform tool to modify a gradient fill.
8. You drag the circular handle on a linear gradient to rotate the gradient.

Session 5.3

1. The native file format for Flash documents is FLA.
2. The file format for published Flash movies is SWF.

3. To get the GIF tab to display in the Publish Settings dialog box you click the GIF Image (.gif) check box.

4. The size report contains information about the published movie such as the number of frames, the total size of the movie, and the size of individual elements in the movie such as each symbol and bitmap.

5. The Publish command publishes files according to the selections in the Publish Settings dialog box.

6. File formats you can export with the Export Image command include JPEG, GIF, PNG, SWF, AI, WMF, and BMP.

7. False. You can also add a SWF file to an existing Web page using Macromedia Dreamweaver or Microsoft Frontpage.

TASK	PAGE #	RECOMMENDED METHOD
Action, add to button	FL 4.25	Select button instance on the Stage, open Actions panel, click Actions, click Movie Control, double-click desired action
Action, add to frame	FL 4.27	Select frame, open Actions panel, click Actions, click Movie Control, double-click desired action
Bitmap, change properties	FL 5.06	Select bitmap in Library panel, click
Bitmap, convert to a vector	FL 5.18	Select bitmap instance, click Modify, click Trace Bitmap, set Trace Bitmap options, click OK
Bitmap, import	FL 5.04	See Reference Window: Importing a Bitmap
Button, add from common library	FL 4.04	Drag button from Button Library panel to the Stage
Button, create	FL 4.11	See Reference Window: Creating a Button
Button, test within program window	FL 4.07	Click Control, click Enable Simple Buttons, click the button on the Stage
Colors, select	FL 2.13	Click Stroke color control list arrow or Fill color control list arrow to open color pop-up window, click desired color swatch
Fill, apply	FL 2.36	Click , select a fill color, select a Gap Size modifier, click the area to apply fill
Flash, exit program	FL 1.42	Click File, click Exit
Flash document, open	FL 1.25	Click File, click Open, select file, click Open
Flash document, modify	FL 2.10	Click Modify, click Document
Flash document, preview in a Flash Player window	FL 1.28	Click Control, click Test Movie
Flash document, preview within program window	FL 1.27	Click Control, click Play; or press Enter
Flash document, preview by scrubbing	FL 1.31	Drag playhead in Timeline header
Flash document, preview in a Web page	FL 1.28	Click File, point to Publish Preview, click default (HTML)
Flash document, test animation	FL 3.29	See Reference Window: Testing a Document's Animation
Flash Movie, display context menu	FL 1.23	Right-click the Flash movie
Flash MX, start	FL 1.24	Click , point to All Programs, point to Macromedia, click Macromedia Flash MX
Frame action, test	FL 4.30	Click Control, click Enable Simple Frame Actions
Frame label, add	FL 4.27	Select frame, type label in Frame Label text box in the Property inspector
Gradient, create	FL 5.24	Click Fill style list arrow in Color Mixer panel, select Radial or Linear, set gradient pointers and their colors
Gradient fill, apply	FL 5.28	Click , select gradient for fill color, click object on the Stage
Gradient fill, transform	FL 5.29	Click , click gradient on the Stage, adjust gradient
Grid, display	FL 2.07	Click View, point to Grid, click Show Grid
Grid, edit	FL 2.07	Click View, point to Grid, click Edit Grid

TASK	PAGE #	RECOMMENDED METHOD
Grouped object, edit	FL 2.13	Select object, click Edit, click Edit Selected, or double-click object
Grouped object, exit edit mode	FL 2.13	Click Edit, click Edit All
Guides, create	FL 2.08	Display rulers, drag guide line from a ruler to the Stage
Guides, edit	FL 2.09	Click View, point to Guides, click Edit Guides
Help, display Contents	FL 1.41	Click Help, click Using Flash, click a Contents category
Help, display Index	FL 1.41	Click Help, click Using Flash, click Index tab, click a letter
Help, display Search	FL 1.41	Click Help, click Using Flash, click Search tab, enter keyword(s), click List Topics, click a topic, click Display
Image, export	FL 2.50	Click File, click Export Image, select location, enter filename, click Save As type list arrow to select file format, click Save
Instance, create	FL 3.18	Drag copy of symbol from the Library panel to the Stage
Internet Explorer, follow a hyperlink	FL 1.14	Click the hyperlink
Internet Explorer, open a Web page	FL 1.12	See Reference Window: Opening a Page Using the Address Bar
Internet Explorer, start	FL 1.08	See Reference Window: Starting Internet Explorer
Keyframe, insert	FL 3.23	Select frame in Timeline, click Insert, click Keyframe
Layer, add	FL 3.11	Click Insert, click Layer, or click ➕⬛
Layer, change properties	FL 3.11	Click the layer, click Modify, click Layer, change layer properties, click OK
Layer, delete	FL 3.11	Click the layer, click 🗑
Layer, select	FL 3.11	Click the layer in Timeline
Library panel, change to Narrow (default) view	FL 3.14	Click ▯ in the Library panel
Library panel, change to Wide view	FL 3.14	Click ▭ in the Library panel
Library panel, open	FL 3.13	Click Window, click Library
Lines, draw with Pen tool	FL 2.40	Click ✒, select colors, drag pointer on the Stage, or click to create points on the Stage
Lines, draw with Pencil tool	FL 2.33	Click ✏, click Pencil mode modifier, set stroke properties, draw on the Stage
Motion Guide layer, create	FL 3.35	Click Insert, click Motion Guide, or click ➕⬛
Objects, align on the Stage	FL 4.20	Select several objects at one time, open the Align panel, click the desired align button
Object, change its position on the Stage	FL 1.40	Drag object with ➤, or change object's X and Y values in the Property inspector
Object, copy	FL 2.42	Select object, click Edit, click Copy, click Paste
Objects, flip horizontally	FL 2.42	Select object, click Modify, point to Transform, click Flip Horizontal
Objects, group	FL 2.12	Select several groups at one time, click Modify, click Group
Object, modify anchor points	FL 2.19	See Reference Window: Using the Subselection Tool
Object, modify with Arrow tool	FL 2.16	Click ➤, drag a line or a corner of the object to change its shape

TASK REFERENCE

TASK	PAGE #	RECOMMENDED METHOD
Object, move	FL 2.16	Click ⬈, select the object, drag the object
Object, scale on the Stage	FL 1.40	Select object with ⬈, change object's W and H values in Property inspector
Object, select with Arrow tool	FL 2.17	Click ⬈, click or double-click the object; or draw a rectangular marquee around the object
Objects, select with Lasso tool	FL 2.21	Click ⬭, click and drag to select objects; or click ⬭, ⬡, click points around objects
Object, transform	FL 2.46	See Reference Window: Transforming an Object using the Free Transform Tool
Oval, draw	FL 2.26	Click ◯, select stroke and fill colors, click and drag pointer on the Stage
Panels, collapse	FL 1.36	Click ▽ on the panel's title bar
Panels, expand	FL 1.36	Click ▷ on the panel's title bar
Panels, open	FL 1.36	Click Window, click desired panel
Panels, set to default layout	FL 1.25	Click Window, point to Panel Sets, click Default Layout
Publish settings, change	FL 5.33	Click File, click Publish Settings, select Type, click a tab, select options, click Close
Rectangle, draw	FL 2.24	Click ▢, select stroke and fill colors, click and drag pointer on the Stage
Rectangle, specify rounded corners	FL 2.25	Click ▢, click ⬀, enter point value, click OK
Rulers, display	FL 2.08	Click View, click Rulers
Snap to Objects, select	FL 2.30	Click View, click Snap to Objects to toggle on and off
Sound, add to a button	FL 4.34	See Reference Window: Adding a Sound to a Button
Stage, move its view	FL 2.06	Click ✋, drag Stage to new position
Stage, show all	FL 1.27	Click View, point to Magnification, click Show All
Stage view, change	FL 2.03	See Reference Window: Changing the View of the Stage
Stroke or Fill properties, copying	FL 2.38	Click ✎, click existing stroke or fill, click another stroke or fill to apply copied properties
Symbol, create	FL 3.17	See Reference Window: Creating a Symbol
Symbol, create duplicate	FL 3.18	Select symbol in Library panel, click ▤, click Duplicate, enter duplicate symbol's name, click OK
Symbol, edit	FL 3.19	Select symbol in Library panel, click ▤, click Edit
Text, create	FL 2.48	Click A, set text properties in the Property inspector, click or click and drag on the Stage to create a text block, type text
Timeline, change its view	FL 3.09	Click ⊞, click desired view
Timeline, close	FL 2.04	Click Window, click Timeline
Tools, select	FL 1.34	See Reference Window: Selecting Tools in the Toolbox
Zoom level, change	FL 2.05	Click 🔍, click ⊕ or ⊖, click an area of the Stage

Macromedia Flash MX File Finder

Tutorial	Location in Tutorial	Name and Location of Data File	Files the Student Creates
Tutorial 1	Session 1.1	Disk1\Tutorial.01\Tutorial\Actions\index.htm	
	Session 1.2	Disk1\Tutorial.01\Tutorial\Actions\sample.htm	
	Session 1.3	Disk1\Tutorial.01\Tutorial\SimpleKite.fla	
	Review Assignments	Disk1\Tutorial.01\Tutorial\SimpleKite.fla	SimpleBalloon.fla
	Case Problem 1	None	
	Case Problem 2	None	
Tutorial 2	Session 2.1	Disk1\Tutorial.02\Tutorial\Sample.fla	Mysample.fla
	Session 2.2		banner.fla
	Session 2.3	Disk1\Tutorial.02\Tutorial\banner.fla Disk1\Tutorial.02\Tutorial\Flounder.htm	banner.gif
	Review Assignments	Disk1\Tutorial.02\Tutorial\banner.fla	banner2.fla
	Case Problem 1	None	spcbanner.fla; spcbanner.gif
	Case Problem 2	Disk1\Tutorial.02\Cases\music.fla	rcmbanner.fla; rcmbanner.gif
	Case Problem 3	None	saclogo.fla; saclogo.gif
	Case Problem 4	None	lfsbanner.fla; lfsbanner.gif
Tutorial 3	Session 3.1	Disk1\Tutorial.03\Tutorial\sports.fla Disk1\Tutorial.03\Tutorial\banner.fla	floundersbanner.fla
	Session 3.2	Disk1\Tutorial.03\Tutorial\floundersbanner.fla	
	Session 3.3	Disk1\Tutorial.03\Tutorial\sports2.fla Disk1\Tutorial.03\Tutorial\floundersbanner.fla	
	Review Assignments	Disk1\Tutorial.03\Tutorial\floundersbanner.fla	floundersbanner2.fla
	Case Problem 1	Disk1\Tutorial.03\Cases\partybanner.fla	partybanner2.fla
	Case Problem 2	Disk1\Tutorial.03\Cases\musicbanner.fla	musicbanner2.fla
	Case Problem 3	Disk1\Tutorial.02\Cases\saclogo.fla	saclogo2.fla
	Case Problem 4	Disk1\Tutorial.02\Cases\lfsbanner.fla	lfsbanner2.fla
Tutorial 4	Session 4.1	Disk2\Tutorial.04\Tutorial\petshop.fla	petshop2.fla
	Session 4.2	Disk2\Tutorial.04\Tutorial\petshop2.fla	
	Session 4.3	Disk2\Tutorial.04\Tutorial\petshop2.fla Disk2\Tutorial.04\Tutorial\bubbles.wav	
	Review Assignments	Disk2\Tutorial.04\Tutorial\petshop2.fla	petshop3.fla
	Case Problem 1	Disk1\Tutorial.03\Cases\partybanner2.fla Disk3\Tutorial.04\Cases\party.wav	partybanner3.fla
	Case Problem 2	Disk1\Tutorial.03\Cases\musicbanner2.fla Disk3\Tutorial.04\Cases\piano loop.wav Disk3\Tutorial.04\Cases\piano1.wav	musicbanner3.fla
	Case Problem 3	Disk3\Tutorial.04\Cases\sonnylogo.fla Disk3\Tutorial.04\Cases\auto loop.wav Disk3\Tutorial.04\Cases\carhorn.wav	sonnylogo2.fla
	Case Problem 4	Disk1\Tutorial.03\Cases\lfsbanner2.fla	lfsbanner3.fla
Tutorial 5	Session 5.1	Disk4\Tutorial.05\Tutorial\floundersnew.fla Disk4\Tutorial.05\Tutorial\cat.jpg Disk4\Tutorial.05\Tutorial\parrot.jpg	flounders.fla petlogo.fla
	Session 5.2	Disk4\Tutorial.05\Tutorial\flounders.fla	
	Session 5.3	Disk4\Tutorial.05\Tutorial\flounders.fla Disk4\Tutorial.05\Tutorial\banner Report.txt Disk4\Tutorial.05\Tutorial\petlogo.fla Disk4\Tutorial.05\Tutorial\sample.htm	banner.swf banner Report.txt petlogo.jpg
	Review Assignments	Disk4\Tutorial.05\Tutorial\flounders.fla Disk4\Tutorial.05\Review\dog.jpg Disk4\Tutorial.05\Review\sample2.htm	flounders2.fla newbanner.swf
	Case Problem 1	Disk5\Tutorial.05\Cases\partylogo.fla Disk4\Tutorial.05\Cases\jellybeans.jpg	partylogo2.fla; partylogo2.swf partylogo2.jpg; partylogo2.html
	Case Problem 2	Disk3\Tutorial.04\Cases\musicbanner3.fla Disk5\Tutorial.05\Cases\trumpet.png Disk5\Tutorial.05\Cases\violin.png	musicbanner4.fla musicbanner4.swf musicbanner4.html
	Case Problem 3	Disk3\Tutorial.04\Cases\sonnylogo2.fla C:\Program Files\Macromedia\Flash MX\Tutorials\FlashIntro\assets\view1.png, view2.png, and view3.png	sonnylogo3.fla sonnylogo3.swf sonnylogo3.html
	Case Problem 4	Disk3\Tutorial.04\Cases\lfsbanner3.fla	lfsbanner4.fla; lfsbanner4.swf lfsbanner4.html